Russia's Liberal Media

This book examines the challenges and pressures liberal journalists face in Putin's Russia. It presents the findings of an in-depth qualitative study, which included ethnographic observations of editorial meetings during the conflict in Ukraine. It also provides a theoretical framework for evaluating the Russian media system and a historical overview of the development of liberal media in the country. The book focusses on some of Russia's most influential liberal national news outlets: "the deadliest" newspaper *Novaya Gazeta*, "Russia's last independent radio station" *Radio Echo of Moscow (Ekho Moskvy)*, and US Congress-funded *Radio Free Europe/Radio Liberty*. The fieldwork included ethnographic observations of editorial meetings, long interviews with editors and journalists, as well as documentary analysis. The monograph makes theoretical contributions to three main areas: (1) media systems and terms of reference; (2) journalism: cultures, role conceptions, and relationship with power, culture, and society; and (3) mediatisation of conflict and nationhood.

Vera Slavtcheva-Petkova is a Senior Lecturer in Communications and Media Studies at the University of Liverpool, UK. She is the author of *Global Journalism: An Introduction* (with Michael Bromley).

Routledge Research in Journalism

For a full list of titles in this series, please visit www.routledge.com.

Russia's Liberal Media
Handcuffed but Free

Vera Slavtcheva-Petkova

Routledge
Taylor & Francis Group

LONDON AND NEW YORK

First published 2018 by Routledge

2 Park Square, Milton Park, Abingdon, Oxfordshire OX14 4RN
52 Vanderbilt Avenue, New York, NY 10017

Routledge is an imprint of the Taylor & Francis Group, an informa business

First issued in paperback 2020

Copyright © 2018 Taylor & Francis

The right of Vera Slavtcheva-Petkova to be identified as author of this work has been asserted by her in accordance with sections 77 and 78 of the Copyright, Designs and Patents Act 1988.

All rights reserved. No part of this book may be reprinted or reproduced or utilised in any form or by any electronic, mechanical, or other means, now known or hereafter invented, including photocopying and recording, or in any information retrieval system, without permission in writing from the publishers.

Notice:
Product or corporate names may be trademarks or registered trademarks, and are used only for identification and explanation without intent to infringe.

Library of Congress Cataloging in Publication Data
CIP data has been applied for.

ISBN: 978-1-138-23728-5 (hbk)
ISBN: 978-0-367-59200-4 (pbk)

Typeset in Sabon
by codeMantra

Contents

List of Tables and Figures

Tables

Figures

Acknowledgements

First and foremost, I would like to thank my family – my parents Yordan and Zoya; my husband Tsvetan; my children Zoya, Nadezhda, and Jordan; my sister Desislava, her husband Kostadin, and my niece Darina; and my mother-in-law Nadezhda for their unwavering support and for putting up with me during all those years.

This project would not have been possible without the financial support of the University of Chester's International Research Excellence Awards Scheme funded through Santander Universities. Special thanks are due to my former colleagues in the Department of Media at the University of Chester and especially my friends from the Journalism programme there as well as the Research and Knowledge Transfer Office. I took inspiration for this book from my colleague Dr Simon Roberts who published a monograph on journalism in the former Soviet republics, so I am especially grateful to him and to my dear friend and colleague Ato Erzan-Essien. I would also like to thank my colleagues at the Department of Communication and Media at the University of Liverpool for their support over the last few months of this project. I am also grateful to the Faculty of Journalism at Lomonosov Moscow State University for sponsoring my visa application and inviting me to deliver a guest lecture to their MA students. Thanks are due to Simon Webb, Mila Burt and Iliya Iliev for their help with the translations.

I would also like to thank my Commissioning Editor at Routledge, Felisa Salvago-Keyes, for her efficiency, her patience, and for putting her trust in this project, and to Senior Editorial Assistant Christina Kowalski for guiding me through the publication process. Special thanks are due to the anonymous reviewers who kindly supported this book and offered invaluable suggestions for improvements.

Last but not least, I would like to express my utmost gratitude to all journalists and editors who agreed to take part in my study and who allowed me to observe their work. Words cannot express how inspired I felt by what I saw during my short stay in Russia. Their courage and resistance are truly admirable, and I hope their efforts will pay off in the long run.

Introduction

"My editor-in-chief called me at 5 a.m. If he calls me at this time, I know that something wrong has happened". Sitting at her desk, casually dressed in a T-shirt and a pair of jeans, with a small kitten sleeping peacefully behind her next to a suitcase hastily prepared for her trip to Ukraine, 35-year-old Russian journalist Nadezhda Prusenkova recalled the events of the past few hours. Something wrong did indeed happen in the early hours of that Monday morning on 12 May 2014. One of her colleagues was kidnapped while covering the uprisings in Eastern Ukraine. Russian newspaper *Novaya Gazeta's* editor-in-chief received an early-morning phone call from a German colleague informing him that special correspondent Pavel Kanygin was kidnapped by activists from the self-proclaimed Donetsk People's Republic. The activists demanded a ransom of $30,000 in exchange for Kanygin's freedom. Editor-in-Chief Dmitry Muratov immediately called Prusenkova and asked her to start making informal inquiries and to accompany him to Ukraine. "We were ready, I flew to Kiev prepared to pay a ransom for him because I wanted to save the life of our correspondent. When terrorists are concerned, if you don't pay, there is no saving him, they will kill him", Muratov (2014, personal communication) explained a few days later after coming back from Kiev. However, on her way to the airport, Prusenkova received another phone call. It was no longer necessary for her to travel to Ukraine – the activists had promised to release Kanygin. With her suitcase in her hands, she caught the train in the opposite direction – now to the newspaper's office where, as managing editor, she was responsible for the next edition. She was also the paper's press officer, so her phone was ringing all day with inquiries about her kidnapped colleague.

In addition to answering phone calls and determining the salience and order of articles, Prusenkova had to take care of a kitten brought by a compassionate reader who asked the newspaper to find a home for the pet. "We placed a notice in the newspaper, and another reader promised that he would come and collect the cat, but she never turned up. Usually, it's calmer than that", she (Prusenkova, 2014, personal communication) summed up her day smiling. Prusenkova then hastily qualified her comment by saying that she shared her editor-in-chief's view that American journalists as portrayed in the HBO series *The Newsroom* were "like children" in comparison with them. And indeed, her experience as a journalist in "the deadliest newspaper in Russia" speaks for itself. In her time at *Novaya Gazeta*, she had witnessed the murders of six of her colleagues as well as numerous acts of brutality – from physical attacks, harassment, and intimidation, to business pressures and spies in the newsrooms. She had personally been harassed on numerous occasions, and she had received threats, including a dead rat with a big knife under her doorstep and a donkey's ears in her post. "I have no fear. Like many of my colleagues, we are not suicidal; we are not crazy adrenaline maniacs. My murdered colleagues did something exact and painful for society. This was the only way. That's why maybe I see it as normal – you can be killed because you do something very important, very needed for all of us. *Novaya Gazeta* couldn't be just a job. It's a way of thinking, it's a way of life really", she (Prusenkova, 2014, personal communication) said.

This book tells the story of Prusenkova and her colleagues – Russian liberal journalists from *Novaya Gazeta* and two radio stations – *Radio Ekho Moskvy (Echo of Moscow) and Radio Svoboda (Radio Free Europe/ Radio Liberty)* – who believe they have an important role to play in their country's thorny road to democratisation. It describes the challenges and pressures liberal journalists currently face in Russia. The monograph presents the findings of a semi-ethnographic in-depth qualitative study, and it also provides a historical overview of the development of liberal media in the country. The book also makes an important contribution to the theoretical development of the field by focussing on three key areas: (1) media systems and terms of reference; (2) journalism: culture(s), role conceptions, and relationship with power, culture, and society; and (3) mediatisation of conflict and nationhood: conflict reporting and nation-building.

The Role of Liberal Media in Russia's Thorny Journey to Democratisation: Recent Developments, Conceptual, and Theoretical Departures

Russia is indisputably one of the most dangerous countries for journalists in the world (Azhgikhina, 2007; CPJ, 2017; Mickiewicz, 2008), and the conflict with Ukraine and Russia's controversial involvement in Syria presented even further challenges for the future of Russian journalism. Although Russia has not been involved in an armed conflict within its territory, it has been ranked among the top 10 countries in the world with the highest number of murdered journalists since 1992 (Azhgikhina, 2007; CPJ, 2017). Key reasons are "the lack of political will to investigate the murders", the "lack of coordination and cooperation" between editorial offices and the authorities, and the lack of cooperation between law enforcement officers and investigators and the judicial structures (Azhgikhina, 2007, p. 1248). *Novaya Gazeta* is the deadliest newspaper because it has the highest number of murdered journalists of all media in the country, including the assassination of the famous investigative reporter Anna Politkovskaya on President Vladimir Putin's birthday in 2006. Putin's reaction to her death was indicative of his attitude towards liberal media. He notoriously said: "Her death caused more damage to the country than her articles" (Azhgikhina, 2007, p. 1259). Russia also has a poor record of impunity (CPJ, 2017).

The country is classified as "not free" by non-governmental organisations such as Freedom House. Commentators pointed out that although "freedom of speech was the first and perhaps the only real achievement of perestroika", this achievement was later "shaken, and then lost" (Azhgikhina, 2007, p. 1249). Russian media's road to democratisation has not only been thorny, but also appears to have taken a turn for the worse. In addition to the physical threats and attacks, journalists in Russia also experience a range of pressures from the state. Putin's tightening grip on Russian media includes overt and covert practices of censorship, persecution, and harassment of journalists who voice alternative views, and a great degree of self-censorship, which has become "endemic" (Oates, 2013, p. 14). Freedom House's 2015 report stated that "Russia's occupation of the Crimean Peninsula and involvement in the conflict in eastern Ukraine helped to drive an increase in propagandistic content in the Russian news media and tighter restrictions on dissenting views". Russian media are indeed kept in the tight grip of the state propaganda machine. Television is the main and the most influential medium of news and political information and the one most strictly controlled by the Kremlin. Most television stations are either state-owned or funded by the state. The state "has also found 'administrative means' to get a grip on the coverage" of private stations, so "all TV stations now carefully adhere to the official line, and hear very quickly from the Kremlin if they wander off message" (Brenton, 2011, p. 35). The press has "more latitude, largely because they are seen as less important", and while "there is no formal censorship, Kremlin 'guidance' is abundantly available to editors" (Brenton, 2011, p. 35). Most newspapers are owned by major companies such as the state-owned gas giant Gazprom, which are "heavily dependent on their links with the Kremlin for their day-to-day activities, and will be careful that their journalistic protégés do not endanger those links" (Brenton, 2011, p. 36). The Kremlin also notoriously closed down or hacked a few opposition websites. Most Russian news media do not just support the government "with biased news", but they are also increasingly "participating in an 'information war' with its perceived adversaries", both at home and abroad (Freedom House, 2015). The European Union even announced the launch of a task force to counter biased Russian news reports. East StratCom Task Force is part of the European External Action Service, and it was set up in 2015 in response to growing concern in Eastern Europe and the Baltic states about the destabilising influence of Russian-language news reports. Its main task is "to address Russia's ongoing disinformation campaigns" (European Union External Action, 2015). A team of 400 experts, journalists, officials, non-governmental organisations (NGOs), and think tanks supports the Task Force by reporting disinformation articles to it.

Only a few media outlets in Russia strive to remain "independent" in this climate of propaganda and self-censorship, but as *Novaya Gazeta's* experience demonstrates, independence comes at a price. Putin's soaring popularity and the elaborate range of tactics used to suppress press freedom are forcing liberal/"independent" media to rethink their mission(s) and identity(ies). The book focusses on some of Russia's most influential liberal national news outlets – "the deadliest" newspaper *Novaya Gazeta*, "Russia's last independent radio station" (Nemtsova, 2014) *Radio Echo of Moscow (Ekho Moskvy)*, and US Congress-funded *Radio Free Europe/Radio Liberty* (known as *Radio Svoboda* in Russia). Most of the fieldwork was conducted in May 2014 in the midst of the conflict with Ukraine. It involved ethnographic research, including observations of editorial meetings as well as interviews with editors, deputy editors, and journalists. Subsequent archival research and analysis of various sources of information as well as additional informal conversations were conducted in the following months up until the submission of the manuscript in December 2017 at a time when the country's role on the world stage was becoming increasingly controversial.

More than a quarter of a century after the fall of the Berlin Wall, most European countries appear to have left their Cold War differences behind and have joined forces as part of the European Union and the North Atlantic Treaty Organization, but Russia's actions in Ukraine, Syria, and the USA come as an acute reminder that the "war" between the East and the West is probably not yet over. The conflict between Russia and Ukraine and the deteriorating relationship between Russia and the West prompted commentators to claim that the Cold War was back. Wikipedia even added an entry called "Cold War II", and commentators disputed whether the world was moving in the direction of a new "hot war". Russia and Putin are permanently back on our television screens, and a key question is: What went wrong in Russia? What happened to the country's journey towards democratisation? This question cannot be fully answered unless we explore more closely the role of the mass media in the country. After all, free media are the backbone of any democracy. Moreover, as Oates (2006) claimed, "the experience of Russia highlights the fact the mass media are critical factors in halting the slide into authoritarianism" (p. 194).

This book makes an important theoretical contribution to the field by focussing on three key points: (1) media systems and terms of reference; (2) journalism: culture(s), role conceptions, and relationship with power, culture, and society; and (3) mediatisation of conflict and nationhood:

conflict reporting and nation-building. Needless to say, the three wider topics are very closely interrelated. First, an attempt towards conceptualisation of the Russian media system is made because it is important to place the empirical findings within the wider context of news media in general and news media in Russian society in particular. Second, the role of the state, culture, and society vis-à-vis journalism and journalistic practices cannot be fully explained unless the relevant journalism culture(s) and journalists' own role perceptions are taken into account as well. Finally, the ethnographic fieldwork took place in the midst of the conflict with Ukraine, so it is also important to consider the media's role in the representation and perception of conflicts, particularly in cases such as the Russian one when the relevant nation-state has a stake in the conflict. Linked to that is the wider issue about the media's role vis-à-vis nationalism, national identities, and nation-building. This topic has been of particular relevance in the Russian context due to Putin's increased efforts in the construction and promotion of a particular type of modern-day Russian national identity. These conceptual issues are investigated in more detail in Chapter 2, but it is important to briefly outline the main points of departure from the onset.

Although there have been a few notable attempts towards operationalisation of the media system in Russia (Becker, 2014; Koltsova, 2006; Oates, 2006, 2013), as Rollberg (2014) argued, it is very hard, "if not impossible" for researchers "to arrive at a lasting analytical consensus about the post-Soviet media sphere" because "media in post-Soviet societies are a moving target, influenced by technological, geopolitical, and cultural developments" (p. 175). This difficulty is in large part due to the fact that, as Kolstova (2006) claimed, lots of researchers use Western concepts, terms, and theories in their attempts to explain the situation in Russia. Commonly used terms are censorship, self-censorship, and transition, but their "undifferentiated use" is problematic because of two key reasons (Rollberg, 2014). First, they reinforce the Cold War dichotomy between the East and the West, democratic countries, and totalitarian regimes (Burrett, 2011; Rollberg, 2014). The reinforcement of this dichotomy is based on the assumption that after 1989/1990, Russian society and media have been in a period of transition from communism/authoritarianism to democracy (Burrett, 2011; Rollberg, 2014). Even if the assumption that Russia was en route to democratisation during and shortly after the perestroika and glasnost years, recent developments in the country clearly show that this is hardly the case anymore. In fact, both Kolstova (2006) and Oates (2013) questioned the extent to which Russian society and media were ever on a linear journey towards democratisation. Koltsova (2006) claimed that the Russian experience demonstrated that "the authoritarianism-democracy axis is not the only one along which societies can change" (p. 5). She proposed a move away from normative theories of democracy to an agency-focussed approach, whereby "the struggle between different power centres" was investigated in more depth in an attempt to explain the development of post-socialist media (Koltsova, 2006, pp. 5–6). Koltsova (2006) argued that the typology of national media systems should be based on different sets of categories such as "power agents, resources, strategies and rules" (p. 227). Second, the terminology is problematic because the exact meaning of these notions can no longer be "taken for granted" since they "originated from totalitarian society models" (Rollberg, 2014, p. 176). Rollberg (2014), for example, demonstrated that none of Siebert, Peterson, and Schramm's (1956) four theories of the press fully operationalised the situation in Russia. Although on the surface it appeared that post-Soviet media had undergone an evolution from a Social Responsibility model to an Authoritarian model in the early 2000s,

> even in the most liberal years of glasnost, Soviet media retained essential features of what Siebert called "the Soviet model," and even in the most intrusive years of the Putin presidency (2002–2003, after 2012), the Authoritarian model contains libertarian and consumer-driven features.
>
> (Rollberg, 2014, p. 175)

This suggests that developments in Russian media and society should not be interpreted through Western lenses and with existing (predominantly normative) Western media theories and concepts.

Instead, commentators (Becker, 2014; Pomerantsev, 2014) claimed that Russia had embarked on its own journey. Koltsova's (2006) power-focussed model went some way towards explaining who the key actors in the web of relationships that encompassed the Russian media system were. Becker (2014) concluded that Russia had "adopted a neo-authoritarian media system that has more in common with similar non-democratic systems around the world than with the Soviet system that once prevailed on the same territory" (p. 191). Similarly, Pomerantsev (2014) argued that "this isn't a country in transition but some form of postmodern dictatorship that uses the language and institutions of democratic capitalism for authoritarian ends" (p. 42). One notable difference is of particular relevance to this book – the types of control imposed to the media and the role of ideology in modern-day Russia are very different from the ones used during the Soviet era (Becker, 2014). This manuscript offers a typology of the controls and restrictions that Russian liberal journalists face, which supports Becker's (2014) claim that "the breadth, depth, and mechanisms of control" (p. 202) are indeed not the same.

This leads me to the second theoretical contribution this book makes, namely in relation to the conceptualisation of journalism as a profession, more precisely in terms of journalistic culture(s) and journalists' own role perceptions. A few seminal studies (Koltsova, 2006; Mickiewicz, 1999;

Oates, 2006, 2013) questioned the assumption that Russian journalists cherished Western values of journalism and would have striven to be "watchdogs" of society if it was not for Putin's repressive practices. Koltsova (2006) showed that the majority of Russian journalists were not simply used as tools in Putin's propaganda machine, but they willingly took part in the process. Oates (2006) went further than that by claiming that the two key factors that "led to the failure of elections to consolidate democracy are the journalistic profession itself and the audience" (p. 192), and the attitude of journalists had been "most destructive" to their profession. Oates (2013) explained that "all segments of Russian society, from politicians to the public to the journalists themselves, perceive the mass media as a political player rather than as a watchdog" (p. 12). She added that self-censorship was "endemic" and that the situation resembled Soviet times – journalists were rarely censored because they were "well aware of the limits of what can be said" (Oates, 2013, p. 14). Oates (2006) also claimed that the audience did not expect journalists to be objective:

> the notion of media freedom and, in particular, the idea of objectivity is not central to Russian watching habits. Rather, Russians often seek something different from their prime television station, notably a sense of pride and nationhood in a troubled and chaotic environment.
>
> (p. 20)

Oates's (2006, 2013) and Koltsova's (2006) studies are mainly of a qualitative nature, so it is worth pointing out that a few surveys have been conducted on the topic. In their survey with 500 journalists, Anikina and Johansson (2013) argued that "modern Russian journalists have taken on several principles that are typical for Western journalistic cultures" (Anikina & Johansson, 2013, p. 84). The top three journalistic duties were "be a neutral reporter, provide information objectively and stand free of special interests" (Anikina & Johansson, 2013, p. 84). These apparent discrepancies in findings are perhaps in large part due to the different methodologies utilised by researchers. The issue of role conceptions is, nonetheless, very relevant to this study, and my book reveals what journalists in liberal media think their role in Russian society is/should be.

This question is also linked to another key issue that I explore in the book: the media's role in the representation and perception of conflicts, which is intrinsically related to the wider question about the media's role in the process of nation-building and national identities. It is important to consider the mediatisation of the conflict with Ukraine because, as Mortensen (2015) argued, "the news media constitute the primary platform for political and military actors to inform the public", and for both official and non-official actors to "gain visibility and voice" as well as seek legitimacy (p. 7). Journalists' role is particularly tricky in that respect because, as Allan and Zelizer (2004, pp. 3–4) pointed out, "any belief that the journalist can remain distant, remote, or unaffected by what is happening 'tends to go out the window'", and the distinction between "patriotism and militarism is central to the problems of reporting war". As already indicated, this topic has been of particular relevance in the Russian context due to Putin's increased efforts in the process of construction and promotion of a particular type of modern-day Russian national identity. Hutchings and Tolz (2015) argued that in Russia, "isolationist popular nationalism" coexisted with "the neo-imperial nationalism of Putin's regime" (p. 9). The conflict with Ukraine presented opportunities for liberal media to provide an "alternative" framing to the overall pro-Putin chorus led by Russian state broadcast media, but it also led to a key challenge for liberal/non-governmental media – the threat of increased marginalisation. Putin's popularity has been soaring in large part due to the strong role he has been perceived to be playing in the process of nation-building and revival of Russia's identity as a superpower on the world stage. A few recent studies (e.g. Cottiero, Kucharski, Olimpieva, & Orttung, 2015; Hutchings & Tolz, 2015) investigated the role of state-aligned television in that process as well as the differences and similarities in framing between state-aligned television and the Internet sphere. Cottiero et al.'s (2015) study showed that the Kremlin's framing of the conflict with Ukraine had been really effective and had influenced Russia's Internet audience, and that the Internet space did not really provide an alternative portrayal of the conflict. An important question that this study explores: What role have liberal media played in the mediatisation of the conflict with Ukraine, and to what extent have they provided an alternative framing to the conflict? Another issue that became apparent during the interviews and the ethnographic observations was that the conflict with Ukraine had also presented "identity" issues for these media because it had further led to their marginalisation due to the often-unpopular messages they spread about Russia's role in Ukraine. Journalists in my sample reported that any story they published about wrongdoings by the Russian forces in Ukraine was interpreted by "ordinary Russians" as "proof" that they were "the voice of the enemy".

To sum up, the main research questions of the study are: (1) What kind of constraints, controls, and restrictions do Russian liberal journalists face, and how do they tackle these challenges? Are the "breadth, depth, and mechanisms" (Becker, 2014) of control very different from the ones used during Soviet times? (2) What role do liberal media play in the mediatisation of the conflict in Ukraine, and to what extent have they provided an alternative framing to the conflict to the one offered by Putin and state-aligned media? (3) What role do liberal journalists believe they (should) play in post-Soviet Putin's Russia? Finally, what do all these trends tell us about the Russian media system and the potential for development of democracy in the country?

The timing for this book is excellent because although a few books have been written about the state of Russian media, most of them pre-date Putin's second and third terms as president, and/or the more recent ones focus on the Internet and state-aligned television. No known recent book or journal article explores the state of liberal news outlets such as the three this book focusses on. A few recent developments within these media outlets, as outlined later, add increased weight to the timeliness and pertinence of the study.

Methodology

This is a qualitative study based on long, semi-structured interviews with journalists, editors, and/or deputy editors conducted during my stay in Russia in May 2014, as well as documentary analysis and ethnographic observations of formal and informal meetings in the editorial offices of the three outlets during that period. Additional and follow-up informal conversations as well as documentary analysis of recent developments were conducted up until the publication of the book. The documentary analysis is based on a range of materials: archives, including past editions/broadcasts, founding constitutional charters, minutes from meetings, mission statements as well as books and articles about key developments in the history of the three outlets. All formal editorial meetings were fully recorded, but I also made copious notes of my observations of informal meetings between journalists. The ethnographic material is presented in a style known as '"women's ways of knowing"' in which "there is no harsh separation between research and life, and where what happens in one realm inevitably informs the other" (Clark, 2012, p. xx). The analysis and presentation of findings is organised around the key research questions, as outlined farther in the text. All interviews were fully transcribed and thematically analysed, namely "the data are read for analytical themes, which are listed" (Fielding, 2001, p. 159). A grounded theory approach guided the analysis. The constant bottom-up comparison method was used (Dye, Schatz, & Rosenberg, 2000; Glaser, 1965). In practical terms, the bottom-up analysis consisted of "at least two phases: initial and focused coding" (Charmaz, 2006, p. 42). In the first stage, "fragments of data – words, lines, segments, and incidents" were examined "closely for their analytical import" (Charmaz, 2006, p. 42). Then, in the second stage, decisions were made "about which initial codes make the most analytical sense to categorise" the "data incisively and completely" (Charmaz, 2006, p. 57).

As already indicated, my sample consists of three of the most influential liberal news media organisations in Russia. Access was easily arranged to *Novaya Gazeta* and *Radio Free Europe/Radio Liberty*, but it was more difficult to get access to *Ekho*. I was allowed to interview any journalists of my choice in *Novaya Gazeta* and *Radio Free Europe/ Radio Liberty* as well as to attend all meetings (formal and informal), but the editor-in-chief of *Ekho* pre-arranged all interviews for me, and I was not allowed to freely move in the building. I aimed for a theoretical sample with both senior and junior journalists and at least one editor or deputy editor in each media outlet. My research was constrained by time and staff availability, but as a whole, I achieved a fairly varied sample at *Novaya Gazeta* and *Radio Liberty*. Given the exploratory and qualitative nature of the study, I was not aiming for representativeness. Participants were given the option to remain anonymous, but most of them (bar one) waived their anonymity (or in fact strongly objected to it). Some of the interviews were conducted in English and some in Russian. The original wording of the interviews conducted in English has been preserved. The project received ethical approval both from my institution and from Lomonosov Moscow State University. As a qualitative researcher, I also have to acknowledge that I am an outsider to Russia, and Russian is not my native language, so as much as I have tried to gain a comprehensive understanding of the Russian context and media, I have been limited by my identity, my language abilities, and my own personal experiences and views of communist and post-communist societies.

Novaya Gazeta – The Deadliest Newspaper in Russia

Novaya Gazeta is the deadliest newspaper in the country, with six murders, including the famous investigative reporter Politkovskaya, and many physical attacks or abductions. One of their Ukrainian correspondents was kidnapped during my visit. The national newspaper is renowned for its investigations of corruption practices and strong criticism of the Kremlin and Putin himself. *Novaya Gazeta* is currently in a precarious financial state, notably exacerbated after Putin's second coming to power. The newspaper was founded by a group of journalists, and the majority shares were in the hands of the paper's editorial staff – they owned "an inseparable pack of shares", as the Head of Press Service Prusenkova (2014, personal communication) explained. The other main shareholder (39%) was the Russian oligarch Alexander Lebedev, who also owned the UK newspapers *The Independent* and *The London Evening Standard*. Former President Mikhail Gorbachev owned the final 10% of the shares. Lebedev announced in early 2015 that he would stop "bankrolling" the paper because "of the expense and the strain" under which it placed him. He explained to *The Times* (2015) that he wanted "some respite", "some time with the kids", and that he had been "left alone" by the authorities after withdrawing his financial support. Lebedev's announcement did not come as a surprise to *Novaya Gazeta* journalists. Almost immediately after buying shares in the newspaper, Lebedev was embroiled in a corruption scandal involving the Federal Security Service (previously Komitet Gosudarstvennoy Bezopasnosti (KGB)). Lebedev himself is a former KGB agent: "It was a big scandal and he lost his business. It was a long story, a story of revenge on the side of the secret service", Prusenkova (2014, personal communication) explained. His withdrawal exacerbated the financial situation of the newspaper and led to an announcement by its editor that they might have to stop publishing the print edition.

The financial difficulties of *Novaya Gazeta* have been a recurring story, but for the first time, the newspaper announced that it may not have a print edition anymore. A key contributing factor was the lack of advertising. Prusenkova explained that the situation was very different during Dmitry Medvedev's presidency. The first interview he gave as president was for *Novaya Gazeta*, and big business saw this "as a sign": "There are always signs, and after this sign, we had many, many commercials", she (Prusenkova, 2014, personal communication) explained. By contrast, when Putin embarked on his second term as president, he immediately convened a meeting with "big business representatives... They were told that there were a few media they are not allowed to give any advertisements to. And we were at the important first place – always first place", Prusenkova (2014, personal communication) said. She gave an example of a drinks' company they had signed a one-year contract with for a huge sum of money. After the meeting with Putin, a representative from the company called the newspaper asking them to withdraw any future advertisements but to keep the money they had pre-paid.

In addition to their exacerbating financial woes, *Novaya Gazeta* could also face closure after receiving two recent government warnings about alleged "extremist" coverage. Russian authorities are entitled to order the closure of a media outlet that has received two extremist warnings within a 12-month period. The newspaper came under increased pressure from the state because of its critical coverage of Russia's role in Ukraine. The first warning served by Russian telecom regulator Roskomnadzor (Federal Service for Supervision in the Sphere of Telecom, Information Technologies, and Mass Communications) was for an article by columnist and *Ekho Moskvy* host Yulia Latynina, titled "If we are not the West, then who are we?" The second one was for a book excerpt allegedly containing an expletive.

Radio Echo of Moscow – Russia's "Last Independent Radio Station" (Nemtsova, 2014)

Radio Echo of Moscow has come under similar pressures from the Russian state. It too was served with a warning by Roskomnadzor in November 2014 regarding a programme about the fighting for Donetsk Airport in which two eyewitnesses offered their accounts of the event. The warning stated: "Information is contained in the given programme which justifies the practice of war crimes" (Venediktov, 2014). The programme was fully transcribed and uploaded on the website. Roskomnadzor requested the transcript to be removed and threatened to close down the website. *Ekho Moskvy* had been labelled as "Russia's last independent radio station" "fighting its last battle" due to its main shareholder's (Gazprom-Media) increasing interference (Nemtsova, 2014). *Ekho* was given as an example of the only "free radio station"/"one of the last endangered species, a dodo that still roams the earth" (Remnick, 2008) that was "allowed to survive as a glorious reminder of the openness and disputatiousness that Russian broadcasting enjoyed at its zenith" (Brenton, 2011, p. 35). What made the radio station "unique" was its editorial independence and its "history of antagonistic relations with Kremlin rulers" (Baysha, 2014).

The radio station was also founded by journalists and had long been renowned for giving voice to critical views about Putin and the Kremlin. Putin himself was once quoted as saying to the Editor-in-Chief Alexei Venediktov: "You pour diarrhoea over me day and night" (*BBC News*, 2012). Baysha (2014) also argued that *Ekho*'s independence "appears paradoxical when one considers that *Echo* is owned by *Gazprom*, an energy conglomerate that is one of the bases of the Kremlin's economic and political power" (p. 2929). The last few years had been especially turbulent. The long-serving CEO (since 1992) Yuri Fedutinov was replaced in 2014 by Ekaterina Pavlova – a former deputy chairman and editor-in-chief at the Russian State Radio Broadcasting Company *Golos Rossii (The Voice of Russia)* who was also married to Alexei Pavlov – deputy chief of the Presidential Press and Information Office. *Ekho*'s editor-in-chief protested against the decision by claiming it was "unjust" and "totally political" (*BBC News*, 2014). Ekaterina Pavlova herself lasted only a few months in the post. She resigned in October 2014 and in December 2014 was replaced by Mikhail Demin – the former public relations director of the Organizing Committee for the Olympic Games in Sochi. Demin was dismissed in March 2015 and replaced by Ekaterina Pavlova, who took over the post in June 2015. This "show" (as the editor-in-chief called it) was only the tip of the iceberg in the long-running attempts to influence the radio station's editorial policy. Most of these attempts have been unsuccessful so far because the editor-in-chief has been holding the fort due to a clever clause in the radio's constitutional charter that stipulates that journalists elect their editor.

Radio Free Europe/Radio Liberty – "The Voice of the Enemy"?

The US Congress-funded *Radio Free Europe/Liberty* has also been under fire from the state, but it has been mainly at the receiving end of administrative and legal measures. *Radio Liberty* and *Radio Free*

Europe played a very important role during the Cold War in a number of countries on the eastern side of the Berlin Wall. *Radio Free Europe* was broadcasting in Eastern Europe and *Radio Liberty* in the Soviet Union. The two corporations merged in 1976. *Radio Free Europe/ Radio Liberty* (n.d.) prides itself on the fact that it played "a significant role in the collapse of communism and the rise of democracies in post-communist Europe". In his book about the history of the radio station, Puddington (2000) claimed that it "was arguably the most influential politically oriented international radio station in history", and its story "stands as one of the most intriguing chapters of the Cold War" (preface). The future of the radio, however, is uncertain after a few new laws/ amendments to existing laws were passed in Russia in the last years. The first one required media companies to cut their non-Russian ownership to 20% by 2016. This prompted CNN to announce that it would stop broadcasting in Russia as a result of this law already it later changed its position. The second one banned "undesirable" foreign or international organisations, defined as any organisation that "presents a threat to the defensive capabilities or security of the state, to the public order, or to the health of the population" (Luhn, 2015). The third one was passed in retaliation to the US demand for *Russia Today* to register under the Foreign Agents Registration Act. It led to the designation of *Radio Svoboda* as a "foreign agent".

Radio Free Europe/Radio Liberty (n.d.) was included in my sample because its mission statement is to provide "uncensored news, responsible discussion and open debate" and to promote democratic values in countries where the media are not free. Moreover, the radio did indeed play a huge role during the Cold War. Despite the clear ideological agenda and the funding from the US Congress, most commentators (e.g. Johnson, 2010; Puddington, 2000; Sosin, 1999) speak highly of the radio's democratising role. In fact, Johnson (2010) even argued that *Radio Free Europe/Radio Liberty* was so effective that lessons could be learnt from its experience about how to promote positive political change in the Muslim world. From an academic perspective, we can also learn important lessons about the Russian media system at present, power relations, and the potential for democratisation. What this book shows is that the contemporary Russian media system cannot really be classified under existing Western frameworks, but nor does it fully resemble the Soviet system. The fact that a broadcaster such as *Radio Free Europe/ Radio Liberty* is allowed to have an office and officially operate from the centre of Moscow is testimony of that. This study reveals how different "the breadth, depth, and mechanisms of control" (Becker, 2014, p. 202) in Putin's Russia are and whether different mechanisms are used for different types of media organisations. By including a unique radio station such as *Radio Free Europe/Radio Liberty*, we would be able to reveal more about these mechanisms but also about Russia's problematic journey to democratisation and the political and media system more than 25 years after the end of communism. The fact that *Radio Free Europe/ Radio Liberty* has not withdrawn from Russia (it withdrew from most other Central and Eastern European countries) and is still investing a considerable amount of money in the country shows the importance it is perceived to be playing in Russian society.

Key Contributions and Overview of Chapters

While events and developments in these three media news outlets have attracted some patchy media coverage in the West, no known academic study provides a detailed account of the history of these outlets or indeed the history of liberal media in Russia, let alone the recent challenges and pressures they face. Most studies about Russian media are based on textual analysis of newspaper articles (e.g. Heinrich & Tanaev, 2009; von Seth, 2012) or discuss the role of state-run television stations (e.g. Burrett, 2011). A few books (e.g. Arutunyan, 2009; Koltsova, 2006; Mickiewicz, 1999; Oates, 2006, 2013; Zassoursky, 2004) offer very useful accounts of the development of Russian national media, but they are either outdated and/or do not fully investigate the plight of liberal media. Similarly, most books about *Radio Free Europe/Radio Liberty* (among others, Johnson, 2010; Puddington, 2000; Sosin, 1999; Urban, 2007) are based on historical and/or insiders' accounts of the two radios and not on their present state. NGOs and Western journalists have been showing a greater interest in these media than the academic community, which may in part be due to the financial and language limitations most colleagues face. By contrast, this book offers a unique ethnographic insight into the daily pressures and challenges Russian liberal journalists face. It fills an important void in the market by providing a rich and insightful account of the history and current state of liberal media in Russia. This is not meant to be an exhaustive outline of the state of all news outlets that claim they are independent. It is an in-depth study of three media outlets, which, when taken together, illustrate the range of challenges Russian liberal journalists face under Putin and the coping strategies they utilise in their attempts to tackle these challenges. The book also makes an important theoretical contribution to the field of Russian media studies.

   This book is divided into nine chapters. Chapter 1 provides a generic historical overview of the development of mass media in Russia after the demise of communism. It looks at the legacy of Gorbachev's perestroika, Boris Yeltsin's largely positive role, and the development of free media prior to and during Putin's terms as president. I draw a distinction between Putin's approach to media interference and development during his first term, and then his second and third terms, as president. Most commentators acknowledge that the grip on Russian media has significantly tightened after Putin's second coming into power.

Chapter 2 sets out the theoretical framework the study is built upon and the potential conceptual contributions it aims to make. It discusses three main topics: (1) conceptualisation of the Russian media system and terms of reference; (2) journalism: culture(s), role conceptions, and relationship with power, culture, and society; and (3) mediatisation of conflict and national identities: conflict reporting and nation-building. First, an attempt towards conceptualisation of the Russian media system is made because it is important to place the empirical findings within the wider context of news media in general and news media in Russian society in particular. Second, the role of the state, culture, and society vis-à-vis journalism and journalistic practices cannot be fully explained unless the relevant journalism culture(s) and journalists' own role perceptions are taken into account as well. Finally, the ethnographic fieldwork took place in the midst of the conflict with Ukraine, so it is also important to consider the media's role in the representation and perception of conflicts as well as more widely in the process of constructing and promoting a shared national identity.

Chapters 3 and 4 are then devoted to *Novaya Gazeta*. Chapter 3 traces the newspaper's history while Chapter 4 focusses on the present. Chapter 3 starts with a brief outline of when and how the newspaper was founded as well as the key developments in the newspaper's early history, including the financial history of the newspaper and the relationship between the Kremlin, the newspaper journalists, and the two main shareholders – Lebedev and Gorbachev. It then moves on to more troublesome developments such as the six murders. Investigative journalist Politkovskaya's murder is by far the most infamous assassination, and I pay particular attention to her case. My account of these events is based on archival research and ethnographic observations. It is interesting to note that eight years after Politkovskaya's murder, her colleagues still kept her desk. I explore the reasons for that in my analysis.

I then present the results of my ethnographic fieldwork in Chapter 4. Given that I was in Moscow in the midst of the conflict with Ukraine, I share my observations on how editorial decisions were made in the reporting of the situation in Ukraine as well as how the senior management team handled the abduction of their correspondent in Ukraine. The abduction of Kanygin was not an isolated case, but it highlighted a common approach the editor and his staff adopt in crisis situations. Physical attacks and abductions are not uncommon for *Novaya Gazeta* journalists. A few of my interviewees recollected their own experiences and described their reactions to them. These anecdotes lead to a much bigger question that this chapter also explores: What role do these journalists see themselves as playing in Russian society? As Prusenkova stated in the quote in the opening paragraph, for most of them, journalism is not a living, it is a way of life, and even though they are not "suicidal", they are prepared to pay a hefty price for their contributions to Russia's democratisation.

Chapters 5 and 6 turn to the history of *Radio Echo of Moscow* and the current pressures and challenges journalists face there. The chapters are organised in a similar way to the previous two chapters – Chapter 5 explores the past while Chapter 6 focusses on the present. Chapter 5 starts with a brief outline of when and how the radio station was founded and the key developments in its early history. Starobin (2012) wrote that *Ekho Moskvy* was "a thorn in Putin's side that he has so far been unable, or unwilling, to extract". This was in large part due to the role the editor-in-chief played, so I explore the key role some veteran figures have played in the history of the radio station. I also explore the role of Gazprom-Media as a majority shareholder and the numerous attempts to tone down any critical coverage of the Kremlin.

In Chapter 6, I then present the findings from my fieldwork in Russia in May 2014 as well as subsequent developments as reported by the media and in follow-up interviews. Although the coverage of Ukraine was a topic on the radio's agenda on air, another topic featured more prominently in my conversations with journalists – the appointment of their new pro-Kremlin CEO and the pressures the editor had experienced as a result of that. A photo Venediktov tweeted during my stay there was indicative of the difficult situation he was placed in – it was a picture of a twisted hand holding a pen in the air. Moreover, the intensified pressure *Ekho Moskvy* has been under since 2012 and in particular in 2014 led to an internal soul-searching (or was it navel-gazing) process that resulted in internal conflicts and the resignation of *Ekho Moskvy's* founder and inaugural Editor-in-Chief Sergey Korzun. These frictions were to a great extent the result of personality clashes, but on a broader level, they revealed some profound disagreements in relation to *Ekho Moskvy's* mission and its role in Russian society. I conclude the chapter by looking at the broader role journalists see themselves as playing in Russian society.

Chapters 7 and 8 trace the historical development and current state of *Radio Free Europe/Radio Liberty*. The first chapter looks back at the founding of the (then) two radio stations and the funding arrangements. It then focusses on the pivotal role the radio station played during the Cold War – not simply as a provider of objective news, but also as a democratising force for the Soviet Union and its Eastern European satellites. In the final section of the chapter, I look at the post–Cold War development of the radio station in Russia. Paradoxically, although the radio now has an official modern office in the centre of Moscow, its headquarters are still in Prague where half of its team are based. Moreover, the radio's influence has significantly diminished, and as a result of that, it has gone through a range of transformations in recent years.

I further look into this "identity crisis" in Chapter 8, which presents the findings from my ethnographic research. The chapter starts by providing a rich empirical account of the daily routine journalists follow, including the virtual editorial meetings with their colleagues in Prague.

The discussions about the coverage of the situation in Ukraine as well as a detailed account of the decision-making process are outlined. Then, in the second part, the focus shifts to some wider issues – the diminishing role the radio plays in Russian society, recent challenges and changes that the editorial staff have experienced such as the ban to broadcast on AM waves, and the new laws that jeopardise the future of *Radio Liberty* in Russia. A recurring theme is journalists' fear that, especially in light of Putin's soaring popularity and the conflict in Ukraine, they are increasingly seen as representing the interests of "the enemy". It is almost paradoxical that at a time when they are allowed to broadcast from the centre of Moscow, they suffer from an identity crisis they have never experienced to the same extent during the "dark ages" of communism when they were operating under cover.

The concluding chapter summarises the common challenges Russia's liberal media face under President Putin and the coping strategies and mechanisms they adopt in their battle to survive and make a difference. It also revisits the theories and concepts discussed in Chapter 2 in light of the empirical findings. The chapter ultimately aims to answer the main research questions of the study. The following is the key concluding question I pose: What is the role of the international community in that situation, and why are news outlets such as *Novaya Gazeta* and *Radio Echo of Moscow* left to fight these battles on their own? After all, the controversial role Russia currently plays in Ukraine, Syria and even the USA reminds us acutely of the need to refocus our attention to a country whose journey to democratisation appears to have come to a halt. This book goes some way towards explaining how the few remaining liberal media in the country still persevere in their efforts to put Russia back on the road to democratisation.

1 The Mass Media in Putin's Russia

"Shame" and "pride": these are the two words that Russian journalist and vice president of the European Federation of Journalists Nadezhda Azhgikhina (2007, p. 1249) used to describe the post-perestroika history of Russian journalism. Azhgikhina (2007) claimed that this recent history was "so accelerated and contradictory that it is hard to believe it all happened in such a short space of time" (p. 1249). She summarised the key trends in one sentence:

> It is widely thought that freedom of speech was the first and perhaps the only real achievement of perestroika, and that it was only later, during the chaos of the "wild market", that that freedom was shaken, and then lost.
>
> (Azhgikhina, 2007, p. 1249)

She also argued that the history of the Russian press was a 300-year history of censorship. Is this indeed the case? What are the key trends in the development of Russian media after the demise of communism?

Chapter 1 tackles this question. It provides a historical account of the development of the mass media in post-Soviet Russia. It is split into three main sections: (1) Mass Media Development after Communism and Before Putin, (2) Mass Media in Putin's Russia, and (3) Russia's Liberal Media. The first section briefly presents the key trends in the development of free media immediately after the fall of the Berlin Wall, including the legacy of "perestroika" and Yeltsin's role. Then, in the second section, the key changes and challenges after President Vladimir Putin came to power are outlined. A distinction is drawn between his first and then his second and third terms as president. Most commentators acknowledge that the grip on Russian media has significantly tightened after Putin's second term as president commenced. Finally, in the third part, the development of liberal media is investigated through a focus on a few common challenges such as propaganda, financial issues, threats and harassment, legal restrictions, and self-censorship.

Mass Media Development after Communism and before Putin

Sheftelevich (2009) claimed that since 1986 the media in Russia had been in a state of transition from "an 'administrative bureaucratic' model toward the market and democratization model" (p. 89). Arutunyan (2009) identified four main stages/models in the development of Russian media in that period. The first stage was the perestroika period of 1986–1990. Mikhail Gorbachev's policy of perestroika and glasnost resulted in the profound transformation of most, if not all, countries on the eastern side of the Berlin Wall. The majority of Russian journalists embraced these new freedoms wholeheartedly (Brenton, 2011), and in many respects, these initial few years were a golden era for Russian journalism. The media in that period were generally free from government and corporate control, and they transformed from an instrument of the propaganda machine into "an instrument of democratization" (Arutunyan, 2009, p. 32). Arutunyan (2009) argued that

> the exuberant press culture that exploded in Russia in the late 1980s and early 1990s, as journalists rushed to unmask the atrocities of the Soviet regime, created an illusion of freedom and independence. But whether or not the press was ever free in Russia, it was hardly ever truly independent.
>
> (p. 29)

In any case, as Becker (2004) argued, President Boris Yeltsin was clearly a supporter of press freedom.

Censorship was officially abolished in Russia when the Mass Media Law was passed in 1991, just two days after the official break-up of the Soviet Union. One "crucial provision" in this new act was that it allowed the establishment of private media (Vartanova, 2012, p. 123). Yeltsin signed the swiftly drafted bill, which was later criticised because despite embodying the essential principles of democracy, the statute's practical provisions for the implementation of these principles were not that well thought out (Sheftelevich, 2009). The law "established freedom of the press and the right of journalists to refuse to write against their own principles and values" (Azhgikhina, 2007, p. 1255). Freedom of speech was also enshrined in Article 29 of the Constitution of the Russian Federation, which was adopted in December 1993. Two main challenges hindered the democratisation process of Russian media in practice: the lack of sustainable new business models that did not include state involvement, and the lack of practical legal provisions that would guarantee the implementation of these core freedoms in practice. These two issues were the defining features of the second and third periods of development of Russian media – from 1990 to 1995 when private independent media were established, and then from 1995 to 1999 – a period marked by the rise of the power of the oligarchs (Arutunyan, 2009).

Economically, the process of privatisation and commercialisation of the media market followed suit. New business models were being developed in the country with a strong reliance on advertising. Vartanova (2012) even claimed that Russia "has become one of the four most rapidly growing advertising markets in the world" (p. 123), with an annual growth of about 30%. The number of media outlets burgeoned with the development of FM radio, tabloids, and private entertainment TV channels (Vartanova, 2012). The structure of the media market was transformed. While the number of newspapers increased from 4,863 in 1991 to 5,758 in 2000, their circulation drastically decreased – from 160.2 million to 108.8 million (Vartanova, 2012). Vartanova (2012) wrote that TV had become "the leading mass medium" since the mid-1990s (p. 125). As she put it, "with the dramatic decline in newspaper circulation has come the replacement of the print media by TV at the top of the media hierarchy" (Vartanova, 2012, p. 125). Lots of media fell in the hands of oligarchs in the early 1990s, who in turn played an active part in the power struggles that plagued Yeltsin's time in office (Brenton, 2011). The state's formal and informal control over TV gradually increased over the next few years (Vartanova, 2012, p. 125). A key problem during Yeltsin's presidency was that media outlets were plunged into "free market conditions in which many were simply not prepared to survive", and as a result they were soon "bought out or taken over by polarized capital" (Arutunyan, 2009, p. 9). The lack of economic infrastructure was a key issue, closely linked to the ownership problems (Arutunyan, 2009). While there were a few media outlets owned by the journalists who worked for them (I discuss this scheme in the empirical chapters), most media organisations were either in private hands or in the grip of the state. Arutunyan (2009) argued that "the Russian media, incidentally, has suffered through the worst that both systems have to offer" (p. 29).

Politically, the situation was very complicated even in the first few years since the passing of the new press law. Sheftelevich (2009) enlisted a range of practical challenges that the law posed, and in her view, one of its most significant flaws was the lack of provisions specifying exactly how power should be allocated among the authorities, most notably the president and parliament. As a result, the passage of the law led to a lengthy battle for control over the media, especially TV (Sheftelevich, 2009). This battle between President Yeltsin and the Russian Duma culminated in the events of the autumn of 1993 when Yeltsin suspended Parliament and forced the mass media to submit their publications for pre-publication approval. As a result of the conflict, 62 journalists and TV staff lost their lives during the bloody battle at the Russian state TV channel *Ostankino*. Nearly a dozen Moscow newspapers were also closed down at the time (Sheftelevich, 2009).

The power for control and the "information wars" during the 1990s election campaigns were the result of Yeltsin's "polycentric" regime and the state's attempts to "restructure its relationship with the media" (Vartanova, 2012, p. 132). The power centres included not just the presidency and the State Duma, but also oligarchs, regional state organisations, and business elites (Vartanova, 2012). Media were pulled in different directions, and some of the informal deals drawn in the process were rather shoddy. Initially, Yeltsin was "tolerant of pluralism on Russian television", but pluralism "did not take the form of objectivity or balance within a single news report, program or even channel. Rather, the national channels rapidly devolved into champions for their sponsors" (Oates, 2006, p. 14). As Brenton (2011) argued, "black propaganda, much of it paid for, became regular fare even in Russia's most respected newspapers" (p. 34).

The 1993 crisis, however, put an end to the plurality period (Oates, 2006). State involvement in the media was often indirect via economic pressures and/or incentives. Vartanova (2012) labelled the 1990s as "the decade of intensive integration of the Russian state and business" – a period in which "political sponsorship and manipulative use of newspapers" was common, because the state bureaucracy was "a major agent of economic life" (p. 126). The result was "'the creation of a hybrid (hyper) capitalism'..., having a clear statist color" (Vartanova, 2012, p. 126). A key aspect of this process was "the rise of the 'media-industrial complex' comprised of several influential clans and driven by new integrated political and business elites backed by the state" (Vartanova, 2012, pp. 126–127). What this meant in practice was that for lots of big media companies, political interests were more important than profit-making (Vartanova, 2012).

A powerful example of the extent to which power wars dominated the 1990s was the role two oligarchs – Vladimir Gusinsky and Boris Berezovsky – played at the time. Gusinsky founded the first private TV channel in Russia – *NTV* – and a number of other media outlets, while Berezovsky controlled *Channel One* – the leading TV channel. Brenton (2011) claimed that the two oligarchs drew a deal with Yeltsin in which they offered their support during the presidential elections in exchange for "lucrative State assets thereafter" (p. 34). He argued that their role was so powerful that they "probably won" the election for Yeltsin. As a whole, Yeltsin's era was characterised by constant power battles in which Russian oligarchs "used their media assets – which included leading newspaper and television stations – as their primary weapons in vicious muckraking campaigns against each other and against Yeltsin's ailing government" (Arutunyan, 2009, p. 9). The most worrying consequence was the dwindling belief among journalists and the public that "the media was finally free in Russia and could go on to forge a meaningful and lasting fourth estate" (Arutunyan, 2009, p. 10). As a result, the "'golden age' of post-perestroika media freedom" ended in 1994–1995 (Arutunyan, 2009).

The economic and political pressures were not the only problems journalists faced in the 1990s. Brenton (2011) argued that murders of journalists were also common in that period, and at least 30 journalists were killed because of their job. As a whole, journalists faced a range of security issues, including "an abundance of threats ... not necessarily because of any direct government clampdown, but due to issues of corruption and crime" (Arutunyan, 2009, p. 10). Corruption was widespread in Russian society at all levels, and the judicial system was so weak that journalists did not have proper protection. Moreover, both pre- and during Putin's regime, the legal system has been "habitually used to limit rather than protect both the ability of journalists to disseminate information and the rights of citizens to receive it" (Oates, 2006, p. 24).

Not all was doom and gloom in that first era of post-Soviet journalism. Becker (2004) wrote that "the press under Gorbachev and Yeltsin made substantial gains compared with the pre-glasnost era" (p. 148). In his view, at that time there was pluralism, examples of investigative journalism and critical reporting of the government. McNair (2000) even claimed that prior to Putin's coming into power, Russia had "a real public sphere through which ordinary people can learn about and participate in political debate" (p. 81). Vartanova (2012) argued that this era also brought about new professional values and practices for journalists, driven by the core belief in freedom of speech. Investigative journalism gained momentum. Arutunyan (2009) wrote that in the period between 1990 and 1995, "the Russian media briefly became the fourth estate, in the sense that as a free institution it had the power to mould politics and society, arguably reflecting the will of the people" (p. 43). The new legal framework allowed editorial staff to gain ownership of their publications, but this process was accompanied by a range of teething problems, most notably the development of new business models and the power struggles of the 1990s.

The Mass Media in Putin's Russia

Putin's inauguration as president in 2000 led to a number of significant changes for Russian media and marked the beginning of the fourth period in the development of contemporary Russian media – "the 'return to a government' model" (Arutunyan, 2009, p. 33), or what Koltsova (2006) labelled "the period of State consolidation" (p. 40). A key principle for Putin and his administration was the belief that the state was "a core of national identity" (Vartanova, 2012, p. 127), and the mass media had a major role to play in that process. A much heavier emphasis was placed on TV, and both state funding (formal and informal) and tightened control were streamlined in the direction of TV. TV played a key role in Putin's rising to power, and Putin quickly seized control over it because he clearly acknowledged the medium's potential (Mickiewicz, 2008; Pomerantsev, 2014). TV was used as a medium for political propaganda, but the nation-building efforts were also accompanied by a process of de-politicisation of Russian journalism and a heavier emphasis on entertainment (Vartanova, 2012). Pomerantsev (2014) summed up the Kremlin's approach:

> The new Kremlin won't make the same mistake the old Soviet Union did: it will never let TV become dull. The task is to synthesize Soviet control with Western entertainment. Twenty-first century Ostankino mixes show business and propaganda, ratings with authoritarianism. And at the center of the great show is the President himself, created from a no one, a gray fuzz via the power of television, so that he morphs as rapidly as a performance artist among his roles of soldier, lover, bare-chested hunter, businessman, spy, tsar, superman. 'The news is the incense by which we bless Putin's actions, make him the President,' TV producers and political technologists liked to say.
>
> (p. 6)

As Vartanova (2012) explained, some researchers (e.g. Butterfield & Levintova, 2011) labelled this era as the period of (re-)etatization, including in relation to media ownership. Estimations (Fossato, 2003, as quoted in Vartanova, 2012) showed that 70% of electronic media, 80% of the regional press, and 20% of the national press fell into state hands in the early 2000s. Putin's relationship with the media was best summarised by him during a press conference in the Kremlin in 2004. "There is a phrase in a famous Italian film – 'a real man should always try, while a real woman should always resist'" (Arutunyan, 2009, pp. 5–6). As Arutunyan (2009) pointed out, "Putin did not indicate which role the press should take", but the widespread interpretation was that "the government, as a man should try, while the press, as a woman, should resist" (p. 6). She even claimed that Putin's media policy was "a form of revenge" (Arutunyan, 2009, p. 49). The overall result, however, was that "television, viewed as a societal institution that could spread the ideas of democracy and civil society in the new Russian state, has become once again a very effective tool for repression and authoritarianism" (Oates, 2006, p. 20).

One of the first battles Putin fought was against "the threat of oligarchic capital" (Brenton, 2011, p. 34). Brenton (2011) argued that he put an end to the "liberal moment", and "the first target was broadcast media" (p. 34). Both Berezovsky and Gusinsky were forced into exile, and their TV stations were appropriated by the state/state-controlled companies, thus "bringing all three national TV networks under State control" (Brenton, 2011, p. 35). Becker (2004) claimed that the attack on Gusinsky's Media-Most empire "reeked of revenge for the editorial views expressed by Media-Most entities", and "few would argue that the government would have taken such an uncompromising approach had Media-Most supported Putin in the 2000 presidential elections and taken a less critical view of Russian military actions in Chechnya" (p. 151). The fate of other critical media outlets was similar. Becker (2004) also wrote that there were instances of journalists sent to psychiatric institutions, detained, or arrested for their critical stance of the government.

Lipman and McFaul (2001) pointed out that "the Kremlin's successful campaign to eliminate critical content from the Media Most media outlets without actually eliminating the media outlets themselves represents the latest and perhaps most consequential phase of consolidating managed democracy in Russia" (p. 116). Under this system, all essential institutions of democracy continued to exist, but they were so stripped of their actual powers that their proper functioning was severely restricted. Lipman (2014) argued that during "Putin's leadership the concentration of media properties significantly exceeded that of Gusinsky's or Berezovsky's holdings in the 1990s", but the main difference was that the new "media magnates ... are fully loyal to Putin" (p. 183). Becker (2004) also acknowledged that similar to Eastern Europe, there was an "interpenetration of politics and economics" as well (p. 152). However, in Russia, "the state clearly rests on top of the food chain" also because all businesses were created in "illegal circumstances" (Becker, 2004, p. 152).

A new ministry was created – the Ministry of Press, Broadcasting and Mass Communication – and a range of administrative measures were used to exert pressure on the few remaining private broadcasters. Vartanova (2012) described a number of state pressures: legal sanctions, libel lawsuits, political appointments of key media executives, a denial of access to information, including a ban on press conference attendance, acquisition of regional media that were then used by local authorities, and informal barter and exchange arrangements.

Nonetheless, despite the fact that "all TV stations now carefully adhere to the official line, and hear very quickly from the Kremlin if they wander off message, particularly at election times", Brenton (2011) argued that "this does not mean that broadcast politics has the dreary consistency it had under Communism" (p. 35). He gave *Ekho Moskvy* as an example of "a free radio station", which was "allowed to survive as a glorious reminder of the openness and disputatiousness that Russian broadcasting enjoyed at its zenith" (Brenton, 2011, p. 35). The challenges *Ekho Moskvy* experiences and the role it plays in Russian society are explored in subsequent chapters. Brenton (2011) also said that print media had considerably more latitude and freedom than they were given credit for in the West, and there were numerous examples of investigative reports, criticism of the authorities, and the use of sarcasm.

Part of the reason for this lower degree of control of print media as opposed to broadcast media was the fact that the press was seen "as being less important" (Brenton, 2011, p. 35). However, even if there was no direct censorship, "Kremlin 'guidance' is abundantly available to editors" (Brenton, 2011, p. 35). A few major companies such as the state-owned Gazprom-Media now control the majority of print publications in the country. As Brenton (2011) rightly pointed out, "these companies are heavily dependent on their links with the Kremlin for their day-to-day activities, and will be careful that their journalistic protégés do not endanger those links" (p. 36).

As a result, one problem that plagues journalists from all types of media is the widespread self-censorship. Oates (2013) argued that "self-censorship is endemic in the journalism industry", and "employees of all media outlets are well aware of the limits of what can be said on air or in print" (p. 14). She compared the situation with Soviet times: "the action of a censor was rarely needed as Soviet reporters understood the party line and the way all stories should be formulated from their first day on the job" (Oates, 2013, p. 14). Arutunyan (2009) wrote that even the way in which journalists reprinted Putin's infamous remark about his relationship with the media "shows the extent to which journalists have internalized their subordinate role" (p. 6). Azhgikhina (2007) enlisted a number of changes that have led to this development: "the strength-ening of the government's 'vertical line of power'", the battle against terrorism, the state's attack on civil freedoms, and the interests of busi-ness, "the virtual liquidation of independent television", the lack of a proper system of self-regulation, and the lack of respect for journalists as professionals, including by high-profile politicians such as the president (pp. 1253–1259).

Arutunyan (2009) traced the origins of self-censorship further back in time. She argued that in their 300-year history, Russian media had been "with few exceptions, directly dependent on the state in terms of funds, means of production and even editorial initiative" (p. 6). Russian journalism had "emerged from its start in 1702 as a top-down, government-sponsored endeavour", and Gorbachev's glasnost policy was successful because it was initiated and supported by Gorbachev himself (Arutunyan, 2009, p. 6). In spite of the range of new freedoms that media in Russia enjoyed during and after Gorbachev's term in power, they inevitably "inherited the same cultural traditions and the same dependence on the state that governed the preceding 300 years of journalism" (Arutunyan, 2009, p. 7). While the state did not directly censor publications, "rather, through its ownership of leading media out-lets and television, it indirectly influences coverage" (Arutunyan, 2009, p. 33). There were taboo topics for journalists, and some media even had "'curators' within the presidential administration who can consult on shaping editorial policy" (Arutunyan, 2009, p. 33). Another big prob-lem for Russian journalists was "the crisis of identification", "purpose and credibility", borne out of the century-long tradition of subservient journalism and the power struggles that have prevented journalists from becoming "independent" (Arutunyan, 2009, p. 77).

As a whole, commentators agreed that the current state of Russian journalism was dire. Azhgikhina (2007) talked of "an aggressive wave of propaganda" (p. 1257), and in her view, the state had "a basic monopoly on the news" (p. 1253). The situation was particularly precarious in the regions where "direct censorship and violations of the Law on Media and the rights of journalists have become common practice" (Azhgikhina, 2007). Non-government organisations recorded dozens of cases each week (Azhgikhina, 2007). Arutunyan (2009) also wrote that "the current media playing field is still a far cry from the Soviet-style control model that some Western observers speak of" (p. 33).

The lack of respect for journalists as professionals was borne out of a combination of factors – public smearing campaigns orchestrated by the political elite and journalists' own controversial behaviour. Azhgikhina (2007) shared an anecdote, which was quite telling:

> Never before have journalists been blamed so much for corruption, bribe-taking, dishonesty, and even collaboration with enemy intelligence services. Nor have they been subjected before to the ridicule and grotesque representation that was evident at Putin's press conference on 1 February 2007. During that event women flirted with the president, openly admiring him and one journalist from the provinces prefaced her question with the bizarre address "Incomparable Mister President!". Many viewers and professionals saw this episode, with its fawning and disregard for serious issues, as symbolic of the country's disturbing condition. Journalists inviting Putin to pay them a visit, stupid questions, frivolous words, sensationalism, and a lack of interest in people's genuine needs and concerns – these were all signs that this was a show prepared and designed in advance by political PR producers.
>
> (p. 1260)

Vartanova (2012) also claimed that journalism became "one of the most publicly criticised professions" because it "lost the moral legitimacy gained in the first years of perestroika" (p. 137). The most apparent contradiction was that while journalists formally proclaimed "the ideals of press freedom", they were informally serving the interests of their owners or sponsors (Vartanova, 2012, p. 137). A key dilemma for Russian journalists has been "whether their role is to serve society or the state" (Butterfield & Levintova, 2011).

Another important aspect is the extent to which journalists themselves have been willing to adopt Western values of objectivity and impartiality. Horbyk (2015) argued that "despite the multifaceted changes of the last decades, even the young generations of journalists inherited the traditional concept of journalism 'as a derivative of power' ... they typically reject the ideas of neutrality and objectivity" (p. 506). Arutunyan

(2009) explained that the structuring of hard news stories according to Western conventions – namely, starting with the five Ws – was not familiar to the majority of Russian journalists. "Hence, the initial concept of objectivity was initially understood to mean printing what had hitherto been suppressed or made taboo" (Arutunyan, 2009, p. 27). This, in turn, led to increased sensationalism. Oates (2013) pointed out that

> all segments of Russian society, from politicians to the public to the journalists themselves, perceive the mass media as a political player rather than as a watchdog that can provide a check on political power for the interest of citizens.
>
> (p. 12)

Rather than attempting to serve the public interest, journalists were used as "puppets", serving the interests of their "masters" (Oates, 2006, p. 6 and p. 192) Arutunyan (2009) wrote that the first newspaper that tried to move away from the tradition of opinionated, literary journalism to a stricter separation between facts and opinion was *Kommersant,* which was launched in 1987. She differentiated between TV, on the one hand, and radio, the press, and Internet, on the other. Quoting Zassoursky, Arutunyan (2009) argued that Russian TV "comprises ... the worst of the Soviet tradition and the worst of the western tradition" (p. 131).

Russia's Liberal Media

Dmitry Medvedev's presidency brought about a marked improvement in press freedom in the country. Medvedev publicly proclaimed his liberal views and support for freedom of expression. Lipman (2014) argued that his message was received by Russian citizens who "began to use freedom of expression more avidly, the media environment grew more vibrant, and a modicum of political liberty emerged even on TV ... In short, the 'ghetto' life grew more intense" (p. 183). Medvedev also embraced the Internet and new technologies to a much greater extent than Putin ever did. *TV Rain (Dozhd)* – the only remaining critical TV station – was launched in 2010, and its history best demonstrates some of the notable differences between Medvedev's and Putin's treatment of liberal media. The channel was founded by journalist Natalia Sindeeva and her businessman husband. *TV Rain* gained prominence with its critical coverage of political topics. It covered the 2011 protests, and it even displayed the symbol of the protests – a white ribbon – next to its logo. *RIA Novosti* claimed that *TV Rain* was the first media organisation Medvedev started to follow on Twitter, but he allegedly stopped following them during the protests. The TV station was broadcast by cable and satellite services in Russia. As Lipman (2014) pointed out, "as soon as Putin returned to the Kremlin, the Medvedev-era flirtations with liberty vanished" (p. 184).

TV Rain's fate changed overnight in January 2014, shortly after the conflict in Ukraine started. *TV Rain* launched a survey about the siege of Leningrad, asking whether the city should have surrendered to the Nazis to avoid loss of life. The reaction was unprecedented: within a month, all cable and satellite services stopped broadcasting *TV Rain*, and it lost 90% of its audience (Dzyadko, 2014). The channel also lost its premises and had to operate out of an apartment in Moscow. Moreover, the Russian Parliament passed a law banning advertising on cable channels, "believed to be aimed at *TV Rain*" (Walker, 2015). Subsequently, its influence dwindled substantially. As of April 2017, it broadcast only online, and it was subscription-based. *TV Rain* was not included in my sample because at the time of fieldwork, journalists who worked for the TV channel claimed that it was "on the edge of extinction" (Dzyadko, 2014). The channel's Deputy Editor Masha Makeeva explained the logic behind the Kremlin's approach: "The authorities didn't want to shut us down, as that would have looked bad. They wanted to create impossible conditions for us so we had to shut down ourselves" (Walker, 2015).

The experience of *TV Rain* is not unique. Other liberal media have been subjected to similar pressures. The situation has especially deteriorated during Putin's second, and then even more so during his third, term as president. Horbyk (2015) claimed that "the policy of media control and screw-tightening has intensified since 2012, during Putin's third term in office" (p. 506). A commonly used strategy of media "taming" was via the manipulation of "advertisement revenues" and "control through ownership" (Horbyk, 2015, p. 506; also Lipman, 2014). Examples of "reshuffles" of top executives at liberally minded media included changes at *RIA Novosti*, *Kommersant vlast*, *Bolshoi gorod*, *Ekho Moskvy*, *TV Rain*, and *Lenta.ru* (Horbyk, 2015). Horbyk (2015) also argued that the media market was divided between two groups – the state-owned Gazprom-Media and the National Media Group "controlled by Putin's personal friends" (p. 506).

Both Horbyk (2015) and Lipman (2014) argued that the situation had significantly deteriorated since the start of the conflict in/with Ukraine. The main TV networks had been actively used by the propaganda machine and "dissenting voices were condemned as natsional predateli ('traitors of the people')" (Lipman, 2014, p. 180). A Ukrainian website (StopFake.org) even collated and published evidence about fake stories disseminated by Russian media, including some very extreme ones such as a broadcast by *Channel One* about a boy allegedly crucified by Ukrainian soldiers (Lipman, 2014). Putin and the Kremlin's concerted efforts in relation to Ukraine are best understood in the context of his nation-building/promotion attempts. Hutchings and Rulyova (2009) argued that Putin's "efforts to install a latter-day version of imperial pride in Russian military achievements" were "at the centre of a national identity project amount to a form of remote control" (p. 3). These efforts

were especially visible during my visit to Moscow when 9th May celebrations were under way, with red flags waving from most buildings in
central Moscow. The journalists I spoke to said that Putin has placed
a much greater emphasis on these celebrations in recent years. Liberal
media often hindered this process, which made them a frequent target
for the authorities. Although the state of Russian journalism was dis-
mal, Arutunyan (2009) saw hope for the future in radio and the Internet, which "hold immeasurable potential that can be combined with a
uniquely Russian penchant for dialogue, criticism and ideology to forge
lasting and powerful media institutions that can prove themselves independent both from the government and from politicised capital" (p. 163).

While Azhgikhina (2007) acknowledged that Russia's "independent
press" was born during perestroika, she traced the origins of liberal media
back to the Soviet era. Azhgikhina (2007) claimed that Soviet journalism
"was not all that bad", and some of its "best traditions" were "service to
the reader, belief in human beings and moral priorities" (p. 1250). She
argued that there were three journalistic cultures at the time: (1) "Official
line" journalism, practised by newspapers such as *Pravda*, (2) "Samizdat"
journalism, practised by oppositional/underground/dissident journalists
in publications such as *A Chronicle of Current Affairs*, and (3) the liberal
press in between these two cultures, practised by *Literaturnaya Gazeta*,
Yunost, *Sovetskaya Rossiya*, and *Komsomolskaia pravda*. "These papers
published the best minds of the era, and educated their readers in civic
awareness, appealing for a better life and awakening a yearning for justice and truth that filtered through the Aesopian language to which the
Soviet eye was accustomed", thus formulating "latently" "all the main
tenets and ideology of perestroika" (Azhgikhina, 2007, p. 1250).

One key aspect of Soviet journalism was journalists' strong connection with their readers (Azhgikhina, 2007).

> People wrote to them about everything. Trusting neither the courts
> nor Soviet organisations, they often appealed to newspapers as a
> last resort for help in establishing the truth. And the newspapers
> were often able to help – to get people their jobs back, to have them
> released from jail, or to reestablish justice in situations where peo-
> ple had suffered injustice. Moreover, a resolution of the Central
> Committee required that there should be a response by the author-
> ities to issues raised in the press, and this ensured the effectiveness
> of these interventions.
>
> (Azhgikhina, 2007, p. 1250)

The growth of independent media was contingent upon the development
of the media market and journalists' own engagement (Azhgikhina, 2007).
However, one of the defining features of contemporary Russian journalism was the lack of solidarity and the low pay journalists received

(Azhgikhina, 2007). A lot of journalists received both an official salary ("white salary") and an unofficial "editor's monthly subsidy", which was yet another way to control them (Azhgikhina, 2007, p. 1258). Journalists also engaged in ethically questionable practices such as black PR and writing paid-for articles, including opinion pieces (Urban, 2007). Moreover, the financial difficulties most publications faced prevented them from investing in investigations or indeed writing critical stories that might upset their sponsors, advertisers, or the political class (Oates, 2006).

Both Arutunyan (2009) and Brenton (2011) pointed out that the Internet had provided a platform for liberal media, but their assessment of the role of the Internet differed. Arutunyan (2009) acknowledged "the liveliness of its often politicised blogosphere", but she argued that a very small proportion of the population had Internet access or used the Internet as a source of political information. She even labelled the Internet "as the most paradoxical media phenomenon in Russia", which in her view was a symptom of

> a perennial problem not just in Russian media but in its politics and civil society – when we do speak of any significant impact or transformation, it more often than not affects the elite exclusively, and only to a small extent the rest of the population.
>
> (Arutunyan, 2009, p. 25)

Oates's (2013) study of the Russian Internet showed that while the Internet had become an important source of political information, the

> Russian government still holds an asymmetrically large amount of power over bloggers, able to deploy controls ranging from informal pressure ... to lawsuits, to even arrest and imprisonment in order to control bloggers who violate the accepted norms of coverage in Russia.
>
> (p. 186)

She found as "most chilling" the way in which prominent bloggers such as opposition leader Alexei Navalny had been persecuted by the state. Navalny had been sued on a number of occasions on libel and embezzlement charges. Navalny was a vocal critic of Putin and his regime. The European Court of Human Rights ruled that Navalny was denied the opportunity to have a fair trial in his embezzlement case and his conviction was "prejudicial" (Agence France-Presse, 2016). The Russian approach to controlling the Internet was what Oates (2013) labelled as "third-generation internet control" – a term coined by Deibert and Rohozinski (2010). This was a "highly sophisticated, multidimensional approach", which involved using the Internet for surveillance purposes and black PR campaigns (Oates, 2013, p. 195). Horbyk (2015) mentioned the good reporting of two websites – slon.ru and colta.ru, which had not only covered the Ukrainian conflict extensively but they had also "exposed the manipulations of mainstream media" (p. 509).

The claim that mainly the elites benefitted from the relative freedom of the Russian Internet (Arutunyan, 2009) was indicative of a wider trend. Liberal media are generally "held in high regard by the country's intelligentsia" but have "little influence over the voting masses" (Bidder, 2012). Lipman (2014) argued that liberal media were small-audience, "'niche' outlets for a critically minded and politically concerned minority" (pp. 181–182). Arutunyan (2009) wrote that "the most popular outlets are not the most influential, while the most influential frequently have a much smaller audience" (p. 22). Tolerating a small number of liberal media targeted at a minority of the population appeared to be a deliberate strategy (among others, Baysha, 2014; Lipman, 2014; Urban, 2007). Scott Shane (2012) from *The New York Times* argued that "Putin devised a new model of media management ... providing a steam valve to the intelligentsia and a display of tolerance to foreign critics". Urban (2007) said that "suppression by the Kremlin of the small-circulation alternative print media would be not only futile in terms of stamping out oppositionist views but also not worth the negative impact such a move would have on international public opinion" (p. 95). Moreover, Kremlin policy included

> constraints on media freedom through the redistribution of media assets, not through the repression of journalists; and allowing a reasonable degree of freedom of expression in smaller-audience media, yet turning it politically irrelevant through tight controls on the political realm.
>
> (Lipman, 2014, p. 182)

Lipman (2014) also wrote that the non-government media of the mid-2000s "were often described as 'ghettos' or 'islands.' And they were, for the most part, preaching to the converted. The 'converted' – roughly speaking, the liberal constituency – may have enjoyed listening to the critical voices, but, just like the rest of their compatriots, they acquiesced to controlled politics and to being denied political participation" (p. 182). Lipman (2010) argued that in today's Russia, "there is no shortage of alternative sources, but rather a shortage of demand" (p. 160).

The experience of the three liberal media this book focusses on is very similar. In spite of the fact that *Ekho Moskvy* was "a flagship of independent quality journalism" (Baysha, 2014, p. 2929), the influential role it played was not matched up by popularity in terms of audience size (Arutunyan, 2009). Remnick (2008) wrote that *Ekho Moskvy* "is one of the last of an endangered species, a dodo that still roams the earth". Arutunyan (2009) pointed out that it was "a unique information radio station, in some sense a beacon that helped launch independent broadcasting in Russia", whose "significance ... lies in its legacy, credibility and pervasiveness as an oft-quoted source of news" (p. 22). Similarly, as already indicated, although allowed to exist, a newspaper such as *Novaya Gazeta* was plagued by economic problems – again typical for most liberal media without foreign funding.

The publishers of liberal media had "limited ability to attract print advertisement revenue" (Urban, 2007, p. 98). Urban (2007) explained that the cost of subscription for *Novaya Gazeta* readers was very high, but they could not really rely on its availability in kiosks either. The prospect of losing advertising revenue had been constantly used as a deterrent both for big and small media. As Lipman (2014) explained, "profitable media outlets can be easily stripped of advertising revenues – no firm would want to displease the Kremlin by placing its ads in a publication deemed unwelcome by the powers that be" (p. 186). She gave one example – *The New Times* magazine, which had lost all its advertisers because of its "uncompromising and daring" articles (Lipman, 2014, p. 186). Another commonly used method of indirect interference was the reshuffling of owners, CEOs, and in some cases even editors. Lipman (2014) enlisted numerous examples of this type of interference, including gazeta.ru, lenta.ru, *Kommersant FM, Ekho Moskvy, Bolshoi Gorod*, etc. A new model tried out by some online bloggers was crowdfunding. The blogs of journalists Oleg Kashin and Arkadiy Babchenko were funded by readers' donations and personal savings (Lipman, 2014). In Lipman's (2014) view, "this model retains the most possible independence and the most critical views in Russia" (p. 509). Babchenko urged his readers to fund him with the slogan "Journalism without intermediaries" ("Журналистика без посредников").

Part of the reason why the majority of Russians have little or no interest in consuming pro-Western liberal media is because of a radical shift in public opinion sentiments towards the West. From a largely pro-Western orientation in the late 1980s, today "Russians' attitude toward the West is almost uniformly negative across all economic and social strata" (Åslund & Kuchins, 2009, p. 100). Moreover, Putin's popularity has been soaring especially since the start of the Ukrainian conflict. Another reason is Russians' acknowledgement that even if corruption and wrongdoing are exposed by investigative journalists, little, if anything, is likely to change as a result of that (Urban, 2007). As Urban (2007) pointed out, "ordinary Russians, even those who are politically attuned, are understandably not eager to follow press debates that remain without perceptible impact on the powers that be" (p. 93).

Another big issue that journalists from liberal media face is the lack of safety and the high number of attacks and murders. Russia is indisputably one of the most dangerous countries for journalists in the world (Azhgikhina, 2007; CPJ, 2017; Mickiewicz, 2008). As Mickiewicz (2008) pointed out, "the killing fields of Chechnya have taken many lives. Death threats and murders of Russian journalists have served as warnings to desist, or to drop their investigative reporting" (p. 31). The Committee to Protect Journalists' (CPJ) Global Impunity Index (Witchel, 2017) placed Russia in the top 10 list of countries "where journalists are murdered and their killers go free". The Index covered murders that took place between 1 September 2007 and 31 August 2017. In a previous report, the CPJ (Witchel, 2015) argued that Russia had "a bleak record of impunity", which made it "the worst country in Europe and the Central Asia region at prosecuting journalists' killers". They claimed that in nearly 90% of murders of journalists in Russia, no one was convicted, which "stands in stark contrast to a statement by Investigative Committee Chief Aleksandr Bastrykin in 2014 that 90 % of all homicides in Russia are solved" (Witchel, 2015). The CPJ also said that even in cases when the killers had been prosecuted and convicted such as the high-profile murder case of investigative journalist Anna Politkovskaya, it did not become clear who actually ordered these murders.

In total, 56 journalists were killed in Russia from 1992 to 2017, which placed Russia seventh on the list of "20 deadliest countries" (CPJ, 2017). Thirty journalists lost their lives in the 1990s, 22 from 2000 to 2010, and six from 2011 to 2017. Two murders were confirmed in Russia in 2017 (CPJ, 2017). In 21% of the cases, the suspected source of fire was government officials, in 36% military officials, in 17% criminal groups, and in 8.6% political groups. Thirty per cent lost their lives in Moscow. Arutunyan (2009) objected to two main misconceptions: (1) Russia was much safer for journalists before Putin came to power, and (2) the government was directly responsible for these murders. She argued that "in cases where it is fairly obvious that a journalist is attacked over what he wrote, what stands out is not the government's involvement, but its inaction" (Arutunyan, 2009, p. 70). Arutunyan (2009) made a very arguable claim, however, namely, that "the ambiguities of the circumstances under which so many journalists are killed make it difficult to view their deaths as an outright attack on free speech" (p. 71). Attacks against journalists directly related to their work are an outright attack on free speech and should not be excused or tolerated.

While the number of murdered journalists has decreased, liberal media faced an increasing number of legal restrictions and prosecutions under Putin. As Price (1995) pointed out, "looking at the development of mass media law in post-Soviet Russia is like examining the wrists of a recently freed prisoner where the marks of the chains are still present" (p. 795). Oates (2013) mentioned some of the constrictions faced by journalists in relation to state secrets and anti-terrorism legislation as well as the regulator Roskomnadzor's very pro-active role in issuing warnings and threating media organisations with closure if they did not tone down their coverage, especially of the conflict in Ukraine. Security and anti-terrorism laws have also been used to curtail journalistic freedom. Brenton (2011) gave the two anti-terrorism laws passed by the Russian Duma in 2006 as examples. They banned "extremist" materials, but the term "extremism" was so vaguely defined that it left too much scope for potentially criminalising "legitimate journalism" (Brenton, 2011, p. 36). For example, the definition of extremism included "public slander directed towards officials fulfilling state duties of the Russian Federation" (Arutunyan, 2009, p. 74).

The numerous prosecutions that took place as a result of this restrictive legislation could be defined as "government-sanctioned posterior censorship" (Arutunyan, 2009, p. 74). The passing of a few new bills that attempted to put an end to the Russian operations of some Western media and human rights' charities was yet another example of Putin's strategy of "managed democracy" (Lipman & McFaul, 2001). The 2011 protests against the elections prompted a revival of repressive measures, including legislation against activists, protesters, and critical journalists (Lipman, 2014). Lipman (2014) succinctly summed up the ideological approach adopted:

> The government's rhetoric increasingly focused on issues such as faith, sex, school curricula, art and culture and condemned "nontraditional" practices. The goal of the new policy was to consolidate the conservative majority and pit it against the modernized minorities. What began as a tactical move aimed at discrediting and neutralizing the excessively modernized trouble-makers has gradually evolved as a new "ideological choice": Russian traditions and morality vs. the decadent and immoral West and its "fifth column" within Russia that included liberals, gays, activists, and protesters. Any criticism of conservative laws and policies came to be seen as unpatriotic and undermining Russia's traditional values.
>
> (p. 185)

Putin's supporters often go out of their way in their attempts to please the president. The Glasnost Defence Foundation records and publishes an online database with all cases of persecutions and attacks against journalists – arrests, censorship, threats, blocking of websites, attacks, criminal investigations, and so forth. For September 2016 alone, there were 25 such cases. Not all violations of press freedom were directly orchestrated by the Kremlin. Arutunyan (2009) argued that:

> Very often, the consequences of a corrupt judicial system are confused with deliberate, centralized attempts to tamp down the press. Journalists do go to jail in Russia, but not as a direct result of the central government's efforts to silence them. Rather, business interests use the leverage with corrupt law enforcement and court officials to literally frame inconvenient reporters, or convict them on fabricated claims.
>
> (p. 76)

To sum up, it is indisputable that media freedom has deteriorated in Putin's Russia, and a lot of the positive developments observed in the perestroika years and in the 1990s have been reversed. Moreover, Putin has clearly tightened his grip on the media, especially since he commenced his second term as president and even more so during his third term. As Becker (2014) put it, there is no doubt that a bad situation is worsening ... The current situation is the most challenging since the Soviet period, with a corrosive market, meddling owners, and an intrusive state that both imposes tremendous punitive actions on journalists and owners, and actively seeks to depoliticize media and the citizenry.

(pp. 205–206)

While the range of measures used against freedom of expression have deterred some journalists, there are still a number of publications that remain undeterred and do an excellent job of holding the powerful into account, including in relation to the conflict in Ukraine.

2 Conceptualising Russian Media and Journalism

A Theoretical Framework

This chapter sets out the theoretical framework and the key conceptual contributions of the study. The theoretical framework is organised around three key topics: (1) Media Systems and Terms of Reference; (2) Journalism: Culture(s), Role conceptions, and Relationship with Power, Culture, and Society; and (3) Mediatisation of Conflict and National Identities: Conflict Reporting and Nation-Building. First, an attempt towards conceptualisation of the Russian media system is made because it is important to place the empirical findings within the wider context of news media in general and news media in Russian society in particular. To this end, a few existing seminal studies on the topic are briefly reviewed (among others, Becker, 2014; Koltsova, 2006; Mickiewicz, 1999, 2008; Oates, 2006, 2013; Rollberg, 2014). As Rollberg (2014) argued, it had been very hard, "if not impossible", for researchers "to arrive at a lasting analytical consensus about the post-Soviet media sphere" because "media in post-Soviet societies are a moving target, influenced by techno- logical, geopolitical, and cultural developments" (p. 175). This difficulty is in large part due to the fact that as Koltsova (2006) claimed, lots of re- searchers used Western concepts, terms, and theories in their attempts to explain the situation in Russia. Another common flaw in Western-centric studies was the assumption that "the authoritarianism-democracy axis" was the only one "along which societies can change" (Koltsova, 2006, p. 5). Both Koltsova (2006) and Oates (2013) questioned the extent to which Russian society and media were ever on a linear journey towards democratisation. Similarly, Rollberg (2014) demonstrated that Siebert, Peterson, and Schramm's (1956) four theories of the press could not fully operationalise the situation in Russia because post-Soviet Russian media did not fit into any of the four models. This suggested that developments in Russian media and society should not be interpreted through Western lenses and with existing (predominantly normative) Western media the- ories and concepts, and this chapter explores in more detail some of the alternative Russian-focussed frameworks (e.g. Becker, 2014; Koltsova, 2006; Oates, 2006, 2013).

Second, the role of the state, culture, and society vis-à-vis journalism and journalistic practices cannot be fully explained unless the relevant journalism culture(s) and journalists' own role perceptions are taken into account as well. The main premise this section is built upon is Waisbord's (2013) argument that journalistic professionalism "should not be narrowly associated with the normative ideal as it is historically developed in the West during the past century" (blurb). The Russian context shows that Russian journalists do not necessarily strive to be "watchdogs" of society, and as Oates (2013) argued, the state of Russian media, journalism, and democracy (or lack thereof) could in large part be explained by journalists' own role conceptions. Oates (2013) explained that "all segments of Russian society, from politicians to the public to the journalists themselves, perceive the mass media as a political player rather than as a watchdog" (p. 12). She added that self-censorship was "endemic" and the situation resembled Soviet times – journalists were rarely censored because they were "well aware of the limits of what can be said" (Oates, 2013, p. 14). Most studies did not focus on the role conceptions of journalists in liberal media, so it will be interesting to see the extent to which these journalists share Western values or whether they too see themselves as political actors but with a different role from their colleagues in state-aligned media.

Finally, the ethnographic fieldwork took place in the midst of the conflict with Ukraine, so it is also important to consider the media's role in the representation and perception of conflicts, particularly in cases such as the Russian one when the relevant nation-state has a stake in the conflict. It is important to consider the mediatisation of the conflict with Ukraine because, as Mortensen (2015) claimed, "the news media constitute the primary platform for political and military actors to inform the public", and for both official and non-official actors to "gain visibility and voice" as well as seek legitimacy (p. 7). Thussu and Freedman (2003) identified three different views on the role media play in conflicts: as critical observer, as publicist, and as "battleground, the surface upon which war is imagined and executed" (p. 4). Closely linked to these debates is the wider issue about the media's role vis-à-vis nationalism, national identities, and nation-building. This topic has been of particular relevance in the Russian context due to President Vladimir Putin's increased efforts in the construction and promotion of a particular type of modern-day Russian national identity, which, as Hutchings and Tolz (2015) argued, combined "isolationist popular nationalism" with "neo-imperial nationalism" (p. 9). While it is neither feasible nor desirable to fully engage with the vast body of literature on media, war, and conflict, some of the key theories and the premises they were built upon (Allan & Zelizer, 2004; Cottle, 2006; Hoskins & O'Loughlin, 2010; Mortensen, 2015; Thussu & Freedman, 2003) are outlined in conjunction with seminal concepts in media and nationalism studies such as Benedict Anderson's (1991) "imagined communities" and

Michael Billig's (1995) "banal nationalism" concepts. A few studies (e.g. Cottiero, Kucharski, Olimpieva, & Orttung, 2015; Hutchings & Rulyova, 2009; Hutchings & Tolz, 2015) that investigated the role of Russian "state-aligned" TV in that process as well as the differences and similarities in framing between state-aligned TV and the Internet sphere are also reviewed.

Media Systems and Terms of Reference

The media system of a country is closely linked to its economic, political, and cultural context. Vartanova (2012) used Hallin and Mancini's (2004) indicators for comparing media systems in an attempt to characterise the Russian media system. The four main comparative dimensions Hallin and Mancini (2004) proposed were:

> (1) the development of media markets, with particular emphasis on the strong or weak development of a mass circulation press; (2) political parallelism; that is, the degree and nature of the links between the media and political parties or, more broadly, the extent to which the media system reflects the major political divisions in society; (3) the development of journalistic professionalism; and (4) the degree and nature of state intervention in the media system.
>
> (p. 21)

Vartanova (2012) explained that after the demise of communism, the Russian media system adopted many of the Western media systems' features such as abolition of censorship, legal provisions for freedom of expression, and privatisation. However, in her view, the political and cultural peculiarities of the Russian context did not allow the media system to achieve a full transformation "as a linear and universal movement toward an imaginary and uncritically understood ideal Western media model" (Vartanova, 2012, p. 121). Some of the reasons behind this development were already discussed in the previous chapter. To sum up, the "sociopolitical context and culture of political communication in Russia were different" not just because of the legacy of communism, but also because the transition period brought about a range of political and economic challenges as well as "a moral crisis in Society" (Vartanova, 2012, p. 126). Institutional and legal changes were accompanied by "old rituals in relations among politicians, new media owners, journalists, and audiences" (Vartanova, 2012, p. 121). Furthermore, although the Russian media context bore similarities with other post-communist media systems in Central and Eastern Europe, there was one fundamental difference – the role of the state (Vartanova, 2012). In Russia, the state while liberating the economic activity in the media was not ready to relax the control over the content. This has produced practically unsolvable tension for the media themselves trying to function both as commercial enterprises and as institutions of the society.

(Ivanitsky, 2009, p. 114, as quoted in

Vartanova, 2012, p. 123)

Becker (2004) shared a similar view. He claimed that "the state remains the most important threat to the emergence of democratic media systems" and it also "retains the greatest potential to encroach upon media autonomy and limit pluralism" (Becker, 2004, p. 158).

Another substantial difference was the role citizens played and the expectations they had of their media. Vartanova (2012) argued that the relationship between the Russian state and its citizens had always been one of subordination. The state was both "alien" and "superior" to citizens, but also "a sacral force, a guarantor of the unity and the very existence of the Russian nation and society" (Vartanova, 2012, p. 131).

The Western European/American idea of a social contract that implied the mutual responsibility of state power and mass media for society had taken in the Russian context a nationally specific form in which the state did not need an intermediary between itself and society and the society did not consider itself as something autonomous and independent from the state.

(Vartanova, 2012, p. 131)

These peculiarities of the Russian context meant that Western perceptions of the mass media as the fourth estate were not applicable in Russia. As Vartanova (2012) put it, "neither the state nor the public have supported clear and transparent rules for the media, as they have for other political and social institutions" (p. 132). Oates (2006) also pointed out that Russians "see themselves as media subjects, without the rights of either media citizens or media consumers" (p. 192).

If the Russian media system clearly differs from Western media systems, then can we argue that it is unique? Scholars differed in their answers to this question. De Smaele (1999) claimed that

the unique position of Russia in between Europe and Asia, and its combination of western (European) and eastern cultural and philosophical principles, might cause Russia to interpret the concept of "Eurasianism" into a Eurasian media model or simply the Russian model.

(p. 186)

Becker (2014) argued that the Russian media system was not unique because it had lots of common features with other neo-authoritarian media systems. Vartanova (2012) wrote that the Russian media model could be defined as "statist commercialized" (p. 142) because its two key features were the centrality of the state and the growing commercialisation. She argued that "the contemporary Russian media model should be viewed as a synergy of different features that might be found in various national contexts" (Vartanova, 2012, p. 140). She also pointed out that this synergy of Western and Asian elements was "sometimes regarded as a distinct Eurasian hybrid system" (Vartanova, 2012, p. 140). Some of the common features that post-Soviet and post-imperial countries as well as the countries in Southeast Asia shared were:

> the existence of a state–market complex and its significant influence on media, formal and informal links between political or integrated political/economic elites and journalists, a specific culture of media audiences and elite–journalist relationships, tolerance on the part of audiences to an instrumental use of media by the state and political clans, and a paternalistic culture of media management.
>
> (Vartanova, 2012, p. 141)

Vartanova (2012) acknowledged that some of these features were present in the Mediterranean countries as well, but the main reason Russia could not be classified under Hallin and Mancini's (2001) Mediterranean model was because of the state–media relationship. The key difference was the "strong relationship between media, journalists, and the state, legitimized by a shared belief – consciously or unconsciously – in the regulatory/decisive role of the state (or state agencies)" (Vartanova, 2012, p. 141). Vartanova (2012) referred to a "statist mentality", which was at the heart of the authoritarian media model described by Becker (2004). The media "still play the role of an innocent and obedient child" (Vartanova, 2012, p. 142). Paternalism and neo-authoritarianism were, therefore, the defining features of the current Russian media system. Another key aspect was "the growing commercialism of the media industry" (Vartanova, 2012, p. 142). This trend went hand in hand with audiences' and journalists' resistance to "values of modernization and knowledge" as well as social and technological inequalities and a mismatch between what the media preach and what they actually practise (Vartanova, 2012, p. 142).

Rollberg (2014) argued it was very hard, "if not impossible", for researchers "to arrive at a lasting analytical consensus about the post-Soviet media sphere" because "media in post-Soviet societies are a moving target, influenced by technological, geopolitical, and cultural developments" (p. 175). This difficulty was in large part due to the fact that as Koltsova (2006) claimed that lots of researchers used Western concepts, terms, and theories in their attempts to explain the situation in Russia. Commonly used terms were censorship, self-censorship, and transition but, their "undifferentiated use" was problematic because of two key reasons (Rollberg, 2014). First, they reinforced the Cold War dichotomy between the East and the West, the democratic countries and the totalitarian regimes (Burrett, 2011; Rollberg, 2014). The reinforcement of this dichotomy was based on the assumption that after 1989/1990, Russian society and media had been in a period of transition from communism/authoritarianism to democracy (Burrett, 2011; Rollberg, 2014). Even if the assumption that Russia was en route to democratisation during and shortly after the perestroika and glasnost years, recent developments in the country clearly show that this is hardly the case anymore.

In fact, Koltsova (2006), Sparks (2008), and Oates (2013) questioned the extent to which Russian society and media were ever on a linear journey towards democratisation. Sparks (2008) argued that the transitology model did not provide a good explanation for the trends observed in Russia. It was based on the assumption that countries such as Russia were in period of "a world-wide transition from dictatorial regimes towards western-style democracy", and two parallel processes took place during this period: democratisation and marketisation (Sparks, 2008, p. 7). However, Sparks's (2008) analysis of post–Cold War political and economic developments in Russia, China, and Poland suggested that in all three countries there had been a strong marketisation, but "this has not correlated with any clear pattern of democratization" (Sparks, 2008, p. 16). In China, the party "retains ideological control of the media", in Russia the media "is dependent either upon the political elite or upon its closest business associates", and even in Poland the media were "intensely politicized and partisan" (Sparks, 2008, pp. 16–17). Sparks's (2008) conclusion, therefore, was that "there is no evidence whatsoever of any correlation between marketization and democratization, at least with regard to the mass media", and "alongside a continuation of marketization, there has been an increase in political control" (p. 17). The alternative theory, which in his view, provided a much better explanation of the trends observed in post-Soviet Russia was that of "elite continuity ... in which the former bureaucratic ruling class attempts to restructure itself as the owners of private capital" (Sparks, 2008, p. 7).

Similarly, Oates (2013) argued against claims that Russia was a "developing" democracy because "there is the appearance of democratic institutions in form, including a range of media outlets with various types of ownership, elections, parliament, and a popularly elected president, but these institutions lack democratic content" (p. 13). In her view, Russia was "an oligarchy or a 'delegative democracy' in which citizens have limited opportunities to effect political change" (p. 184). Koltsova (2006) also claimed that the Russian experience demonstrated that "the authoritarianism-democracy axis is not the only one along which societies can change" (p. 5). In her view, media development under Mikhail Gorbachev and Boris Yeltsin was described as democratisation, but under Putin, it was described as "authoritarionization" because Putin's strategy of state consolidation was "less favourable for the West and, therefore, has to be to a certain degree delegitimized as shifting towards authoritarianism" (Koltsova, 2006, pp. 227–228). She claimed that the role of the media in election coverage, for example, was not much different during Yeltsin's presidency, but "the difference in the degree of determinacy and institutional consolidation between Yeltsin's and Putin's Russia is, however, apparent" (Koltsova, 2006, p. 228). Unlike most scholars analysing mass media development in Putin's Russia, she saw "stabilizing tendencies" such as "routinization of new journalistic practices, professionalization of sources, consolidation of resources by state agents, and development of 'satellite' businesses, such as advertising and audience research" (p. 228).

This leads us to the second main reason why Cold War Western terminology and models should not be automatically applied to the Russian context. The "exact meaning" of these notions and theories can no longer be "taken for granted" since they "originated from totalitarian society models" (Rollberg, 2014, p. 176). Rollberg (2014), for example, demonstrated that none of Siebert, Peterson, and Schramm's (1956) four theories of the press fully operationalised the situation in Russia. Although on the surface it appeared that post-Soviet media had undergone an evolution from a Social Responsibility model to an Authoritarian model in the early 2000s, "even in the most liberal years of glasnost, Soviet media retained essential features of what Siebert called "the Soviet model", and even in the most intrusive years of the Putin presidency (2002–2003, after 2012), the Authoritarian model contains libertarian and consumer-driven features" (p. 175). This suggests that developments in Russian media and society should not be interpreted entirely through Western lenses and with existing (predominantly normative) Western media theories and concepts because Russia has embarked on a slightly different journey (Becker, 2014; Koltsova, 2006; Pomerantsev, 2014). However, Western concepts should not be completely discarded because, as both Vartanova's (2012) and Rollberg's (2014) accounts suggested, the post-Soviet Russian media sphere displayed some features evident in Western countries as well. Rollberg (2014) claimed that "most post-Soviet media, are above all, geared towards reinforcing the status quo while gaining maximum profit" (p. 177), thus echoing Vartanova's claim that the two main features of the contemporary Russian media system were statism/neo-authoritarianism and commercialism.

Becker (2014) also defined the Russian media system as neo-authoritarian, and in his view, it had "more in common with similar non-democratic systems around the world than with the Soviet system that once prevailed on the same territory" (p. 191). However, he clearly differentiated between totalitarian systems such as the Soviet one and neo-authoritarian ones, "particularly with regard to the degree of relative autonomy vis-a-vis the state, the breadth of negative and positive control, the degree of pluralism and the mechanisms of control, not to mention ideological context" (Becker, 2004, p. 144). The main defining feature of neo-authoritarian systems was the "tactical choice that many modern authoritarian leaders make: to allow some elements of openness and contestation in exchange for greater legitimacy both domestically and internationally" (Becker, 2014, p. 194). Similarly, Pomerantsev (2014) argued that "this isn't a country in transition but some form of postmodern dictatorship that uses the language and institutions of democratic capitalism for authoritarian ends" (p. 42).

As already pointed out, the types of control differed significantly from Soviet times "in terms of breadth, depth, and mechanisms of control, and the role of ideology" (Becker, 2014, p. 191). Becker (2014) argued that media were controlled in more "subtle" ways. The focus of control fell on the most popular forms of communication, namely, TV, "while allowing relative autonomy in media that have a more limited reach and impact" (Becker, 2014, p. 195). The most commonly used mechanisms of control were already outlined in the previous chapter – rules on government ownership, "mutually beneficial relations with owners, who often have a symbiotic relationship with the political leadership", subsidies and advertising for friendly media, intimidation, imprisonment, exile, restrictions on foreign ownership, and a range of "quasi-legal" and tax measures against "independent" media (Becker, 2014, p. 195). Moreover, Becker (2014) claimed that Putin's tightening grip on Russian media was motivated by his fear of revolutions similar to the ones that took place in Ukraine, Serbia, and Georgia, and that, with his actions, Putin was "setting an example for authoritarian regimes around the world" (p. 191). He gave examples of other similar neo-authoritarian media systems in Yemen, Ethiopia, Singapore, and Venezuela where "leaders pay homage to the importance of freedom of expression and attempt to bask in the glow of democratic legitimacy while at the same time supporting an environment that fundamentally undermines political competition" (Becker, 2014, p. 197).

A key difference between the neo-authoritarian and the Soviet media system is the lack of an "all-encompassing ideology" in neo-authoritarian Russia – "while there may be a cult of leader, there is no guiding ideology, no claims to truths that are scientifically determined and which can transform human history" (Becker, 2014, pp. 196–200). The subtler methods of control are a reflection of this lack of "ideological straightjacket" (p. 206). Hutchings and Rulyova (2009) used the "remote control" metaphor to explain the situation:

> What we find, then, with respect to our protagonist is neither
> the complete capitulation to ruthless state control mechanisms

portrayed (or at least implied) in many western accounts of the
Russian media environment, nor the brave resistance to manipulation depicted in romanticized western depictions of the "semiotic
guerrilla", but rather something altogether more subtle, and more
complex: something perhaps best conveyed in the subtitle of our
book: a submission (which can only ever be partial) to a control
(which must always remain remote).

(p. 217)

Nonetheless, the lack of an all-encompassing ideology does not mean
that the Russian government does not have an information policy –
on the contrary. Koltsova (2006) argued that one of the fundamental
changes that marked Putin's presidency was Kremlin's information
policy, which involved a range of strategies – from the "concealment
of negative information" to "professionally created positive information flow" such as news about official visits and meetings, statements,
and photo opportunities even during the Chechnya war (p. 40). In
spite of the range of repressive measures used against independent/
critical/liberal media, overall the levels of diversity and pluralism
were much higher than during communism. There were still topics
and/or media that were tightly controlled, but other forces also played
a role. Becker (2014) claimed that market forces influenced media
coverage, and there were also "windows of pluralism" in media "in-
dependently owned (by individuals, parties, or foreign corporations),
relatively autonomous, accessible to the population, and highly critical of the regime, in spite of periodic harassment, violence and clo-
sures" (p. 196). Moreover, in comparison with other authoritarian
regimes, the Russian state has adopted a more liberal approach to
Internet regulation. Mathews (2010) summed up the Kremlin's approach as "essentially pragmatic rather than ideological – the rule of
thumb is that newspapers like *Novaya Gazeta* or radio stations like
Radio Ekho Moskvy are allowed to be critical, as long as they are not
too widely listened to or circulated".

Finally, Koltsova (2006) identified a wider problem that prevented
scholars from thoroughly and comprehensively conceptualising the
Russian media system. In her view, a lot of the concepts and theories used
were normative and predominantly focussed on the macro-institutional
level. Koltsova (2006) proposed a move away from normative theories
of democracy to an agency-focussed approach, whereby "the struggle
between different power centres" was investigated in more depth in an
attempt to explain the development of post-socialist media (pp. 5–6).
She claimed that typologies of media systems should, therefore, be based
on categories such as "power agents, resources, strategies and rules"
(Koltsova, 2006, p. 227). Koltsova (2006) said that it was wrong of

scholars to constantly ask the question "Does Russian government still pressure the media?" because journalists were not "'innocent' objects of 'evil' external pressure" but

> ...players who initiate relations with other actors to gain access to those resources which are controlled by the latter and which, without their mediation, are not available to journalists. In other words, media representatives show themselves no less power maximizers than anybody else.
>
> (p. 226)

In her view, this question should be reversed because in the 1990s, media departments were actually pressuring state agents. Koltsova (2006) argued that the question that should be asked was: "Who pressured whom in Russian media production of the 1990s, and with what result?" (p. 226). She even claimed that "Russian journalists, while obviously more controlled, seem less dominated, or, perhaps, more sincere in their statements than their western colleagues" who were less willing to report instances of external pressures (Koltsova, 2006). One major difference between the Soviet and the post-Soviet media systems was precisely the proliferation of different agents who played a role in the process as opposed to one dominant agent (Koltsova, 2006). So, what role do Russian journalists actually play in their society and how can we conceptualise their role in light of existing theories on journalism as a profession?

Journalism: Culture(s), Role Conceptions, and Relationship with Power, Culture, and Society

Waisbord (2013) argued that journalistic professionalism "should not be narrowly associated with the normative ideal as it is historically developed in the West during the past century" (blurb). Before looking at Russian-specific studies, it is worth reiterating what this normative ideal is. Waisbord (2013) explained that "as a normative concept, professional journalism is typically associated with the kind of reporting that follows the ideas of modern, "Western", particularly US, journalism, such as objectivity, fairness and public interest" (p. 7). These quality standards/ethical principles not only guide the work of journalists, but also potentially define their professional identity. The proponents of professional journalism see it as epitomising "the ideals that should guide press performance in democracy ... that fit the needs of citizens" (p. 7). However, as Waisbord (2013) pointed out, critics saw "professional journalism" as "problematic for democratic expression" because

It is a thinly veiled attempt to control expression, a self-serving justification of the prominent role of journalists in the mediated public sphere, a myth that hides the reality of a profoundly undemocratic news industry. By establishing a cadre of "news experts" who decide what information reaches the public, it closes off expression to average citizens and builds journalism as a fortress separated from citizens.

(p. 7)

While it is undeniable that the ideals of "professional journalism" as promulgated by the USA and the UK have been globally spread, it is also clear that these values and ideals have not been universally endorsed by journalists from around the world (Waisbord, 2013). Waisbord (2013) argued that no model has "a paradigmatic position" (p. 15) because of the diversity of journalistic ethics that guide journalism practice.

Russia is a good example of the processes that often take place in countries with historical traditions and contextual conditions different from those of the established democracies of the West, but which nonetheless interact with/are exposed to "professional journalism" as known in the West. Historically, during communism, "propaganda for the policy of 'the Party and the government' and upbringing of 'decent citizens of the Soviet society' was the most significant task of Soviet journalists'" (Koltsova, 2006, p. 24). Moreover, the style of writing was very different. Instead of following the Anglo-American inverted pyramid structure, most Russian journalists wrote in a more literary tradition. Arutunyan (2009) pointed out that

in those times, every intern, even when writing about a fire at a poultry plant, strove to demonstrate the talent of a columnist. That was why news articles so often started off with a lyrical digression, with historical or philosophical allusions.

(p. 28)

A quote from a Russian journalist best summarised the key difference:

...I remember, we, provincial journalists, were taught impartial journalism at courses in Moscow. The teacher, who during all life worked in English newspapers tried to include into our heads that in the newspaper there should be only one genre – the information. And therefore all materials should be built according to only one scheme: first a lead paragraph, then a description of the fact, then two different points of view of specialists and experts on the given question. And – nothing from me, only one person in the periodical has the right to state own position – the columnist. [...] I have left the courses with certain belief that it is not for us and not for our readers. The Russian journalists have accustomed the Russian readers

(and, maybe, on the contrary, our reading public always demanded
it from a writing community?) to other press. To other newspapers
and articles, in which the author's position is present. And emotions
are present too – not necessarily in the form of exclamations and
naming of villains as villains.

(Lebedeva, 2007, p. 25, as quoted in
Korkonosenko, 2011, p. 168)

This journalist was from a liberal newspaper – *Novaya Gazeta* – a
newspaper that has generally endorsed many of the values cherished in
the liberal democracies of the West, but despite that, she did not feel that
the values that underpinned the dominant journalistic tradition in these
democracies served the needs of journalists and citizens in her country.

Another key difference between Western and Russian journalism was
"the importance of actuality" (Korkonosenko, 2011, p. 165). Korkonosenko
(2011) claimed that while "for Western journalists actuality is one of the
most prominent news values. For Russian journalists it is only of mar-
ginal relevance" (p. 165). One particular genre – "otcherc" – exemplified
this trend. There is no precise translation in English of this genre, but it is
something between an essay and a treatise (Korkonosenko, 2011). "The
classical Russian otcherc is an attentive look to the external world inhab-
ited by unique persons", who can either be "outstanding figures" or "ordinary people" (Korkonosenko, 2011, p. 165).

While some Western values were embraced in the 1990s as the
historical outline showed, this was not a linear and long-term process.
Although an attempt was made for facts to be more clearly separated
from commentary, "this separation would remain, however, as little
more than a vulnerable fine line, so superficial that it was frequently
crossed" (Arutunyan, 2009, p. 28). Arutunyan (2009) argued that objectivity as a concept was initially misunderstood as focussing on anything
that had "been suppressed or made taboo", which led to the rise of sensationalism (p. 27). The Russian context shows that Russian journalists
do not necessarily strive to be "watchdogs" of society, and, as Oates
(2013) argued, the state of Russian media, journalism, and democracy
(or lack thereof) could in large part be explained by journalists' own role
conceptions. Oates (2013) wrote that "all segments of Russian society,
from politicians to the public to the journalists themselves, perceive the
mass media as a political player rather than as a watchdog" (p. 12). She
added that self-censorship was "endemic" and the situation resembled
Soviet times – journalists were rarely censored because they were "well
aware of the limits of what can be said" (Oates, 2013, p. 14). Pasti,
Chernysh, and Svitich (2012) argued that one key dimension had not
changed – the degree of "political subordination" of journalists (p. 267).

Nonetheless, it will be a gross oversimplification to claim that all
journalists in Russia feel their main role is not to hold the powerful

to account but to serve political and business interests. Butterfield and Levintova's (2011) study showed that there was an ideological split even among journalism educators in Russia's most prestigious university – Lomonosov Moscow State University. Two parallel schools educate journalism students there – the Faculty of Journalism and the School of Television. The two schools formally split in 2007–2009, and political factors were believed to be key motivation behind the split (Butterfield & Levintova, 2011).

> There are numerous accounts of the split within the journalism department that paint a picture of intellectual and academic struggle between adherence to Western standards, on the one hand, and more patriotic state-supporting journalism, on the other. Newspapers noted that, while the new broadcast journalism department is pre-paring cadres for the state-run TV and radio channels and is being sponsored by Channels 1 and 2 (ORT and RTR), the students of the traditional journalism department intern and subsequently find employment in private opposition newspapers, including Novaia Gazeta {sic}.
>
> (Butterfield & Levintova, 2011, p. 331)

The School of Television allegedly has close ties to the Kremlin and

> is explicitly and unapologetically patriotic and pro-governmental and is more interested in cultivating a uniquely Russian journalis-tic perspective than following the western models. The traditional department, on the other hand, praises itself for the adherence to the Western standards and maintains close ties with Western foun-dations and universities.
>
> (Butterfield & Levintova, 2011, p. 331)

Furthermore, the results from the 2012–2016 Worlds of Journalism (2017) representative survey showed that there were a range of roles that Russian journalists found important. The list of roles which Russian journalists found extremely or very important was topped by the follow-ing: "report things as they are" (78.7%), "educate the audience" (75.4%), "provide advice, orientation and direction for daily life" (66.4%), "ad-vocate for social change" (66.2%), "provide analysis of current affairs" (63.3%), "tell stories about the world" (61.8%), "be a detached ob-server" (61.3%), "let people express their views" (59.2%), "promote tolerance and cultural diversity" (58.2%), and "support national devel-opment" (51.9%) (Anikina, Frost, & Hanitzsch, 2017). However, other roles that "Western journalists" found extremely or very important were not wholeheartedly embraced by their Russian colleagues. For ex-ample, only 28.5% said that to monitor and scrutinise political leaders was extremely or very important, and only 23.8% felt the same way about monitoring and scrutinising business. Moreover, only 18.2% of Russian journalists said that setting the political agenda was extremely or very important for them. Similarly, to be an adversary of the government was extremely or very important for 17.2% of Russian journalists. Nonetheless, contrary to claims in the literature about Russian journalists' "subservient" mentality (Arutunyan, 2009, p. 77), to convey a positive image of political leadership was extremely or very important only for 10.3% and to support government policy for 11.3% of Russian journalists. We should not forget that these questions were quantitative and the answers journalists provided were not necessarily a reflection of the practices they engaged in also because of the alleged mismatch between what the media preached and what they actually practised (Vartanova, 2012). However, providing an overtly generalised and potentially oversimplified view of Russian journalists is not what this book is aiming for. The qualitative nature of the study would allow us not just to outline liberal journalists' own role conceptions, but also to unpack the reasons for these conceptions and the extent to which journalists practise what they preach.

A range of factors affect journalists' role perceptions, and while we outlined the main ones in the previous chapter, it is worth mentioning three interrelated issues that have clearly affected journalistic values and professionalism in Putin's Russia. The economic difficulties, the widespread corruption, and audiences' expectations of and attitudes towards journalists have played an important role. Lipman (2010) argued that "the independent media can only work as an instrument of public accountability if the public demands that the government be held accountable", and that "if the public is generally indifferent and atomized, independent media will remain politically ineffective" (p. 163). She argued that this was exactly what the situation in Russia was like at the moment – "the media cannot *generate* activism that is not there" (Lipman, 2010, p. 163). A representative survey conducted by the Levada-Center in February 2017 showed that the majority of Russians (53%) did not know who political activist and opposition leader Alexei Navalny was. Of those who had heard about him, only 3% felt respect towards him, 4% felt sympathy, and 9% had "nothing bad to say about him". Another public opinion survey conducted in October 2016 demonstrated that the majority of Russians were actually in support of Internet censorship (Levada-Center, 2016a). In all, 60% said that censorship was necessary, including the blocking of websites or Web materials. Furthermore, 44% did not think that censorship or restrictions of the online activities of social activists were an infringement of their civil rights and freedoms.

Another issue of concern is that most media in Russia are not economically sustainable and rely on subsidies to survive, which in turn leads to dependencies and high levels of corruption. Out of 900 publications in St. Petersburg, only 150 covered their expenses. "The remaining 750 relied on various subsidies from the state, corporations, and solvent clients" (Pasti et al., 2012, p. 268). In a 2008 survey with 796 Russian journalists, 52% admitted that they had produced a news piece "in return for extra payments during the last 12 months", and the practice was "especially prevalent among younger journalists" (Pasti et al., 2012, p. 274). More significantly, the majority of journalists did not really disapprove of such practices – only 22% among those who entered the profession prior to or in 1991 disapproved of these practices as opposed to 10% of those who joined the profession between 1992 and 1999, and 14% of those who started working as journalists in/after 2000. The Worlds of Journalism 2012–2016 survey showed that more than a quarter of Russian journalists said that accepting money from sources was justified.

All in all, the quality of Russian journalism appears to be in decline, and commentators claimed that its reputation in society has suffered as a result of that. The head of the Russian Union of Journalists said that no more than 15% of the content media produced was news. Overall, there has been a notable decline in ethical standards, which in turn has led to the inability of journalists to "meet the public needs" (Pasti et al., 2012, p. 268), and ultimately an erosion in the general trust in journalists:

> One of the biggest problems posed by corrupt journalistic practices was that the journalists themselves stopped believing in any possibility of a journalistic ethic... Even today allegations of journalistic corruption are still the most common and easiest means to put pressure on journalists... Today, rare is the journalist who has never been accused of printing or broadcasting paid-for material... If in Soviet times it was mostly the dissidents who distrusted the press and learned to read between the lines, in today's Russia, journalists in general suffer from a poor reputation and the value of what is printed can be questioned arbitrarily.
>
> (Arutunyan, 2009, pp. 79–80)

However, representative surveys with Russian audiences show a slightly different picture. TV still remains the most trusted source of information for them. A 2015 Levada-Center survey showed that 59% trusted the information they received about current world affairs on the main TV channels either "entirely so" (11%) or "for the most part" (48%) – an increase of 12% since 2012. When it comes to the Internet, 31% said they trusted the information "for the most part" and 6% "entirely so" – an increase of 8% since 2012. Nonetheless, journalists' own levels of trust in the news media were lower – 28.7% said they had "complete trust" or "a great deal of trust" in the news media (Anikina et al., 2017). Most studies and surveys did not focus on the role conceptions of journalists in liberal media, so it will be interesting to see the extent to which these journalists share Western values or whether they too see themselves as political actors but with a different role from their colleagues in state-aligned media.

Mediatisation of Conflict and National Identities: Conflict Reporting and Nation-Building

The ethnographic fieldwork took place in the midst of the conflict with Ukraine, so it is also important to consider the media's role in the representation and perception of conflicts, particularly in cases such as the Russian one when the relevant nation-state has a stake in the conflict. As Mortensen (2015) argued, "the news media constitute the primary platform for political and military actors to inform the public", and for both official and non-official actors to "gain visibility and voice" as well as seek legitimacy (p. 7). Thussu and Freedman (2003) identified three different views on the role of the media in conflicts: as critical observer, as publicist and as "battleground, the surface upon which war is imagined and executed" (pp. 4–5). Cottle (2006) and Mortensen (2015) used the term "mediatisation" to describe the process. As Deacon and Stanyer (2014) argued, the term mediatisation had two commonly used definitions: as either an "institutionalist" or a "social-constructivist" process. The former conceptualised mediatisation "as a process in which non-media social actors have to adapt to 'media's rules, aims, production logics, and constraints'", whereas the latter places an emphasis on mediatisation "as a process in which changing information and communication technologies (ICTs) drive 'the changing communicative construction of culture and society'" (Deacon & Stanyer, 2014). Mortensen (2015) wrote:

> Conflict *is* thoroughly mediatized on communicative, organizational, strategic, and operational levels: from the great involvement of the press in all aspects of conflict; to the professionalized communication of political and military actors; to participants in conflict taking advantage of social media and the news media to inform, mobilize and propagate their cause.
>
> (p. 41)

She claimed that mediatisation had two main interrelated dimensions: elite actors (state, military) and non-elite actors (outside the institutions). The media were essential because they "constitute an important platform for actors from the two dimensions to push their diverging claims about and representations of the conflict in question" (Mortensen, 2015, p. 42).

However, as Cottle (2006) pointed out, the media's role was by no means neutral or passive. In Cottle's view (2006), the term mediatisation offered a more suitable explanation of the role of the media than the term mediation because the media were not simply reporting and representing conflicts but they were "actively 'doing something' over and above disseminating ideas, images and information" (p. 9). The mediatisation of conflict is a complex process involving a range of actors. It is a much more suitable framework for explaining the empirical trends observed in a country such as Russia because it allows us to capture the complexities of the context in a more thorough way than Herman and Chomsky's (1988) "manufacturing consent" paradigm, which is considerably more simplistic. As Cottle (2006) argued, "the propaganda model appears to short-circuit the complexities and dynamics of conflict-driven representations unfolding through time, as well as the strategic struggles informing media production and the cultural mediations inflecting their reception" (pp. 19–20). However, there is one aspect of the propaganda model, which is useful to this study – the focus on economic and political/state power, and "how media performance is often subservient" to it (Cottle, 2006, p. 20). It seems undeniable that the state plays a very strong and, to a large extent, dominant role in the Russian context. We should not forget, however, that as the previous section demonstrated, journalists are not passive actors in the process, and we will not be able to capture the role of liberal journalists without acknowledging the range of dimensions and actors that influence the process.

An essential part of the mediatisation process as far as journalists are concerned is the balancing of the conventional rules of reporting (whatever they are in the relevant contexts) with/against journalists' own national identities. Allan and Zelizer (2004) argued that reporters' "very commitment to some rendering of national identity, even patriotism ... is likely to engender a change in journalistic work", which "may entail a migration toward vague word choice, the absence of a broader perspective, the lack of explicit images, even the wearing of flag pins" (p. 4). The relationship between media and nationalism has been well documented in the literature. Anderson's (1983) "imagined communities" concept was built on the premise that the nation was "an imagined political community" because "the members of even the smallest nation will never know most of their fellow-members, meet them, or even hear of them, yet in the minds of each lives the image of their communion" (p. 49). In Anderson's view (1983), the key driver behind this process of imagining was print capitalism, namely, "the development of print-as-commodity" (p. 52). Billig (1995) argued that the media "flag" the nation in a banal way through the daily reproduction of "ideological habits":

> The national flag hanging outside a public building in the United States attracts no special attention... Daily the nation is indicated, or "flagged", in the lives of its citizenry. Nationalism, far from being an intermittent mood in established nations, is the endemic

condition... The metonymic image of banal nationalism is not a flag which is being consciously waved with fervent passion; it is the flag hanging unnoticed on the public building... In routine practices and everyday discourses, especially those in the mass media, the idea of nationhood is regularly flagged. Even the daily weather forecast can do this.

(Billig, 1995, pp. 6, 8–9)

The concepts of imagined communities and banal nationalism are highly relevant to this study because Putin's presidency has been marked by a pronounced strategy of nation-building and promotion in which the media (especially TV) have played an instrumental role. Hutchings and Rulyova (2009) described Putin's national identity vision as "a latter-day version of imperial pride in Russian military achievements" (p. 3). They argued that Putin had used his "unchallenged authority over the media as an opportunity to use TV as a propaganda tool with which to promote his agenda of rebuilding popular belief in a militarily strong, self-confident, stable and united nation" (p. 10). Similarly, Hutchings and Tolz (2015) wrote that in Russia, "isolationist popular nationalism" coexisted with "the neo-imperial nationalism of Putin's regime" (p. 9).

In relation to the conflict with Ukraine, Roman, Wanta, and Buniak's (2017) study examined a year's worth of news stories about the conflict broadcast on the highest rated TV news programme – Channel One's *Vremya*. The analysis showed that during the first four months, the conflict was framed as a "'punitive operation' of 'Kyiv's authorities' against their own people", and "several stories during the period of the study stressed that there were no regular Russian troops in Eastern Ukraine and that the war is a 'local conflict, and Russia has nothing to do with it'" (Roman, Wanta, & Buniak, 2017, p. 13). Moreover, the Russian channel "relied heavily on Second World War symbolism", including words such as "fascists" and "extremists" to describe the Ukrainian volunteer battalions (Roman, Wanta, & Buniak, 2017, p. 17). Similarly, another study analysing the *Vesti Nedeli/Вести Недели (News of the Week)* show on Russian state TV found that two key frames were used to explain the conflict – World War II-era fascism and anti-Americanism (Cottiero et al., 2015). Moreover, the authors' subsequent analysis of search query histories on Yandex and Google showed that these two frames "have had lasting impacts on Russian Internet users" (Cottiero et al., 2015, p. 533). Their conclusion was that "state television has a strong impact in setting the agenda for the Internet and society as a whole" (p. 533).

Therefore, Cottiero et al. (2015) claimed that the Kremlin's efforts in shaping public opinion had been successful and as a result had boosted "Putin's legitimacy as Russia's leader" (p. 533). Hoskins and O'Loughlin (2010) were indeed right in claiming that the mediatisation of war and conflict "matters because perceptions are vital to war", and it is "through media that perceptions are created, sustained or challenged" (p. 5). In the Russian context, the majority of the population supported the annexation of Crimea. When asked "Do you support Crimea joining Russia", 86% of Russians said "definitely yes" or "probably yes", both in May 2014 and in May 2016 (Levada-Center, 2016b), despite the fact that the majority defined the situation in Eastern Ukraine as "tense" (66%) or "critical, volatile" (17%). Another key principle applies in the Russian context – the process of mediatisation of conflict is multifaceted because "war and conflict are drivers of the form media take, of how media are controlled and of what information reaches them" (Hoskins & O'Loughlin, 2010, p. 6). The Russian media regulator Roskomnadzor has been particularly proactive in that respect. It has blocked websites or issued warnings threating to block various websites, including the websites of the Ukrainian Crisis Media Centre, Forbes Ukraine, the Ukrainian Institute of National Memory, and Russian media websites.

Crucially, the framing of the conflict in Eastern Ukraine in terms of World War II-era fascism and anti-Americanism and the high level of support for Putin's nationalistic project and the annexation of Crimea presented both a challenge and an opportunity for Russian liberal media. On the one hand, this was an opportunity for liberal media to provide an "alternative" framing to the overall pro-Putin chorus led by Russian state broadcast media. On the other hand, liberal media faced the threat of increased marginalisation because any attempts to present the conflict in an alternative (more neutral and objective) way could easily be dismissed as anti-patriotic US propaganda. Putin's popularity has been soaring in large part due to the strong role he has been perceived to be playing in the process of nation-building and revival of Russia's identity as a superpower on the world stage. The Soviet era legacy still lives on. Moreover, the process of othering plays an important part in the national identity revival project. Hutchings and Tolz (2015) argued that "state-aligned media … construct Russian identity in relation to a western, as well as an 'ethnic', 'other'" (p. 7). *Vesti Nedeli*, for example, presented the war in Ukraine "as externally evoked by 'the West,' and in particular, by the USA, and thus portrays it as an act of aggression directed against Russia" (Cottiero et al., 2015, p. 541). Any critical voices questioning Russia's alleged right to self-defence or indeed its greatness as a nation were bound to be met with a great degree of hostility. Russia's involvement in Syria further exacerbated these trends. Exploring liberal journalists' strategies gives us invaluable insights into the role they see themselves as playing in Russian society.

3   Russia's Deadliest Newspaper
The History of *Novaya Gazeta*

"The murder that killed free media in Russia" (Walker, 2016b). This was how *The Guardian* described the most (in)famous murder of a Russian journalist – that of *Novaya Gazeta's* investigative reporter Anna Polit-kovskaya who was an outspoken critic of the Second War in Chechnya as well as of President Vladimir Putin himself. Politkovskaya was murdered in broad daylight on 7 October 2006 – Putin's birthday. This led to spec-ulations about the president's potential involvement in her assassination. However, in his interview with me, the editor-in-chief of *Novaya Gazeta* made it explicitly clear that he did not believe that Putin was behind her murder. The president himself reacted to the murder by infamously saying that her death was "more damaging to the current authorities, both in Russia and the Chechen Republic, than her activities" (Filipov, 2017). This chapter explores the reactions to Politkovskaya's murder and the outcomes of the trial that concluded precisely at the time when I was completing my fieldwork in Russia. It traces the historical development of Russia's deadliest newspaper – *Novaya Gazeta* (Table 3.1).

The chapter is organised around two main headings: (1) Founding of the Newspaper and Early Years, including financial pressures and difficulties and (2) Threats, Risks, and Landmark Cases: international reputation and the six key murders, with a particular focus on Anna Politkovskaya's assassination. It starts with a brief outline of when and how the newspaper was founded and the key developments in the early history of *Novaya Gazeta*. In the first part, I also explore the on-going financial difficulties that the newspaper had been facing over the years, to a large extent, as a result of its marked anti-Kremlin stance. The chapter then moves on to more troublesome developments such as the murders of five of its journalists and lawyer Stanislav Markelov. Inves-tigative journalist Anna Politkovskaya's murder is by far the most infa-mous assassination and particular attention is paid to her case.

This focus on the six murders is not coincidental. The six murders are not merely an indication of the dangers liberal journalists face in Russia, but the story of each of these journalists also reveals the values underpin-ning the work of all journalists in the newspaper and the broader mission it purports to be playing in Russian society. The findings presented in

Table 3.1 *Novaya Gazeta*: Timeline

Year	Milestone
1993	First issue comes out
1994	The inaugural Editor-in-Chief Sergei Kozheurov resigns
	Vladimir Lepekhin elected as editor-in-chief
1995	Dmitry Muratov elected as editor-in-chief
2000	Special projects department editor Igor Domnikov murdered
2003	Deputy editor and MP Yuri Shchekochikhin murdered
2006	Investigative journalist Anna Politkovskaya murdered on Putin's birthday
	Muratov considers closing down the newspaper
2009	Lawyer Stanislav Markelov, trainee reporter Anastasia Baburova, and correspondent Natalia Estemirova murdered
2015	Main shareholder Alexander Lebedev stops "bankrolling" the newspaper
	Muratov announces that print edition might be terminated
2017	Muratov does not stand for re-election
	Sergei Kozheurov elected as editor-in-chief

this chapter are based on my interviews with *Novaya Gazeta* editor and staff and on documentary analysis. I read and analysed all articles published about the five journalists and lawyer Markelov and their murders on the newspaper's website. I also explored the brief historical section on the website and read through all the articles published by these journalists. I also draw upon some secondary sources – reports by news organisations, state authorities, non-governmental organisations (NGOs), and international organisations. Given that some of the claims made are highly contentious, all sources are duly acknowledged in the text and quoted in the bibliography.

Founding of the Newspaper and Early Years

Novaya Gazeta was founded in 1993 after a group of around 40 journalists decided to leave another newspaper – *Komsomolskaia Pravda* – because they wanted to create "a different newspaper … for everyone and without orientation towards any political party" (Klimentov, 2010). Moreover, they were not happy with the direction *Komsomolskaia Pravda* was taking. The first editor-in-chief of *Novaya Gazeta* was Sergei Kozheurov, who, until November 2017, was *Novaya Gazeta's* CEO and first deputy editor-in chief. In November 2017, he was elected as editor-in-chief again after Dmitry Muratov decided not to stand for re-election but to continue working for the newspaper as chairman of the board of directors and the editorial board. Kozheurov was a deputy editor-in-chief in charge of politics at *Komsomolskaia Pravda*. In an interview for the website slon.ru, reprinted as the only document in the history section of *Novaya Gazeta's* website, Kozheurov explained that the split was prompted by the different vision the journalists who left and those who stayed had about "what a newspaper should be about, what principles it should uphold" (Rostova, 2010). In his view, what followed after the coup was a period of "spiritual and ideological pause" and "disappointment" (Rostova, 2010). The two opposing views held by *Komsomolskaia Pravda* journalists at the time were that they should either maintain their identity from the late 1980s and early 1990s of a sociopolitical newspaper independent from those in power or they should commercialise the newspaper to appeal to a mass audience. There did not appear to be much scope for compromise between the two warring factions.

The newspaper also changed its ownership structure by splitting the shares between the editorial staff. After the restructuring process was completed, a meeting was convened with the aim of electing a new editor-in-chief. The incumbent editor who supported the more "pragmatic approach" won, and this prompted the opposing faction to leave *Komsomolskaia Gazeta* in order to set up their own newspaper (Rostova, 2010). Nearly half of the senior editors left the newspaper. As the current editor of *Novaya Gazeta*, Muratov explained: "Those who stayed wanted to produce a tabloid newspaper, and we did not want to produce a tabloid" (Kashin, 2011). *Novaya Gazeta*'s journalists themselves elected their editor –Kozheurov – who served as editor-in-chief until June 1994.

The split was relatively amicable, and initially the newspaper was called *Novaya Ezhednevnaia Gazeta* (*New Daily Newspaper*), but the word "*Ezhednevnaia*" (daily) was later dropped from the title. In the first few months the newspaper was not issued daily, but weekly. However, they could not register the newspaper title without the word "daily" in it because *Novaya Gazeta* was already registered as a trademark by the workers of a cement factory who never actually published such a newspaper. The issue was eventually resolved and the title of the newspaper was changed.

The first issue came out on 1 April 1993 with a circulation of 100,000 copies. The main principle that *Novaya Gazeta* advocated in its mission statement published in the first edition was that of "духоподъемным", which is perhaps best translated as soul-uplifting. The guiding aims were to achieve political and business honesty and integrity, and independence from power (Rostova, 2010). Kozheurov explained that Russian society was split at the time, and it was important for *Novaya Gazeta* to declare that they would not be taking sides and that their position would be one of "non-alignment" (Rostova, 2010). However, this did not mean that they would aim to be detached observers. The newspaper's editorial position on key issues was formulated by the editorial staff, whom the first editor defined as "poor but proud" people "who could afford not to make any compromises" (Rostova, 2010). They were interested in "other, new people", and as an example, Kozheurov gave the excellent relationship they had with the Russian United Democratic Party Yabloko (Rostova, 2010). Yabloko (2017) was a liberal party "in favour of socially oriented market economy, equality of starting opportunities, inviolability of private property, competition in politics and economy, strengthening of democratic institutions, the rule of law, law-governed state and citizens' control over the government." The party's founder was Grigory Yavlinsky. Later, Yavlinsky sponsored the newspaper at a very difficult financial time.

The history of *Novaya Gazeta* in terms of topics covered, journalists' shared values and role conceptions, and even the general approach to handling financial issues, broadly reflects this romantic vision as initially put forward by the founding mothers and fathers of the newspaper. By Muratov's own admission, in the beginning they did not seriously consider the financial costs and implications because that was not really a concern for them when they worked at *Komsomolskaia Pravda* – a newspaper with an alleged circulation of 22 million copies at the time. *Novaya Gazeta*'s first edition was financed by contributions of around £1,000 from the journalists themselves and from a few friends and supporters. For a long time the journalists did not receive any salaries. They occupied three rooms in the editorial offices of another newspaper – *Moscow News*. The editor of *Moscow News* – Len Karpinsky – "graciously" allowed them to use these rooms for free (Kashin, 2011).

Another donor of the newspaper (and later a shareholder) was the former Soviet leader Mikhail Gorbachev. Gorbachev used some of the money he received for his 1990 Nobel Peace Prize to purchase the first computers for the newspaper. Muratov and Gorbachev knew each other from *Komsomolskaia Pravda* after Muratov and another journalist invited Gorbachev to contribute to a monthly column called "Once a month with Gorbachev". Kozheurov recalled that Gorbachev himself approached Muratov with an offer to help as soon as he heard about the launch of the new paper:

> He had said that for him it was a matter of honour that we could make such a newspaper that we felt was necessary and that he would do whatever he can to help us (Although, I note, he himself was an opponent of our departure from *Komsomolskaia Pravda*). And he helped – in the beginning with computers. But the most important thing is that at that time he was and still is like a source of optimism for us: he himself believed we would succeed, and we thought so too.
> (Rostova, 2010)

Kashin (2011) argued that the early editions of the newspaper in 1994 did not create the impression that it was a "poor publication" because it went to print daily and it had a lot of supplements. According to Muratov, this was "a show-off". The buzz word at the time was capitalisation, and they played that game very well. The financial troubles cost Kozheurov his post as editor-in-chief although he still stayed at the newspaper as

CEO and deputy editor-in-chief. Kozheurov recalled that in June 1994, his colleagues forced him to resign because they had high hopes that another colleague would solve their financial issues. Vladimir Anatolievich Lepekhin, who was also a State Duma deputy, initially joined the newspaper as an observer. His stint at *Novaya Gazeta* was very short. There were two different versions explaining why he left his post so soon after he took it up. According to Kozheurov (who did not name him explicitly in his interview), Lepekhin had promised subsidies for the newspaper that he did not provide. According to Lepekhin's website, however, he left the newspaper because of disagreements over the newspaper's editorial policy on Chechnya. Either way, he left *Novaya Gazeta* in February 1995. That was a very difficult time for the newspaper because, at that point, it had accrued such a huge debt that they had to stop printing in Moscow because they could not afford the running costs. The temporary halt led to the resignation of some of the journalists who joined other editions.

Muratov became editor-in-chief at the end of February 1995 and has led the newspaper until November 2017. Muratov was democratically elected by his colleagues. This policy of electing their own editors-in-chief was adopted by the newspaper staff at the time when they initially founded *Novaya Gazeta*, and it is still in place. Muratov managed to secure some funding and thus, with the help of generous donors, the paper resumed printing in August 1995. Among their sponsors was a goldsmith, a bank consultant, and the opposition politician and economist Yavlinsky. The gifts the newspaper received were not just monetary – they were also given their first two cars.

Kozheurov explained that he did not really want to assume his previous role as editor-in-chief again:

> Why would I do that? At this point in time we had a person who was capable of taking up this post. Muratov. Back at *Komsomolke* {*Komsomolskaia Pravda*} I considered him to be my student. But students grow and outgrow – myself and many others.
>
> (Rostova, 2010)

Chechnya and Novaya Gazeta's "Relationship" with Putin

In spite of its on-going financial battles and the fact that it could not offer any financial incentives, the newspaper recruited a few prominent journalists from other newspapers. One of the new recruits was army Major Vyacheslav Izmailov who did not just become the newspaper's military columnist/observer but he also fought in Chechnya. Muratov said that one of the newspaper's main achievements was the release of 171 soldiers and hostages in Chechnya in the course of a couple of years and with the help of the attorney general's office (Kashin, 2011).

Chechnya has indeed been one of the key topics the newspaper had focussed on. The interviews conducted on the topic clearly suggested that journalists did not aim to cover Chechnya in a neutral and dispassionate way. In his interview with me, the editor explained what prompted this focus on Chechnya and why this is an approach the newspaper had consistently adopted, including in its coverage the recent conflict with Ukraine (a topic I will explore further in Chapter 4):

> In this country we need peace and tranquillity. We need a new generation that thinks that we should not be firing gun shots, we shouldn't be fighting, invading and killing, or like in Afghanistan or Chechnya pillaging, but who thinks that we need peace and tranquillity. Our opponent Putin, I mean the President, thinks that Russia needs grandeur, not tranquillity, he wants grandeur. As Gorbachev once said: I brought peace back to Russia and peace brought Russia back. This is very important for us – to become a global nation, which will preserve its identity and its honour. But what we currently observe is how our children go abroad to places they do not want to live in or to study. If we accept peace, then we won't experience this attitude of people being very negative towards us, treating us like bandits and fighters.
>
> (Muratov, 2014, personal communication)

It is notable that in his interview with me, Muratov referred to Putin as "our opponent", but in an earlier interview, he argued that they did not deliberately set out to "go for Putin" but sovereignty was an important issue they felt they had to defend (Kashin, 2011). From the very beginning, *Novaya Gazeta* took a tough stance against the Chechenisation of Russia. Muratov himself was a war correspondent reporting from Chechnya, Nagorno-Karabakh, and Central Asia.

All in all, the relationship between Putin and *Novaya Gazeta* can best be described as a cold war. Soon after he became president in 2000, two journalists from *Novaya Gazeta* conducted an investigation into the dealings of the mayor's office in Saint Petersburg at the time when Putin and his "friends" worked there. Their attempts to receive a formal response from Putin were futile. In fact, all attempts by the newspaper to request an interview with Putin had been refuted politely, and *Novaya Gazeta* journalists had rarely been allowed to report on press conferences organised by the Kremlin. The fundamental and irreconcilable difference between Putin and *Novaya Gazeta's* editorial staff is the opposing vision they hold for Russia's future and its role on the world stage. According to Muratov (2014, personal communication):

> Putin is a person who dreams about the happiness of his country. He loves Russia deeply, in a fantastic way. But he envisages Russia as a country in which power and rule do not change. I don't envisage

Russia as an authoritarian country – I see it as a democratic country. Putin thinks that patriotism is about fighting. I think patriotism is when people like living in their country and are not scared of each other. These are fundamental differences. Moreover, I think that our country has fought a lot. A few million people have died in combat – during the First World War a hundred years ago, during Stalin's repressions who no one apologised for – they don't even pay repression pensions. Tens of millions of people died during the Second World War for our great nation. In fact, one of our observers recently read that Russia had lost 360 million people in the wars in the last century, which is 2.5 times the population of Russia at the moment. We all know that lots of people die in wars. Our country burnt in wars. As one of our great writers wrote, the price we paid for victory was very high, terribly high.

It becomes apparent from Muratov's words that the mission of *Novaya Gazeta* was not for its journalists to be detached watchdogs of society and those in power. The newspaper's editor had a clear vision for the future of his country and for the role its president should play both at home and abroad. *Novaya Gazeta* journalists did not pretend that they would cover Putin's activities in an objective way, but they had an agenda, which was clearly articulated by their editor. As Muratov (2014, personal communication) pointed out, he believed in democracy and he was targeting precisely those liberal-minded people who shared similar values. This focus on democratic values and on investigations about wrongdoings and corruption, including in the regions, has turned into the signature style of *Novaya Gazeta* since its inception. This is also the reason why despite the on-going financial difficulties, the newspaper has managed to attract and sustain a loyal audience and (occasional) financial support from like-minded donors. However, it is precisely the coverage of these topics that has come at the highest of prices for the newspaper – the loss of human lives.

Threats, Risks and Landmark Cases

Six Murders

Five *Novaya Gazeta* journalists and one of their lawyers were murdered in the course of their duties: (1) Igor Alexandrovich Domnikov (died on 16 July 2000 at the age of 41). (2) Yuri Petrovich Shchekochikhin (died on 3 July 2003 at the age of 53). (3) Anna Stepanovna Politkovskaya (died on 7 October 2006 at the age of 48). (4) Lawyer Stanislav Yurievich Markelov (died on 19 January 2009 at the age of 34). (5) Anastasia Eduardovna Baburova (died on 19 January 2009 at the age of 25). (6) Natalya Khusainovna Estemirova (died on 15 July 2009 at the age of 51).

Igor Domnikov

Igor Domnikov was a reporter and an editor of the Special Projects Department at *Novaya Gazeta*. On 12 May 2000, a gang of killers followed Domnikov from the building of *Novaya Gazeta* to his block of flats. They attacked him in the corridor and beat him up with a hammer "no less than 10 times into the head" (Markin, 2013). A neighbour found Domnikov lying unconscious on the floor and covered in a pool of blood. He was then admitted into hospital where he was in a coma for two months, and subsequently died on 16 July 2000. The five gang members were identified and convicted in 2007 by the Supreme Court of the Republic of Tatarstan. They were members of a gang of 16 people who were standing trial for a series of killings and abductions. They were given lengthy prison sentences – from 18 years to life imprisonment. The Committee to Protect Journalists' Executive Director Joel Simon welcomed the verdict by saying:

> Justice has been served in a journalist murder for the first time since President Vladimir Putin took office in 2000. We commend the court in Tatarstan for this ground-breaking step in the fight against impunity in the killing of journalists. The authorities must now go further, and find and prosecute the masterminds of Igor Domnikov's brutal murder.
>
> (CPJ, 2007)

Prosecuting the masterminds of Domnikov's murder proved to be a much more challenging task. *Novaya Gazeta's* own investigation into the murder pointed in the direction of the former vice governor of the Lipetsk region – Sergei Dorovsky. Domnikov had published five articles criticising the economic policies of Dorovsky, and *Novaya Gazeta* claimed that Dorovsky should be prosecuted. Dorovsky was indeed eventually charged with solicitation of deliberate infliction of grievous bodily harm to a victim due to his/her professional activity, but this happened in April 2015 after the case was passed to the Moscow Main Investigations Directorate. According to the authorities, Dorovsky had persuaded his friend – the businessman Pavel Sopot – to arrange the attack on Domnikov and inflict "grave harm to his health" (Milashina, 2015). Sopot himself was convicted in 2013 for inciting the murder by recruiting gang members to commit it. He was sentenced to seven years in prison, and he was also ordered to pay compensation to Domnikov's wife. However, Dorovsky vehemently denied the charges and he did not really face justice. The case against him had to be dropped because the crime's 15-year statute of limitations expired on 12 May 2015.

Domnikov's articles about Dorovsky were written in a very distinctive style – they were indeed very critical of the region's economic policies and a range of facts were presented to back up Domnikov's points, but the style of writing was much more light-hearted, humorous, and narrative than in a conventional (Western) investigative piece. One of the articles had the following headline "Lipetsk woke up: All in the economic miracle". The subhead read: "Grandmother, what cold hands, hot heart and red head you have!" This use of a fairy tale (The Red Riding Hood) allegory in the headline was indicative of the peculiarities of Domnikov's writing style.

Novaya Gazeta's deputy editor Khlebnikov even wrote an article about Domnikov's distinctive style, which also revealed a great deal about the kind of journalism practised at *Novaya Gazeta*. He described Domnikov's writing as "effortless, laid-back and lengthy" regardless of what topic he was covering, but also always exploring the different dimensions of life – with its "paradoxes and colourfulness". Khlebnikov (2001) defined his style as verging on prose:

> Special journalism still to be found today in Russia alone. Non-computerised, infinitely remote from dry information. This kind of journalism can only be born in this country, which is a home to great literature, great and free (don't laugh, don't laugh) language and the complete lack of civil liberty.

Khlebnikov (2001) explained that this tradition had been continued after Domnikov's death and that a special department named after him had been created at the newspaper for that purpose. He also claimed that foreigners who visited their editorial office found it really hard to understand this style of writing. "This probably reaffirmed their opinion that we are savage Asians who like building mausoleums", Khlebnikov (2001) said.

Even when covering Domnikov's murder, his colleagues often adopted a similar style of writing. A year after his murder, *Novaya Gazeta* published an article pleading with the Minister of Internal Affairs to assist the murder investigation in whatever way possible because the investigators did not appear to have made much, if any, progress. The piece was mocking the efforts of the police. Here is an excerpt:

> That's the conversation I had with Captain Panferov at the end of last week.
>
> – "Volodya, this is contract killing, isn't it?
> – Maybe.
> – Do you need anything?
> – No, we have everything we need."
>
> But I disagree with Panferov. His operative group has been overwhelmed by the numerous cases accumulated over the past year, they have to investigate dozens of murders that have come to their attention over the last very long year.
>
> (Rozhnov, 2001)

However, the tone of writing was much more sombre when the newspaper announced Domnikov's death. The obituary said:

> You start losing the meaningfulness of the profession when all of a sudden you feel your own helplessness. When we found out about the death of our friend – the editor of the special projects department of Novaya Gazeta Igor Domnikov, we thought: is what we are doing really necessary if we have to pay such a price.
>
> (*Novaya Gazeta*, 2000)

This was the first time when the editor and his colleagues were faced with this question, but it was unfortunately not the last time.

Yuri Shchekochikhin

Three years after Domnikov's assassination, another journalist – Yuri Petrovich Shchekochikhin – died in mysterious circumstances at the age of 53. Shchekochikhin was a deputy editor at the newspaper and an MP at the State Duma from the liberal Yabloko party. He died from an acute allergic reaction to an unknown substance. His relatives and colleagues said they believed that he had been poisoned to "prevent him from further uncovering the truth about a high-level corruption case involving officials from the Federal Security Service (FSB) and the Prosecutor General's Office" (CPJ, 2003).

On 17 June 2003, while on a business trip and just days before he was due to fly to the USA in relation to an investigation he was working on, Shchekochikhin suddenly fell ill with flu-like symptoms – fever, headache, body aches, and a burning sensation all over his skin. He returned to Moscow, and in the next four days, his condition deteriorated so rapidly that he started losing his hair and his skin started peeling off his body. The journalist was hospitalised on 21 June 2003, and according to *Novaya Gazeta*, the first diagnosis he received was poisoning. The subsequent official diagnosis was "acute toxico-allergic reaction – epidermal necrolysis, Lyell's syndrome" (*Novaya Gazeta*, 2008a). According to *Novaya Gazeta*, the representatives of the chief prosecutor's/attorney general's office insisted on this diagnosis, and they also used it to defend their decision not to open a criminal investigation into the case.

His colleagues claimed that he aged by 100 years in the course of a few days. A report about his condition stated: "In the next 12 days, the journalist's organs failed one by one – his skin literally peeled off his body; he lost all of his hair; his lungs, liver, kidneys, and, finally, his brain stopped functioning" (CPJ, 2003). The two prosecutors dealing with the case in 2003 and 2006 argued that Shchekochikhin had developed a rare disease as a result of a viral infection, the self-prescribed medication, and the food supplements he was receiving at the time. *Novaya Gazeta* contacted a team of UK doctors and professors and showed them Shchekochikhin's list of medications. According to the UK medics, the medication and food supplements could not have caused his disease. The allergen that actually caused the deadly reaction was never identified. Moreover, Shchekochikhin's clinical test results were classified as "a medical secret" and were not revealed either to his family or to his colleagues (CPJ, 2003; *Novaya Gazeta*, 2008a).

Shchekochikhin died on 3 July 2003. His family and colleagues called for a murder investigation into his death. For years, the prosecutor general's office refused to open a criminal investigation because of the alleged lack of evidence. Eventually, in April 2008, the Investigations Bureau Chief Alexander Bastrykin ordered an investigation into the suspected murder. In an editorial published on Shchekochikhin's birthday in 2008, the newspaper's scepticism was apparent: "No one really wanted to uncover the circumstances surrounding his death – the cases Shchekochikhin dealt with as a deputy and as a journalist were way too serious" (*Novaya Gazeta*, 2008b). Moreover, the editorial claimed that the people who had obstructed the investigation had recently left the security forces and had joined the Federation Council and the State Duma (*Novaya Gazeta*, 2008b).

However, the case was closed a year after it was opened – on 6 April 2009. "Impunity is becoming a norm of life in Russia", Reporters Without Borders said at the time (Glasnost Defence Foundation, 2009). The deputy editor of *Novaya Gazeta*, Sergey Sokolov, explained in an article that this decision came as no surprise to them because so much time had passed since the journalist's death and so many mistakes had been made along the way that it was impossible for experts to find traces of the substance that had killed their colleague. The newspaper made numerous attempts during the years to conduct its own investigation, including by sending samples abroad, but they did not possess enough forensic evidence to be able to do that themselves. Finally, on 3 July 2013 – 10 years after Shchekochikhin's death – Sokolov wrote an article in which he announced that the newspaper would put an end to its attempts to find out exactly how their colleague was poisoned. Sokolov explained at great length the efforts they had gone into were of no avail. "10 years ago, Yuri Shchekochikhin died. We know – it was a murder, but to prove it, is no longer possible, because for many years the Prosecutor's Office did everything they could to remove any traces of the crime" (Sokolov, 2013).

One thing that was very clear, as the article pointed out, was that whoever ordered the murder had a very strong reason to do that. There were numerous versions as to why they might have done so. Shchekochikhin had received a number of death threats shortly before his death. Sokolov (2013) claimed that his colleague worked on a long list of dangerous assignments:

1   He sought removal from office of two of the deputy attorney generals because he claimed that they allegedly hindered the investigations of high-profile criminal cases. The decision as to whether the

State Duma should demand their resignations was to be reached two months after Shchekochikhin's death, but after he passed away, the motion did not progress any further.

2   He also investigated corruption allegations linked to the minister of atomic energy, who was later convicted.

3   He also revealed "the fate" of the money allocated for the reconstruction of Chechnya. Shchekochikhin strongly objected to the war in Chechnya, and he wrote numerous articles on the topic.

4   He worked on a money-laundering case, involving corrupt officials allegedly depositing money into a US bank.

5   His investigations into the connections between high-ranking FSB (previously KGB) officials and organised crime gang members had led to the resignation of the Moscow bureau chief.

The most recent investigation often quoted as the main suspected reason for his death was into a smuggling and corruption case that involved a Moscow furniture store. The smuggling of furniture had allegedly involved high-ranking FSB officials who had used the furniture business to launder money through a US bank. As a member of Russia's parliament, Shchekochikhin interviewed officials and gained access to documents related to the case (CPJ, 2003; Sokolov, 2013). Shchekochikhin claimed in one of his articles that the attorney general's office in Russia had received $2 million in bribes to stop a corruption investigation into the case (CPJ, 2003). As an MP, Shchekochikhin tried to also enlist the president's help in the re-opening of the investigation. He obtained a US visa and intended to travel to the USA to further probe the US connection in the case and to talk to FBI officials about it. The last article he published on the topic was printed a month before his death (CPJ, 2003).

The brief overview of the range of investigations he worked on clearly showed Shchekochikhin's on-going battle for justice, his bravery, and his resistance. He used both his political and his journalistic power to expose various wrongdoings. In an obituary published in *The Guardian*, his colleagues were quoted as saying that he was "naive in his striving for justice, but it was this very naivety that turned out to be his best weapon against evil" (Corley, 2003). The founder of the Washington-based *Demokratizatsiya: The Journal of Post-Soviet Democratization* Fredo Arias-King (2004) described Shchekochikhin as "fascinating, offbeat, thoroughly laid back, and always generous with his time and company", and yet "Russia's most renowned investigative reporter, specializing in abuse and corruption by a system that could produce little else" (pp. 157–158). He argued that his colleagues "would boast that Yuri was the best known person inside Russia, and perhaps they were right" (Arias-King, 2004, p. 157).

His journalistic qualities and his significance were recognised by both Gorbachev and Putin. *Novaya Gazeta* reprinted the birthday wishes they sent him for his 50th birthday. Gorbachev (2000) called him: "a famous journalist", "a moralist", "a hardcore democrat", "a fighter against the mafia", and "a very reliable Person". The tone of Putin's (2000) birthday card was considerably more restrained. He said that millions of Russians were familiar with Shchekochikhin's journalistic style, and that he was very energetic and demanding towards himself and towards others. "Your sharp, lively pen reminds people of the great values of true democracy (народовластия)", Putin (2000) said.

Arias-King (2004) also praised the deceased journalist for his role in the democratisation process, but he was very critical of Putin's own role in the process:

> Yuri was truly a remarkable pioneer in the democratization of the USSR and a brave critic of what transpired in Russia later. His absence is heartbreaking. This journal lost Galina Starovoitova in 1998 and now loses another one of those irreplaceable, historically towering figures and friends. There is perhaps no more apt an allegory for Vladimir Putin's Russia than the death of Yuri Shchekochikhin.
>
> (p. 159)

Finally, the fact that Shchekochikhin's political and journalistic careers seemed to go hand-in-hand shows that the kind of journalism he practised was very different from the normative ideal advocated in the West. Shchekochikhin (Filippova, 2003) himself described his vision of journalism in an unpublished interview for a student newspaper that was posthumously printed:

> First, I was taught that I should not lie to anyone and I should not be afraid of anyone. Second, write what you yourself feel. Your opinion, no matter how old you are, is very important for understanding life and history as unfolding in front of your eyes. Third, learn how to write well. This is very difficult ... Another rule ... If you are working on a special operation – do not ever mislead the people who are telling you about themselves. Do not provide their names, surnames. It's dangerous for them.

Shchekochikhin also advised younger colleagues to rely on each other because journalism was "a mass profession – they can help you, and you can help them" (Filippova, 2003). However, the most important task for a journalist, in his view, was to protect his or her name and reputation, and to always convey the experiences of the people they were writing about (Filippova, 2003). The general outlook on life that Shchekochikhin shared was summed up by his colleague Gutiontov (2003):

> In the apartments where he lived, the chairs or forks might not have been enough, but the endless stream of people who did not have

enough forks and chairs was always there. And there was always an endless blather "about life" and fierce arguments, and the guitar was being passed from hand to hand.

Anna Politkovskaya

The most notorious murder of a Russian journalist was arguably that of investigative reporter Anna Politkovskaya. Politkovskaya was killed on Putin's birthday – 7 October 2006. She was found shot dead in a lift in her apartment block in Moscow. A pistol and four bullets were found near her body. Politkovskaya was a prominent journalist and human right activist who was very critical of Putin and the Kremlin's policy in Chechnya.

Novaya Gazeta's senior editorial team immediately reacted to the murder by claiming that it was definitely linked to her work. This is an extract from the article they published about her:

> She was threatened, intimidated, subjected to surveillance, raids and searches. "Our" paratroopers arrested her in Chechnya and threatened her with shooting. She was poisoned when she flew to Beslan. She pulled through ... Many, including *Novaya Gazeta's* well-wishers would at times say: "Well, your Politkovskaya – it's too much". No, it wasn't too much! She always wrote the truth. It is quite another thing that this truth was often so terrible that the consciousness of many could not begin to comprehend it. Which is why, they resorted to this defensive reaction of "It's too much". Sometimes – even in our editorial office. Probably the most difficult thing for an ordinary person is not to shun away from danger. But if you look the evil in the eye, it does not stand a chance. Anna looked the evil in the eye. And, maybe, that's why she emerged victorious from the most difficult situations ... For us, she remains alive. We will never accept the death of our Anna ... We will search for her murderers. We can guess where they might be ... While *Novaya Gazeta* exists, her killers will not sleep peacefully.
>
> (*Novaya Gazeta*, 2006)

As this extract suggested, Politkovskaya was known for her relentless determination to expose wrongdoings and corruption, but she was not simply a conventional investigative journalist who did that in a detached and objective way. Politkovskaya was also a human rights activist. She explained that her commitment to social justice was driven by her interest in "reviving Russia's pre-revolutionary tradition of writing about social problems" (Hearst, 2006). The articles written by her colleagues about her revealed how determined she was to help everyone who sought her help even if that involved dangerous interventions. In 2002, for example, she took part in the negotiations with the Chechen terrorists who held 912 hostages in a theatre in Moscow. The terrorists demanded the withdrawal of Russian forces from Chechnya and an end to the Second Chechen War. Politkovskaya defended her decision to intervene:

> Yes, I went beyond my journalistic role. But it would be quite wrong to say that doing so was a bad move from a journalistic point of view. By setting aside my role as journalist I learned so much that I would never have found out being just a plain journalist, who stands in the crowd along with everyone else.
>
> (Meek, 2004)

Politkovskaya did not shy away from danger even when explicitly warned to do so. In February 2001, while investigating rapes, beatings, and murders allegedly committed by the Russian military, she was arrested and held for three days. She received death and rape threats, and later that year, she had to be evacuated to Vienna. Upon her return to Moscow, she continued reporting on Chechnya (International Women's Media Foundation, 2002). Her colleague Ruslan Dubov (2014, personal communication) recalled how determined and even stubborn she was:

> We argued a lot. I found out about her murder from TV. My Mum gave me a ring – I was at a football match at the time. I couldn't believe it. In the beginning I just couldn't believe it. It was Putin's birthday. But after 5 seconds it started to sink in. She received lots of threats because her position was very critical of the ruling authorities. The editor-in-chief did all he could to try to persuade her not to write about Chechnya. He pleaded with her. He assigned very different topics to her which she wrote about – about dogs, etc. But she was like a drug addict – she was engulfed into the topic. When one works for a long time on a given topic, you become an insider. It's like when you are in love with somebody.

Dubov (2014, personal communication) said that all murders of journalists in Russia were political to an extent because "the criminal money is linked to politics". In his view, it was hard to tell, however, whether Politkovskaya's murder was simply a criminal matter or was intended as a political symbol or sign. "Even the former President and the current President discussed this topic. If the situation was better, maybe that would not have happened", Dubov (2014, personal communication) said.

While no one seemed to suggest that Putin had any direct involvement in Politkovskaya's murder, his reaction to it was highly controversial. The president did not immediately react. Two human rights groups issued a statement two days after the murder in which they urged him to publicly condemn it. Consequently, after a phone conversation on the matter with US President George Bush, the Kremlin issued a statement in which Putin condemned the murder and called it a "tragic death" (*Radio Free Europe/ Radio Liberty*, 2006). Then on October 10, during a visit to Germany, Putin said that the killing was "a disgustingly cruel crime that cannot go unpunished" (Rostova, 2006). In response to a question by a German journalist, the president also notoriously said: "In this regard, I think one of our newspapers today correctly stated that for the current authorities in general and for the Chechen authorities in particular, the murder of Politkovskaya caused much more damage than her publications" (Rostova, 2006). *Novaya Gazeta* immediately took issue with Putin's reaction. The editor published an article in which he expressed his anger at Putin's attempt to give his version of the murder. Muratov (2006) said:

> The President of the country had every right not to love A. S. Politkovskaya. A. S. Politkovskaya, as we know, had mutual feelings for him. The President presumably had his reasons to express his attitude towards Anna's publications in Germany. I think that he made a mistake. When the leader of a country whose security services are subordinate to him offers in the first hours and days of an investigation his personal version – the version of the president and the chief commander: about the fact that the killers are foreign enemies of Russia, officers might interpret this as an order by the chief commander and might forget about any other lines of inquiry. Service journalists have already done that.

Muratov (2006) explained that Putin presented the murder as an attack on him because it took place on his birthday. In his interview with me, Muratov made it clear that he did not think that Putin was behind the murder. The president's irritation with the murder and the interpretation he gave of it almost as a nuisance had persisted over time. When I presented my research project at UNESCO's World Press Freedom Day in May 2017 in Jakarta, a representative from the Ministry of Communications and Mass Media of the Russian Federation said: "Why do you all keep talking about Politkovskaya's murder? The murder has been successfully solved. Why do people still talk about it? Can you give me an example of another President who, like Putin, regularly drinks tea with editors?" I discuss the three claims made by the Russian official representative in more detail in this and subsequent chapters.

To start with, he was right in saying that the international reaction to Politkovskaya's murder was indeed very strong. The murder was covered by publications from around the world. Heads of state and international organisations strongly condemned it, including the US President George W. Bush, the UK Prime Minister Tony Blair, the German Chancellor Angela Merkel, the French President Jacques Chirac, the Finnish President Tarja Halonen, and the Georgian President Mikheil Saakashvili. Rallies were organised in Finland, Germany, France, and the UK. Demonstrators voiced strong concerns about the situation in Russia and on Putin's policies. *Novaya Gazeta* reprinted an open letter addressed to Putin by the leader of the Alliance of Liberals and Democrats for Europe in the European Parliament Graham Watson, calling on the president to guarantee freedom of expression in the country and a fair and independent judicial inquiry into Politkovskaya's murder. Watson (2006) also condemned the "increased entrenched lawlessness" in Russia. The European Parliament later adopted a resolution in which it called European Union member-states to put democracy, human rights, and freedom of expression at the heart of any new agreement with Russia. During a visit to Russia, US Secretary of State Condoleezza Rice met Politkovskaya's son Iliya and *Novaya Gazeta's* editor Muratov and gave an interview for the newspaper in which she said that Politkovskaya was "a heroine for her". She also reiterated the importance of freedom of expression for democracy.

It is also true that Politkovskaya's killer and his accomplices were indeed eventually sentenced at the end of the trial that took place during my fieldwork in Russia in May-June 2014. However, it was never revealed who ordered the murder. Politkovskaya gave an interview for *Radio Free Europe/Radio Liberty* just two days before she was murdered. The interview was about Chechnya's Prime Minister Ramzan Kadyrov who had just turned 30 that day, which meant that he could now run for president. Politkovskaya called Kadyrov "a Stalin of our times" (*Radio Free Europe/Radio Liberty*, 2016). She explained that over the past few days she had worked on an investigation about torture in "Kadyrov's prisons" and she claimed that there were people who were abducted and died "for completely inexplicable reasons ... as part of a PR campaign" (*Radio Free Europe/Radio Liberty*, 2016). Politkovskaya said that no other newspaper had written about these abduction cases and that she had only "one dream for Kadyrov's birthday" – for him to face trial for the crimes he had committed (*Radio Free Europe/Radio Liberty*, 2016).

The last article Politkovskaya was working on was indeed about abductions and tortures in Chechnya – a topic she had extensively covered. It described the torture of two terror suspects by Chechen security services. Politkovskaya claimed that innocent people, wrongly accused of being terrorists, were held on trumped-up charges and were being tortured in order to admit to committing crimes they had no involvement in. It contained a quote from a group of young convicted Chechens who said: "This penitentiary colony has turned into a concentration camp for Chechen convicts. They are discriminated against on ethnic grounds. They wouldn't let them leave their single cells and penal isolators" (Politkovskaya, 2006). The article was accompanied by shots from a video that showed how two men were tortured – a knife was sticking out of one man's ear, and another one was lying lifeless on the ground, covered in blood. The two torturers were heard swearing and lamenting how difficult it was to kill these two men.

In an editorial published by *Novaya Gazeta* (2006) two days after Politkovskaya's murder, the newspaper said that they did know who killed their colleague or why, but there were two main lines of inquiry: (1) that the murder was ordered by Ramzan Kadyrov because of the many articles she had written about him and his activities and (2) that the murder was ordered by those "who want suspicion to fall on the current Chechen prime minister", who given that he had just turned 30 could now become president (which is precisely what happened). Kadyrov had always denied any involvement and had defended the thesis that the murder was indeed ordered by people who wanted him to be framed for it. Kadyrov (2006) said, "Politkovskaya's materials did not disturb me at all, they did not influence my work or my activities, quite the contrary, they helped me so I did not have any reason to pursue her. She was a woman and I would never have fallen that low as to actually arrange the destruction of a woman ('разборки с женщинами')." In a press conference, he explained that women were sacred for Chechens and anyone who killed a woman was "not a human being and does not believe in the Most High". Kadyrov also urged the law enforcement agencies to bring to justice those involved in the murder of Politkovskaya.

Military observer Viacheslav Izmailov (2006) wrote an article about his murdered colleague, in which he explained that from the moment she joined the newspaper in 1999, Politkovskaya had always worked on dangerous assignments and she could have died at any moment. The focus of her work had been on fighting injustice by exposing wrongdoings and helping ordinary people. Izmailov (2006) argued that many innocent people had been rescued from adversities such as the war in Chechnya, thanks to her efforts. He recalled how she was poisoned in 2004 while flying to Beslan. Izmailov also claimed that Politkovskaya had told him and other colleagues how she feared that Kadyrov might try to kill her. She met him in 2004, and he allegedly threatened her during that meeting. Moreover, another *Novaya Gazeta* journalist who previously worked in Chechnya was forced to leave the country and settle in the West because his life was in danger.

Five days after the murder, the main shareholder of the newspaper and State Duma deputy at the time – Alexander Lebedev – announced that they would offer 25 million Russian rubles to anyone who came forward with information that might reveal who had ordered and executed Politkovskaya's murder. In an editorial, *Novaya Gazeta* said that although the newspaper would be conducting their own investigation into the murder, they would not publish information about any of the lines of inquiry they worked on because they did not want to impede the official investigation.

The official investigation itself was fraught with difficulties. It took nearly eight years and three trials for her killer and his accomplices to be sentenced and sent to prison, but the instigator of the murder was never identified or prosecuted. Ten months after the murder, Russia's prosecutor general announced that 10 people had been arrested in connection with the assassination. He claimed that a Moscow criminal gang was to blame, but the gang had also received operational support from the Federal Security Service (FSB). The trial itself did not start until 19 November 2008, after a few major setbacks such as the demotion of the chief investigator into the case and the disappearance of the alleged killer Rustam Makhmudov. Makhmudov had escaped abroad and was not present during the first trial. Initially, the judge announced that the trial would be held in closed session because the jury had requested that, but a juror gave a radio interview in which he denied that this was the jury's request. As a result, the judge had to back down and hold the trial in an open court.

Four men were on trial in Politkovskaya's first murder trial – the suspected killer's brothers Dzhabrail and Ibragim Makhmudov, the former Moscow policeman Sergei Khajikurbanov, and the FSB lieutenant colonel Pavel Ryaguzov who was persecuted on related charges. The trial went on for three months, and all four defendants were acquitted at the end of it. Commentators described the judicial process as "chaotic and frequently amateurish" (Harding, 2009). Important pieces of evidence disappeared during the trial, and there seemed to be key discrepancies such as the fact that the assassin caught on camera as entering Politkovskaya's apartment block appeared to look considerably slimmer than the main suspect.

The prosecution appealed, and the appeal was upheld by the Supreme Court. As a result, a new trial was ordered. The defendants in the new trial were the three Chechen brothers and their uncle Lom-Ali Gaitukayev as well as the former police officer Sergei Khajikurbanov. Gaitukayev was accused and eventually found guilty of organising the murder. He was "a Chechen underworld boss with a long criminal record" (Shmaraeva, 2014). Another former police officer Dmitry Pavlyuchenkov was also found guilty of helping organise the murder, but he was sentenced to 11 years in prison in a separate court case in 2012.

The final trial took place in 2014, and the guilty verdict was passed on 9 June 2014. Gaitukayev and his nephew Rustam Makhmudov were sentenced to life imprisonment. Makhmudov's brothers were given 12 and 14 years in prison, while Khajikurbanov received 20 years in prison. According to the prosecution, Pavlyuchenkov bought a gun and handed it over to Rustam Makhmudov. Makhmudov was driven to the murder scene by his brother Jabrail in a green Lada Riva. The Makhmudov brothers were found to be in the vicinity of Politkovskaya's apartment block on the day of her murder, and they had also used their mobile phones repeatedly – shortly before and after she was shot.

In spite of the fact that Pavlyuchenkov struck a deal with the prosecution and promised to reveal who ordered the investigative journalist's murder, he did not actually do that. He explained that his role was to organise surveillance, while Gaitukayev and Khajikurbanov had to organise the actual murder. The overall price paid was $150,000. Gaitukayev was in prison at the time of the murder, but the prosecution showed how he was able to use his mobile phone in prison to arrange the murder. Pavlyuchenkov explained how he met Gaitukayev back in July 2006 in a cafe in Moscow and gave him Politkovskaya's address and car registration number as well as the £150,000 for the contract killing (Shmaraeva, 2014).

Shmaraeva (2014) argued that the official indictment in Politkovskaya's case described the client who ordered the assassination as an "unidentified person, displeased with Politkovskaya's critical publications". All five defendants pleaded "not guilty", but they were all found guilty. Politkovskaya's family and colleagues were not happy with the outcome of the trial. On the anniversary of her death in 2016, *Novaya Gazeta* posted "a video protest" and an article by the deputy editor, Sokolov, entitled: "Do not dare say that the murder has been solved". Sokolov (2016) wrote that he and his colleagues felt "fury" because the "client" in Politkovskaya's contract killing had not been revealed. In the video itself, *Novaya Gazeta's* editorial staff and Politkovskaya's son were filmed holding posters in which the main stages in the investigation of her murder were outlined. One poster kept reappearing throughout the video with the words: "Заказчик не найден" (the person who had ordered the murder had not been found). Sokolov (2016) also said in the article that a lot of time had been wasted in Politkovskaya's investigation because the main organisers and those who had protected them had deliberately perpetuated the wrong thesis, namely, that the Russian oligarch Boris Beresovsky was behind the murder. Moreover, after the end of the final trial, only one investigator had continued working on her case, but even he had recently retired, which meant that in practice the investigation appeared to have been discontinued.

Finally, it is worth pointing out that Politkovskaya has indeed turned into a symbol for the strife for independent journalism in Russia. In addition to the awards she received while still alive, she was also the recipient of a few posthumous awards. *Novaya Gazeta* has also received a number of awards in recognition of their work. Upon receipt of the Reporters Without Borders 2006 award, the newspaper published an article that said:

> Posthumously, she became a symbol in the West of the free Russian press. And Novaya Gazeta was presented as the newspaper in which Anna worked. Her death shocked colleagues abroad and forced them to pay attention to the state of the free press in Russia, to raise the alarm, to learn more about our newspaper and appreciate our work, to express support and solidarity.
>
> (Mineev, 2006)

Politkovskaya's own perception of journalism was best summarised by her in her acceptance speech for the International Women's Media Foundation's Courage in Journalism award:

> It is customary to believe that journalists go to places where wars and catastrophes break out because people and the world want to know the truth and the news about these events. In Russia things are just the opposite today. The people do not want to know the truth about the ongoing war. They have been subjected to a powerful ideological brainwash and were led to believe that the events in Chechnya are nothing but an anti-terrorist operation, and they do not want to know what really takes place there. They do not wish to hear about the crimes committed by the military, about the sufferings of the civilian population or about the thousands of victims on all the sides. So, the courage of a journalist under such circumstances consists in giving this information to the people, much against their will, and make them think about the tragedy that the country is going through, think that this must be stopped.
>
> You may ask, why? Why, if people do not want that?
>
> The answer is simple: this is our duty, the duty of a journalist. A doctor performs an operation. A journalist operates on the public opinion. The need to risk is part of the profession here. If you are tired and cannot take the risk any more, you have to leave. As for me, I am not tired yet.
>
> (International Women's Media Foundation Courage in Journalism Award, 2002)

Stanislav Markelov and Anastasia Baburova

While Politkovskaya's first trial was under way, on 19 January 2009, a human rights lawyer who had worked with her and had also defended opponents of the pro-Kremlin government in Chechnya and a young trainee journalist were murdered in broad daylight on a busy Moscow street. Markelov was 34 years old and Anastasia Baburova was 25 years old. Markelov left behind a wife and two young children. Markelov and Baburova were walking towards the underground station when a man shot Markelov in the head with a pistol with a silencer. Baburova tried to chase the killer, but he turned and shot her in the head. She died in hospital later that day.

Novaya Gazeta reacted to the murders with an article saying: "No fear ... This is not terror anymore, this is a war" (Milashina, 2009). In a follow-up article, Estemirova (2009) asked: "The murder of Markelov is a declaration of war. Now the question is – whose side is the state on?"

Deputy Editor Sokolov (2009) wrote that after Politkovskaya's murder, many people were waiting for "clear words and visible actions" by the authorities but the signal sent had been clearly received not just by them, but also by "all fascist bastards". Sokolov (2009) also wrote that the murderers felt no fear because they knew they would not be punished, but the victims felt no fear either because "when you defend others, you stop feeling fear". Sokolov (2009) called Markelov and Baburova "people with an absolutely precise understanding of such abstract concepts as 'good' and 'bad'".

Special Projects Editor Elena Milashina described Markelov as "a unique lawyer" who took on "hopeless and life-threatening cases". He was a Moscow lawyer who "constantly worked in Chechnya, representing the interests of the victims of extrajudicial killings and tortures" as well as the victims of fascism. Milashina (2009) wrote that he had "defended those who were killed and humiliated by the state". Sokolov wrote that Markelov defended Chechens from Russian military men and the Russian military men from corrupt commanders. Markelov was *Novaya Gazeta's* lawyer, including in Anna Politkovskaya's civil cases and he also defended "the heroes of her publications" (Milashina, 2009). He also represented Igor Domnikov's family in their attempts to force the authorities to launch a criminal court case against the person who had ordered his murder.

Novaya Gazeta (2009a) described Markelov as "a hippie", a person who "could give his life for his friends". Markelov was a left-wing social democrat who was interested in the history of the left movement and the traditions of political advocacy. He even took part in the founding of the Left Historical Club as part of the Human Rights Centre Memorial. His work with Memorial took him on his first visit to the Caucasus in 1994. Markelov worked on a range of dangerous cases, and he received death threats because of his work. One of the text messages he received said:

> You brainless animal … interfering again in Budanov's case??!!! Idiot, could you not find a quieter suicide method??? Go quickly to the translplantology centre, maybe your internal organs will be useful for somebody … although you will not die in vain … maybe they will give more money...
>
> (Estemirova, 2009)

He had also been targeted by neo-Nazis. He was beaten by five men in 2004.

In his first article about the murder, Sokolov speculated on the possible motive. He argued that the assassination could be in retaliation for any of the cases Markelov had worked on. Particularly dangerous was the Budanov case the text message referred to, which involved the rape and murder of an 18-year-old Chechen woman by a drunken Russian army colonel. Budanov was released from prison just a week before Markelov's murder. A few hours before he was killed, Markelov had said that he planned to appeal his release (Harding, 2009). Another dangerous case mentioned by Sokolov was that of Russian officer Sergei Lapin who was sentenced to 11 years in prison for illegally arresting, torturing, and killing a 22-year-old Chechen man. Sokolov wrote that the murder "might have come from Chechnya" because Markelov also took up the case against the secret prison in the village of Chechnya's President Ramzan Kadyrov. Izmailov (2009) wrote that the last case Markelov worked on was about the abduction of Mohmadsalah Masayev. Originally from Chechnya, Masayev gave an interview in which he claimed that for almost four months he had been held hostage by Kadyrov in one of the military bases in a village in Chechnya. Shortly after the publication of the article, Masayev was kidnapped again. An official case was opened into his disappearance, and Markelov represented his family in the case. Markelov claimed that the abduction of Masayev was "an attempt to ruin the unprecedented criminal case about the secret prison organised by Chechnya's leadership" (Izmailov, 2009). As already indicated, Chechnya's president (and former prime minister) had previously been accused of being involved in Politkovskaya's murder – a claim he had always vehemently denied.

Baburova and Markelov had known each other for years. The young trainee journalist joined *Novaya Gazeta* only a few months before her murder – in October 2008. Sokolov (2009) described Baburova as "a romantic rebel – an anarchist, a participant in the anti-fascist movement and the March of Dissent". He praised her for her attempts to stop the killer and said that not many in Russia would have done what she did. In her work, Baburova wanted to focus on investigating crimes committed by neo-Nazis. Donskih (2009) wrote that Baburova was one of the few people in the country who understood the importance of working on this topic about the spread of neo-Nazism and who was very knowledgeable about it. He also said that her fellow students and work colleagues were shocked by her death.

In contrast to the lengthy investigations and controversial court cases in the previous three cases of murdered journalists, Markelov's and Baburova murders were swiftly solved. A 31-year-old neo-Nazi and his 26-year-old girlfriend were convicted in 2011 at the end of a trial that lasted three and a half months. Nikita Tikhonov was 29 and Yevgeniya Khasis was 24 at the time of the murders. They were both involved with the far-right group Russky Obraz (Russian Image) and with the Battle Organisation of Russian Nationalists (BORN) – "a single brand for several autonomous clandestine groups" – which were very active online (*Novaya Gazeta*, 2011a). Tikhonov also had a personal motive to kill Markelov. A search warrant was issued for him in connection with the killing of a 19-year-old anti-fascist activist whose family was represented by Markelov. The court heard that the pair was arrested in November

2009 after three pistols and a Kalashnikov were found at their flat. Initially, Tikhonov confessed to the murders and detailed his actions on the day, but later, both he and his girlfriend denied any involvement. Before the court case, *Novaya Gazeta* (2011a) wrote that the trial would be:

> ...a political process – an open trial against Russian fascism which – under the amiable supervision of the authorities – has developed from street clowns and snotty lowlifes stabbing Tajik street cleaners to combat terrorist groups whose sole purpose of existence is to create situations of chaos and terror in the country by killing public figures, journalists, lawyers, judges, prosecutors, law enforcement and other public officials.

The article also described how less than a month after the murders of Markelov and Baburova, the newspaper had received a threating email message from BORN. In the message, Markelov and Baburova were called "odious enemies of the Russian nation" and their deaths were described as "the latest warning to all anti-Russian human right defenders, journalists, anti-fascists, cops and civil servants" (*Novaya Gazeta*, 2011a).

The prosecution claimed that Tikhonov and Khasis had carefully prepared Markelov's murder. Khasis assisted Tikhonov on the day of the murders by observing Markelov's movements and reporting to Tikhonov. One of the main witnesses in the trial was Ilya Goryachev – the leader of Russky Obraz. Goryachev was under police protection because he testified against Tikhonov. He claimed that Tikhonov had confessed to him that he had killed Markelov and Baburova. Tikhonov was sentenced to life imprisonment and Khasis received an 18-year prison sentence for "helping co-ordinate the attack" (Parfitt, 2011). Parfitt (2011) reported that the "killers laughed and smiled as the sentence was read". Both *Novaya Gazeta* and the victims' families were satisfied with the outcome of the trial and praised the judge for the way in which the trial was conducted.

Natalia Estemirova

Another human rights activist and *Novaya Gazeta* correspondent who exposed the tortures and abuses in Chechnya was also killed in 2009. Natalia Estemirova was the first recipient of the Anna Politkovskaya prize founded in honour of the investigative journalist who also died because of her work on the North Caucasus. Estemirova was a good friend of both Politkovskaya and Markelov. An article about her said that almost every time Politkovskaya went to Grozny, she stayed with Estemirova. The article also described how the human rights activists exposing the tortures and abuses in Chechnya were a very "narrow" circle of people whose lives do "not cost a kopeika" {a penny} (*Novaya Gazeta*, 2009b). Estemirova was perhaps the "most famous human rights campaigner" in Chechnya who, whilst driven by a strong sense of justice, frequently comforted the families of the tortured, killed, or abducted and challenged those in power – from the army generals to "the all-powerful dictator Kadyrov" (*Novaya Gazeta*, 2009b). For security reasons, some of her last articles in *Novaya Gazeta* were signed with a pseudonym. In an obituary in *The Guardian*, Lokshina (2009) recalled how "she felt that she owed it to 'Anya' {Politkovskaya} not to quit". Estemirova (2009) even wrote one of the articles about Markelov's death in which she praised his efforts in Chechnya. She wrote: "The murder of Markelov is a declaration of war. Now the question is – whose side is the state on?" Lokshina and Estemirova attended Markelov's funeral and "stayed up all night, talking about Markelov and Politkovskaya and wondering who would be next in line" (Lokshina, 2009).

In fact, Estemirova was next in line. She was abducted from her home in Chechnya's capital Grozny on 15 July 2009, and was found shot dead later the same day near the village of Gazi-Yurt in neighbouring Ingushetia (Lokshina, 2009). The 50-year-old human rights campaigner and journalist was a single mum who left behind a 15-year-old daughter. Natalie – or Natasha as she was known by her colleagues and friends – was half-Russian and half-Chechen. She had a degree in history and had worked as a teacher for most of her life. She became a journalist and human rights activist in the last 10 years of her life. Her last job was at the human rights organisation Memorial. Her daughter raised the alarm about her disappearance by going to Memorial's office after her mum did not respond to her calls all day. It turned out that a neighbour had seen how Estemirova was dragged into a car in the morning, but she was too frightened to do or say anything about it. An article in *Novaya Gazeta* explained that the reaction of this neighbour (or the lack of it) was indicative of the culture of lawlessness in Chechnya. The article said: "In present-day Chechnya, people try not to look at such things. Power structures are often behind these abductions who as a rule mercilessly punish any witnesses who are prepared to come forward" (*Novaya Gazeta*, 2009c). The murder was described as "cold, cruel, quick" (*Novaya Gazeta*, 2009c). The Russian Union of Journalists condemned it and launched a national campaign against the violence against journalists. They also called for an end to impunity and complimented President Dmitry Medvedev for his swift condemnation of the murder. They claimed that this was "the first time in many years for the leader of the country to immediately react" to such a tragedy (*Novaya Gazeta*, 2009c).

The best portrayal of Estemirova was made by human rights activist Elena Sannikova (2009):

She demanded only one thing from the authorities: to abide by the law. Not to abduct people but to detain them legally. Not to torture them, not to kill them without a proper judicial investigation and trial by throwing dead bodies on the side of the road but to persecute them if there are real grounds for that. I observed with fear the circumstances in which she worked, the unbearable information constantly passed through her conscience. Only a strong-willed person with iron nerves could have worked in the way Natasha worked. We learned a lot of flagrant facts about crimes against humanity through her. Many of Anna Politkovskaya's reports were published thanks to her. And many people were saved from extrajudicial executions as a result of Natasha's efforts. Everyone knew that as a person she was strong-willed, forthright and fearless. But that doesn't mean that simple human feelings were alien to her. She was compassionate, delicate and feminine.

Milashina (2009b) wrote that many people trusted her and came looking for her in Memorial's office on a daily basis, but only about 100 turned up for her funeral – mainly colleagues and relatives. The main reason for that was the general atmosphere of fear in Grozny. She even recalled how on the day of the funeral, well-wishers whispered to Estemirova's daughter not to talk about politics and not to mention Ramzan Kadyrov. Milashina (2009b) explained that Estemirova did not consider Kadyrov as her personal enemy, but her position was principled. She gave a couple of examples of the extent to which her deceased colleague stuck to her principles. For instance, as soon as an avenue in Grozny was named after Putin, she stopped walking down that avenue. She also refused to wear a headscarf as the Chechen government demanded.

In an interview she gave about herself, Estemirova said that at times she felt fear but that if "you are scared of feeling fear, you shouldn't practice this profession" (*Novaya Gazeta*, 2009d). She also explained what her understanding of journalism was and how she reconciled the fact that she was both an activist and a journalist. She said that in her view, "the time for neutral, detached and impartial journalism has ended" because it was important for journalists to raise any issues related to the protection of people in every single situation and this should actually be their main task (*Novaya Gazeta*, 2009d). Estemirova saw as her main task the need to protect people, especially vulnerable ones. She was a history teacher when she first starting writing articles. She was concerned that journalists were not covering the real situation in her republic and the threats facing people, so she decided that it was her duty to do so.

Subsequently, she left teaching as a vocation and opened a local office of Memorial. Her NGO job actually provided her with "invaluable materials" for her journalistic articles. Estemirova drew parallels with the role of non-fiction in the nineteenth century when Russian literature played a moral educational role by instilling feelings of sympathy, promoting good deeds and civic awareness. In Estemirova's view, this is the role that should be played by journalism in contemporary Russia.

Journalism should "educate, be the tuning fork, teach goodness and ... defend the interests of ordinary people and their rights" (*Novaya Gazeta*, 2009d). She also talked of the misguided understanding of the meaning of patriotism in contemporary Russia, which often led to very public demonstrations of support for people such as Putin and Kadyrov. Moreover, she said that journalists should be led by strife for justice. She gave examples of her own practice that had made a positive difference to people's lives despite the very difficult circumstances and various challenges faced due to the overall culture of lawlessness in her region.

Estemirova's killers, however, did not face justice despite demands for an open and thorough investigation into her case by her colleagues, fellow human rights activists, and Western politicians such as the European Parliament President Jerzy Buzek. Nobody was prosecuted for her murder, but the head of the human rights group she worked for was persecuted for allegedly defaming Chechnya's president by accusing him of personal involvement in Estemirova's murder. Hours after the murder, Orlov allegedly said:

> I know, I am sure who is guilty of Natalya Estemirova's murder. We all know this person. His name is Ramzan Kadyrov ... We do not know if he gave the order himself or if his close associates did so to please their superiors. But evidently [Russian] President [Dmitry] Medvedev is happy having a killer run one of the Russian Federation's regions.
>
> (BBC News, 2011)

Kadyrov himself condemned the murder and denied any involvement in it, but he also took Orlov to court, initially launching a civil case against him, but later there was also a criminal defamation case against him. Kadyrov won the civil case but lost the criminal one because the court concluded that Orlov had been speaking of Mr Kadyrov's guilt "not in the criminal sense, but in the social and political sense" (BBC News, 2011).

A year after Estemirova's murder, her colleagues gave a press conference in which they urged the authorities to speed up the investigation. They also sent an open letter to President Dmitry Medvedev in which they objected to the main version the investigation was working on – that the murder was committed by the insurgent Alkhazur Bashaev, who had his personal grievances against Estemirova because of a case she had worked on. Bashaev himself was not alive – he was shot a few months after Estemirova's murder. The letter explicitly reminded Medvedev that the murdered journalist and human rights activist was personally threatened by Kadyrov who had also publicly denounced the activities of Memorial by calling those working for the NGO "enemies of the people, enemies of the law, enemies of the state" (*Novaya Gazeta*, 2010).

One of Estemirova's colleagues explained during the press conference that the last case she worked on was about the abduction and extrajudicial killing of villager Rizvan Albekov for allegedly giving a sheep to the rebels. An article published nearly two years after the murder said:

> Based on the materials of the criminal case on the murder of Natalia Estemirova, it is absolutely clear that one of the main versions about the involvement of Chechen law enforcement officers in the kidnapping and execution of the human rights activist has not been investigated. Two years after this loud political assassination, the investigation has not yielded any results. But, I believe, the reason for this is the inviolability of the Chechen security forces. The special status of Ramzan Kadyrov is the wall which Russian law has hit.
>
> (Milashina, 2011)

On the second anniversary of Estemirova's murder, *Novaya Gazeta* conducted a joint investigation together with Memorial and the International Federation for Human Rights. The results were published by the newspaper and sent to the president. The journalists used materials from the criminal case, but they also commissioned DNA tests and conducted a range of interviews. The main conclusion of the report they published was that the "evidence base" did not support the official version about Alkhazur Bashaev's alleged involvement into Estemirova's abduction and murder. Moreover, the article claimed that the investigators had not closely examined any of the other versions, especially about the alleged involvement of state departments/security forces in the journalist's murder (*Novaya Gazeta*, 2011b).

The article was a prime example of the kind of investigative journalism practised by *Novaya Gazeta* journalists. It was a very detailed report of the main lines of inquiry into Estemirova's murder and the evidence used in the case, but the article was not simply based on evidence obtained from the official investigation. It included the results of DNA tests by Swiss and Russian experts commissioned by the newspaper. The journalists' actions were clearly motivated by the pursuit for justice:

> The investigation has been delayed, the materials on the case are protected due to the "confidentiality of the investigation", the people who ordered the murder and the killers are at large. This is the typical outcome of the investigations into almost all political contract murders committed in contemporary Russia. We consider this situation unacceptable. The main goal of our joint report is to breach the "confidentiality of the investigation", to inform the Russian and international public that the official investigation is deliberately going down the wrong path.

We believe (and prove) that the investigation into the murder of Natalia Estemirova deliberately went away from the search for the real killers.

We are confident that this crime could be solved in hot pursuit. For this, the case has all the necessary evidence. We believe that the delay and the "confidentiality of the investigation" are only necessary in so far as the real culprits in Natasha's death can remain unpunished.

(*Novaya Gazeta*, 2011b)

Seven years after her death, Estemirova's murder still remained unresolved, which prompted the Council of Europe Commissioner for Human Rights to intervene as a third party in the legal case against the Russian Federation in the European Court of Human Rights. The commissioner stated that Estemirova's murder "should not be viewed in isolation but as part of a broader pattern of killings and intimidation of human rights defenders in the North Caucasus and, in particular, the Chechen Republic" and that "the Russian authorities have failed to prevent and to react appropriately" (Commissioner for Human Rights, 2016, p. 10). He condemned the reaction of President Ramzan Kadyrov who in response to Estemirova's murder said in a radio interview: "Why would Kadyrov kill women that no one needs? She never had any honour, dignity or sense of conscience" (Commissioner for Human Rights, 2016, p. 6). The commissioner also reminded the court that after Estemirova's murder, the NGO she worked for had to close down its offices in Chechnya "due to serious concerns for the lives and security of its staff members" (Commissioner for Human Rights, 2016, p. 9). Estemirova's death did not put an end to the violence against human rights activists and journalists in the region, and the commissioner provided a few recent examples of attacks and intimidations.

Conclusion

The history of *Novaya Gazeta* and the six murders of its journalists and lawyer is a story of resilience and determination in the face of numerous adversities. It is also a story of the different types of journalism practised at the newspaper in comparison with the one endorsed on a normative level by their Western colleagues and indeed by most of their Russian colleagues. On a normative level, the journalism practised at *Novaya Gazeta* is underpinned by a similar commitment to public service, namely, the pursuit and publication of stories that are in the public interest and/or hold the powerful to account. However, in practical terms, their understanding of public service journalism appears to be very different because for some it actually involves exposing wrongdoings and helping the powerless at any cost. The lengths to which some journalists go to in their efforts to get to the bottom of an issue or a crime (be it the murder of their colleague) are extraordinary. Journalists often do the job that the authorities should be doing – they conduct criminal investigations themselves by obtaining DNA samples, carrying out forensic-style interviews, and obtaining access to classified information. Their actions are often motivated by a desire to expose sophisticated cover-ups and to ultimately get justice even if that involves fighting battles on many fronts against much more powerful opponents. The five murdered journalists and lawyer Markelov also believed in the rule of law across all republics. They devoted their lives to the fight for justice. As deputy editor-in-chief Vitalii Yaroshevsky (2014, personal communication) said, the main reason for the deaths of his six murdered colleagues was "first of all an honest fulfillment of their professional duties", but their murders were also political murders not because the Russian authorities were directly involved in them but because they "did nothing to protect their work and guard their safety. So, they are indirectly responsible for these deaths".

As their colleagues made it clear, those murdered journalists were no saints. Politkovskaya was a notoriously difficult person to work with who had been repeatedly warned that her life would be in danger if she continued working on Chechnya, but the numerous threats and intimidations she received did not deter her. Neither did her death deter her colleagues from persevering with their work despite the fact that their editor wanted to close down the newspaper because he felt it was too dangerous for his staff. Fundamentally, the actions and practices of *Novaya Gazeta* journalists were driven by the different vision of Russia they shared in comparison with their main "opponent" Putin. Like Putin, they too claimed that they were driven by a sense of patriotism if we define patriotism as "love for or devotion to one's country" (Merriam-Webster Dictionary, 2017). However, as Muratov (2014, personal communication) said, their understanding of patriotism was very different from the one Putin promulgated. It was underpinned by the belief that Russia's future should be of a global, democratic, and peaceful nation and should not involve the invasion of foreign territories or indeed the imperial grandeur of the past.

4 *Novaya Gazeta* Today

Challenges, Practices, and Role Perceptions

While there have been no recent murders of *Novaya Gazeta* journalists, the tragic deaths of their colleagues have left a permanent mark on the newspaper's journalists' current routines, practices, and role conceptions. This chapter presents the findings from my fieldwork in Russia in May 2014, as well as subsequent analysis of developments up until the submission of the manuscript in December 2017. It is organised around four key headings: (1) Ethnographic Observations, (2) The Coverage of Ukraine – Liberal Ideology and/or Split Loyalties, and (3) A Living or a Way of Life: Common Challenges and Coping Strategies, and (4) *Novaya Gazeta's* Role in Russian Society – Journalists' Perceptions. The chapter starts by providing an in-depth account of the daily routine *Novaya Gazeta's* journalists follow.

While the actual fieldwork in the newsroom lasted for only a few days, my observations even during the first day of my visit to the newspaper revealed a great deal about the newspaper's mission and ethos. My first meetings at *Novaya Gazeta* were cancelled because the editor and the managing editor had to urgently travel to Ukraine because one of their correspondents was kidnapped the previous night and his abductors demanded a ransom from them. The chapter explains how the newspaper handled the situation. It also reports the findings from my observations of a few editorial meetings in which the senior editorial staff made decisions about how to cover the situation in Ukraine. Journalists' views on the role they were and should be playing in relation to the conflict in Ukraine are also outlined. Then, in the third part, I explore other issues and challenges that journalists currently face – from verbal and written threats and harassment to physical attacks. Finally, the last section delves deeper into journalists' motivations and the role they see themselves as playing in Russian society. The salaries they received were at least three times lower than the average salary in the sector, but most journalists claimed this was not a major issue because, for them, this was a way of life, not a living. The ethnographic material is presented in a style known as "women's ways of knowing" in which "there is no harsh separation between research and life, and where what happens in one realm inevitably informs the other" (Clark, 2012, p. xx). I use the first person singular much more often in this chapter because of the nature of the work I conducted in Russia and the subsequent interpretation of my observations, which is inevitably influenced by my own perceptions.

Ethnographic Observations

As a person coming from a former communist country, I approached my trip to Russia with mixed feelings. On the one hand, I was excited by the prospect of experiencing the grandeur of Moscow first-hand and I was pleasantly surprised by the welcoming attitude of my contact at *Novaya Gazeta*. I could not yet believe that I would be allowed access to what was considered to be the deadliest newspaper in Russia – a newspaper I had read so much about in Western media. On the other hand, I was extremely nervous. The topic of my study was very controversial. I arrived in Moscow at a historic time – at the heat of the conflict with Ukraine. I was aware of the fact that I had to be extremely cautious because my work might attract undue attention, although a part of me thought that the Russian authorities and the Federal Security Service (FSB, formerly Komitet Gosudarstvennoy Bezopasnosti (KGB)) machine could not possibly be interested in the work of an academic. One of the key questions playing on my mind was: Is the situation in *Novaya Gazeta* as bad as described by Western media? Is it indeed that dangerous for the journalists working for the newspaper or is the Cold War legacy still influencing Western media's perceptions of Russia? I soon received a very definitive answer to this question.

My contact was the head of press service at the newspaper Nadezhda Prusenkova (see Figure 4.1), who was also the newspaper's court correspondent and managing editor on the day I arrived. My first meeting with her was at lunchtime on Monday, 12 May 2014, so I waited impatiently in front of the newspaper's offices in downtown Moscow for her to arrive. There was no direct entrance to the building as far as I could tell. I could see that there was a security gatehouse and then a backyard leading to what looked like a side entrance of the building. A few minutes before my meeting with Prusenkova, I received a text message from her, which said that she had to cancel her meeting with me because something urgent had come up. Given the limited time I had in Moscow, I could not just go back to my hotel, so I quickly texted her and asked her whether I could go in and start talking to her colleagues. Luckily, Prusenkova agreed, and a few minutes later, I was in the building. The security guard got so used to my presence in the next few days that he soon started treating me like a member of staff and would just let me in at any time without asking any questions.

The journalist who greeted me showed me to her office first where I interviewed her. It was during my interview with her that I realised that Prusenkova could not meet me because one of *Novaya Gazeta*'s correspondents in Ukraine had been kidnapped the previous night and she

Figure 4.1 Nadezhda Prusenkova: *Novaya Gazeta*'s Head of Press Service.

was on her way to Kiev with Muratov. After a tour of the building and a few conversations with other journalists, they took me to Prusenkova's office. Prusenkova shared a very spacious room with a young court reporter. The third inhabitant in the room was a tiny kitten lying on a blanket behind Prusenkova's desk. Her colleague explained to me that a compassionate reader had brought the kitten into their office in the hope that the newspaper would find a new home for the cat. There was also a sofa with a blanket in the room, which, as I noticed later, was used by other journalists as well. Some would come for a sit-down and a chat with colleagues, while others would use the sofa for their afternoon nap, which seemed to be a routine practice.

Prusenkova's colleagues explained to me that she was actually going to come back soon because while she was on the train to the airport, she received notification from Muratov that their colleague had already been released and it was not necessary for her to travel to Kiev anymore. A few minutes later, the 35-year-old journalist turned up as expected, with a huge smile, which never left her face even when she was discussing very serious topics. She was casually dressed in a T-shirt and a pair of jeans, and she was wheeling a big suitcase, which she left next to the kitten, who at that point was already peacefully sleeping on the floor. She explained that she did not have enough time to go back home to leave her luggage because she was the managing editor for the newspaper's next issue.

"My editor called me at 5am. If he calls me at this time, I know that something wrong has happened", Prusenkova (2014, personal communication) recalled the events of the last few hours. Something wrong did indeed happen in the early hours. One of her colleagues – Pavel Kanygin – was kidnapped while covering the uprisings in Eastern Ukraine. *Novaya Gazeta's* editor-in-chief received an early morning phone call from a German colleague informing him that special correspondent Kanygin was kidnapped by activists from the self-proclaimed Donetsk People's Republic. The activists demanded a ransom of around $30,000 in exchange for Kanygin's freedom. Muratov immediately called Prusenkova and asked her to start making informal inquiries and to accompany him to Ukraine. Muratov explained a few days later after coming back from Kiev:

> We were ready, I flew to Kiev prepared to pay a ransom for him because I wanted to save the life of our correspondent. When terrorists are concerned, if you don't pay, there is no saving him, they will kill him
> Muratov (2014, personal communication)

However, on her way to the airport, Prusenkova received another phone call. It was no longer necessary for her to travel to Ukraine – the activists had promised to release Kanygin. With her suitcase in her hands, she caught the train in the opposite direction – now to the newspaper's offices where, as managing editor, she was responsible for the next edition. She was also the paper's press officer, so her phone was ringing all day with inquiries about her kidnapped colleague. In addition, she had to consider what to do with the kitten. "We placed a notice in the newspaper and another reader promised that he would come and collect the cat but she never turned up. Usually, it's calmer than that", she summed up. Prusenkova (2014, personal communication) then hastily qualified her comment by saying that she shared her editor's view that US journalists, as portrayed in the HBO series *The Newsroom*, were "like children" in comparison with them.

The story of her kidnapped colleague in Ukraine was a case in point. As soon as he was released, Kanygin, in an article published in their next edition, described what had happened. The headline was: "This is not a ransom, this is your contribution to our war". The subhead was: "The story of the abduction of our special correspondent Pavel Kanygin, as he himself tells it without emotion or judgement" (Kanygin, 2014). Kanygin was having dinner in a pizzeria with his German colleague Stefan Scholl from *Südwest Presse* when four men entered the restaurant and sat at their table demanding an explanation from Kanygin about his articles on the referendum on Crimea's independence that took place in March 2014. "We had read your materials. What do you mean by, 'These ballot papers look as if they have been printed on a printer?'", they asked him. They argued that his claim that hardly any people turned up was a lie (Kanygin, 2014). They also explained what their main demand was:

> Okay bro, you just have to realise that all of you, the press, this is our weapon. What are we without you? The fact is, your writing is murky, bro. You need to write more simply, so that they can all understand

that the Banderites are putting pressure on us here, and we are just normal people, not terrorists; we stand for the truth, in short.

(Kanygin, 2014)

"Banderites" is a colloquial term denoting the members and supporters of the Organization of Ukrainian Nationalists led by Stepan Bandera as well as sometimes, more broadly, members of pro-Western democratic parties. "The term has been used pejoratively in Soviet propaganda and to denote the Ukrainian underground during and after the Second World War, as well as all Ukrainian nationalists and all those in Ukraine opposed to Soviet nationality policy" (Internet Encyclopedia of Ukraine, n.d.).

After the brief conversation in the pizzeria, the four men asked Kanygin to accompany them to the main square of Artemivsk – a city in Eastern Ukraine. There he got surrounded by a bigger group of people who took issue with the fact that he had called them "separatists" in an article. The German journalist tried to talk the crowd out of continuing the confrontation, but they threatened to shoot him if he did not stop his plea. Kanygin described his encounter with the crowd as "lynching":

Although there were few armed militia there, ordinary people were coming to the "lynching." But to explain anything to them, turned out to be useless; people did not want to listen. As if I were a spy, they wanted confessions that I was working for Right Sector. Someone said that they should get a repentance from me and that it should be re-corded on video. Someone else said that I had to publicly announce a retraction [of what I wrote] right there on the spot. My crimes were becoming more fantastic by the minute, and the intentions of the people in the crowd were getting more and more serious. They would not let me explain. About fifty people had gathered around. Finally, the people on the square started saying that I worked for the SBU [Security Service of Ukraine], the CIA, the USA, and the person who took my press card said that I was an American who has mastered the Russian language and had forged my *Novaya Gazeta* identity card. Someone grabbed me by my backpack. I covered my hand with my hands, and they rained blows on me from different directions, wherever it was possible to reach, and I sank to the ground. I was being beaten by women and men. Someone said that it was "revenge for their sons who were dying for freedom in Sloviansk and Kramatorsk." People shouted that no one listens to them and that "no one has heard them all these years." One of them hit me and said, "What kind of terrorists are we, you bitch!".

(Kanygin, 2014)

Kanygin's ordeal then continued in the car they forced him into and in a tent in a nearby village where they forced him to take his clothes off and to give them his computer password so they could look through the files on his laptop. The original intention of Kanygin's abductors was to take him to the armed militia's headquarters in Sloviansk where there were 14 other captives, including five Ukrainian journalists. However, they never got as far as Sloviansk. Instead, they took him to another tent where they passed him onto his "new keepers" whose task was to transfer him to Sloviansk in the morning. "They did not want to do that at all. Someone suggested that they hide me there and demand a ransom. They named an amount of US $30,000", Kanygin (2014) wrote. Kanygin offered to call his colleagues in Moscow, but his abductors did not trust him to do that. Instead, they decided to take everything he had and to call his German colleague and ask him for more cash. They allowed Kanygin to speak to Scholl, and a meeting was arranged for 4 a.m. at the hotel. Kanygin was told that "this isn't a ransom, it's your contribution to our war", (Kanygin, 2014). He was promised that if everything went "smoothly", he would be in Donetsk in the morning. One of the abductors told him: "You should thank us for not handing you over to Sloviansk", and I asked what would have happened [to me] in Sloviansk. "Your FSB and Chechens are there. They wouldn't be talking. At best you'd be sitting in the basement, at worst…well you understand" (Kanygin, 2014).

The militants then took the journalist to a hotel where they waited for his German colleague to come and pay the ransom they demanded. Kanygin was not released immediately after Scholl paid the requested amount. He was taken back to the car they previously travelled in, where he was given mineral water to drink. Kanygin had no recollection of the next few hours, but he ended his article by saying that he woke up in a hotel room in Donetsk where the manager told him that

> people had brought me in a car, I was not drunk but looked like a sleepwalker, walking on my own. Shoes without laces, jeans without a belt, my sim card was on the table and my rummaged bag was lying on the floor.
>
> (Kanygin, 2014)

The way in which Kanygin's colleagues reacted to his abduction was indicative of the way crisis situations were usually handled at *Novaya Gazeta*. Immediately after his abduction, his German colleague managed to get in touch with Muratov who, in the next few hours, frantically tried to establish who had kidnapped his correspondent and what they wanted from him. "The first thing we did is to start negotiating with his abductors who endangered our journalist's life", Muratov (2014, personal communication) explained. They used the services of a mediator from President Vladimir Putin's political party United Russia. They also turned to the special services – both in Russia and in Ukraine as well as the Russian Ministry of Internal Affairs. Muratov said that they did not really expect much from the authorities. He recalled how he had previously tried notifying the Ministry's Centre Against Extremism that one of their journalists was endangered in relation to a story about the Caucasus. "We received a reply from them saying that we haven't sent it to the correct address. We then asked for the correct address and they told us that this is a professional secret/classified information. This is a true story", Muratov (2014, personal communication) said. His deputy editor-in-chief Sergey Sokolov still kept the correspondence on this matter. In cases when they hit a brick wall with the authorities, they simply relayed the facts to the public, Muratov (2014, personal communication) explained.

This lack of trust in the authorities was a recurring theme in my conversations with *Novaya Gazeta* journalists – especially those of them who had been exposed to dangers. For all of them, the first port of call in a dangerous situation was their editor-in-chief. As the editor of the sports department, Ruslan Dubov said, whenever he received a threat, he would always talk to Muratov about it first:

– This is the main rule. In case of threats, the best defence/protection is to inform the editor-in-chief. He has a mechanism in place to protect the journalist, which if need be, involves informing the authorities but by overcoming some of the bureaucratic obstacles which one would inevitably face if following the official channels. The story with Pavel Kanygin is a good example of that. Muratov personally went there. Ukraine is a dangerous place and Muratov personally dealt with the issue to save his life.
– And this is the most effective way?
– Yes.

                                      (Dubov, 2014, personal communication)

Muratov (2014, personal communication) himself explained the rationale behind his actions:

I flew to Kiev prepared to pay a ransom for him because I wanted to save the life of our correspondent and then publicly announce it. When terrorists are concerned, if you don't pay, there is no saving him, they will kill him. Our first aim is to get our colleague back alive and then put up a show and deal with the public. The most important thing for us is to save the life of our colleagues, not to allow our brother to die. We can't turn the death of a journalist into a sensation. We don't need this type of sensation. His murder will not be a sensation. We need him alive... We mobilized our forces but we have to praise the dignified behavior of our colleague as well. They tried to poison him and he was unconscious for a while but the important thing is that he stayed alive. We didn't waste any time.

The use of the word "brother" was not coincidental. Dubov (2014, personal communication) explained that Muratov and his deputy Sokolov were "very close friends, they are like relatives", and, as a whole, the newspaper was like "a big family – brothers, fathers in a good sense...We share the good and the bad moments. We've been together for a long time". The fathers in this family were Muratov and his deputy Sokolov whom journalists turned to, not just when in danger, but also for advice on various other issues (Dubov, 2014, personal communication).

This sense of a collective, family-like atmosphere with a shared history and a clear, but not very rigid, hierarchy behind it was evident during the newspaper's regular editorial meetings that I observed. As Yaroshevsky (2014, personal communication) explained,

> We have a vertical hierarchy of power ever since the newspaper was founded – an imitation of the way Russia is run. Our editor-in-chief has his own policies – do this, show an interest in this, you have missed this or that. This is not censorship.

Every morning at 11 a.m., the senior editorial staff and some junior journalists gathered for their daily planning meeting, but journalists could go and see the editor at any point without any prior appointment or without getting permission from their line managers. Muratov kept his keys on the outside of his door, so that everyone knew when he was in. The meetings took place around a table set under the portraits of their six murdered colleagues (Figure 4.2). This was not

Figure 4.2 A Regular Editorial Meeting at *Novaya Gazeta*, Moscow, May 2014.

the only reminder of the tragic deaths. Eight years after Anna Polit-kovskaya's death, they also kept her desk and her chair in her office (Figure 4.3). Other historical documents and objects were also kept in glass cabinets in the corridor just by the entrance. When I asked Muratov (2014, personal communication) why they still kept Polit-kovskaya's desk and chair, he said: "I don't know. This is what we decided. What do you suggest – that we open a bar in her office? It's not a working office...Anna's computer is in a museum. Anna's chair is there". However, when I went into the office, there was a second desk in it and another woman was working there.

a

b

Figure 4.3 Anna Politkovskaya's desk, Moscow, May 2014.

Younger reporters who have not met Politkovskaya or any of their other murdered colleagues offered their own interpretations as to why her desk and chair were still kept. Olga Prosvirova (2014, personal communication), a correspondent in the Web department, said that she had always been "a huge fan" of Politkovskaya and that was why she had always wanted to work at *Novaya Gazeta*. She said that she often heard stories about her, and "it seems like you know her because people here talk about her like she's still alive". In her view, her colleagues still kept the murdered journalist's desk because "it's always hard to say goodbye... I can't imagine this particular newsroom without her desk. It's part of us" (Prosvirova, 2014, personal communication). She said that she knew that Politkovskaya was a difficult person to work with and she often argued with her editors, but "this spirit of freedom in her is still alive" (Prosvirova, 2014, personal communication).

This spirit of collegiality coupled with sometimes passionate and heated discussions was what I observed too during the daily editorial meetings. One topic dominated all the editorial discussions – Ukraine. The atmosphere was not as sombre as the setting in which these editorial meetings were taking place. Each of the meetings I observed lasted for less than 15 minutes, and although the topics discussed were of a very serious nature – the situation in Ukraine, the abduction of their correspondent, sanctions against Russia, sanctions during previous wars, and so forth – the atmosphere was actually comparatively jovial and there was a lot of humour, laughter, and positivity in the room, especially on the day when their colleague was abducted in Ukraine and subsequently released. Incidentally, the editor-in-chief was not present during this meeting because he was in Kiev at the time. The meeting I observed led by him was not as jovial, but as his deputy editor-in-chief Vitalii Yaroshevsky (2014, personal communication) explained, the tone of these meetings was very often dictated by the mood Muratov was in, and on, that particular day he was not in a very good mood. "There are not many reasons for being in a good mood nowadays", Yaroshevsky (2014, personal communication) said.

The Coverage of Ukraine: Liberal Ideology and/or Split Loyalties

The discussions journalists had were not just about specific articles and assignments, but also about the wider role Russia played on the world stage and their own duties as journalists. The coverage of Ukraine represented a major challenge for the newspaper because the focus adopted in some of the articles often led to accusations of treachery and betrayal of the national interest. The conversations I observed and the interviews I conducted suggested that there was no strict editorial policy on the issue. All journalists and their editors were driven by what they believed was a strife for balance in a very complicated situation. Prusenkova (2014, personal communication) explained that they tried to give voice to the two sides in the conflict, but she also recognised the fact that in the eyes of the Russian public and authorities, they were

> the enemy of Russian authorities – they think about us as enemies. It's a very complicated situation for us because we need to find the balance between the different parts of Ukraine, and between Ukraine and Russia too... It's dangerous for our journalists.

Regional correspondent Ivan Zhilin (2014, personal communication) described the situation in Ukraine as "hell...a big pain".

Prusenkova (2014, personal communication) said that some people got so angry when reading their articles that

> they decide that if a journalist writes something that they disagree with, they can beat him, they can kidnap him, they can do anything. And the problem is many people are twisted there and no one can do anything about that.

Kanygin's abduction was an example of this phenomenon because, according to Prusenkova, the representatives of the so-called Donetsk People's Republic claimed that they were not behind his abduction, but in reality, there were many small military groups associated with them that did not necessarily operate in an organised or coherent way. Although officially they did not assume responsibility for the abduction, they managed to quickly find Kanygin and secure his release, Prusenkova (2014, personal communication) said. "They don't need a conflict and a scandal with journalists. We are official Russian journalists so it's very bad for them", she (Prusenkova, 2014, personal communication) said.

What became clear from my conversations with editorial staff was they did not all share the same vision about how the conflict should be covered or indeed whether and whose side they should endorse (if any) in that conflict. A few themes (with some overlaps between them) emerged.

Bias vs. Balance

A key question journalists discussed was the extent to which they should provide balanced and comprehensive coverage of the conflict. There was no doubt that this was a priority topic. The only clear-cut policy was ensuring that a good number of their own journalists were sent to Ukraine because the newspaper should not rely on secondary reports. One of their correspondents was permanently based in Kiev, but she received back-up from four other colleagues who covered the different regions, and a photo journalist. As a *Novaya Gazeta* journalist, who wanted to remain anonymous, said, they mostly relied "on what our correspondents tell us, what they write, what they see because they are there, they are in Ukraine and from there they understand the situation better". Dubov (2014, personal communication) explained that their materials were not corrected according to the information they received, but they were only stylistically edited because "we trust them completely – no one else. We print what they have seen".

In the view of a journalist who wanted to remain anonymous, there was no clear-cut editorial policy on how the conflict should be covered, but the underlying belief underpinning the coverage was "to minimise the number of victims and to not let the war to happen. That's the main idea". Zhilin (2014, personal communication) also said: "I want to live in a peaceful world". This generally pacifist ideology was in itself evidence of the fact that not all journalists shared the view that the conflict should be covered in a balanced way. This was a bone of contention in the newspaper, and according to Irina Gordienko, in the absence of a unilateral editorial policy, it was a matter for individual correspondents to decide how to cover the conflict. Some journalists like Gordienko herself felt the newspaper's coverage of Euromaidan was too favourable. Does this lack of consensus on how the conflict should be covered also reveal a more general lack of consensus on the issue of what role journalists should play in times of war and conflict or, in fact, the even wider issue of what roles journalists should play in their societies? I come back to this question later in this chapter when discussing journalists' role perceptions.

Pacifism, Sovereignty, and Russia's Role in the Conflict

A key reason why there appeared to be a disagreement on this issue was because journalists' views on who was right and who was wrong in that conflict and whether Russia and the West should have interfered differed. A few journalists were adamant that no external forces should have interfered at all – "neither Russia nor America or Europe" (Dubov, 2014, personal communication) – because the sovereignty of an autonomous state such as Ukraine was paramount. As a journalist who wanted to remain anonymous put it,

> It's a hard question but I guess right now we are at a point where it's very hard to say who's right and who's wrong. I understand that Russia played a major role in making this conflict bigger and harder and stronger but at the same time I wouldn't say that the Western countries reacted absolutely correctly. My personal wish is that there is no war. And that there are no victims because what is happening right now is terrible because there are people who die. And that's much more important than the political ideas that are being followed here.

Prosvirova (2014, personal communication) said that the eastern parts of Ukraine were "a complete mess", and even in Crimea, there were groups that felt so strongly against the Russian government that they were

> ready to take guns and go protect themselves...It's very harsh but I personally see no exit and I don't think that in this situation there are right sides. Like Russia's right or the United States. I think the best way is to stop playing this Cold War and war of media all over the world and just discuss what's going on. Otherwise we are going to ruin the whole country.
>
> (Prosvirova, 2014, personal communication)

Prosvirova covered the referendum in Crimea, and what she observed there made her rethink her newspaper's stance on the issue:

> It felt like you are visiting a great holiday because people were really happy. It's strange when sitting here and thinking: "It's wrong" – like Putin's doing something wrong. And when you go there, you just see all these people that speak Russian, write in Russian, they sometimes don't know Ukrainian and it really feels like it's a great holiday for them. Strange, the contrast is huge. I personally have no opinion of Crimea because I know historically it was part of Russia and my close relatives live there. Of course, I am happy that we live in the same country. I don't like how it was done. Like we are stealing something. Like we are saying: Don't touch, Ukraine. Crimea is ours. I don't like the moves that Putin made. But I agree somehow that Crimea is intrinsically part of Russia. It's very complicated.
>
> (Prosvirova, 2014, personal communication)

A journalist who wanted to remain anonymous acknowledged that in the main her newspaper criticised the measures taken by the Russian government because they were infringing Ukraine's sovereignty. She said:

> They are in the Ukraine, they have their own government, their own people, their own journalists and it's actually up to them how to build their country. As for us, well, it's our government, it's our country who made these decisions and it was actually Russia who interfered into the inner life of another country.

That was precisely the view shared by the editor-in-chief who felt very strongly about the stance his newspaper should take in the conflict. As already indicated in the previous chapter, Muratov took issue with Putin's general approach to foreign policy making – the very idea that Russia should achieve "grandeur" even if that involved military interventions:

> If we accept peace, then we won't experience this attitude of people being very negative towards us, treating us like bandits and fighters. Putin didn't take our army to Ukraine. Our army is not there but what he did is something terrible. In every country where Russian people live, they are now seen as a threat. What he did with the referendum in Crimea – talking about a fifth column – this is unacceptable. The consequences of what he did are catastrophic. 82% of the population is ready to vote for Putin. This is what it has come to – this is what ordinary Russians think. I love my country but this is an unnecessary conflict, a communist conflict. People will start saying that we are not fighting against Ukraine and the propaganda machine will say: "Yes, it's a brotherly nation". A few months ago it was impossible to even contemplate the possibility of that. It's the same as even contemplating the possibility of a war between the North and the South, between Canada and the USA, or Belgium and Luxembourg. This is impossible. But this is how far we have got. We reached a point when Russia received a phone call from Berlin with a plea not to bomb Kiev. Berlin is doing its best to guarantee that Russia will not fight against Ukraine. And this is in the year when we celebrate the victory jubilee. How is this possible? The Russian peace has collapsed, the cultural, the human aspects, everything: Let's fight against everyone, let's win against everyone.
>
> (Muratov, 2014, personal communication)

Muratov's perspective on the conflict was very clear. He said that the role Russia played was very negative and that Putin should not have interfered in the affairs of another sovereign country. He touched upon an important issue that was also mentioned by his colleagues – that of split loyalties – on the one hand, the journalists' love for their country, and on the other hand, the liberal ideology underpinning the journalism practised at *Novaya Gazeta*. However, when Muratov (2014, personal communication) described what kind of issues his newspaper focussed on in their coverage, it also became clear that due to these liberal values, journalists were strongly encouraged to work on investigations that exposed the atrocities that ultra-nationalists were committing in Ukraine. As Muratov (2014, personal communication) put it,

> I don't care what their cause is but people who set fires or kill because of their ideas are fascists, extreme fascists. I am strongly against the separation of Ukraine into regions but I don't care that these people fight for a united Ukraine, because they are murderers. And their ideology is a felony. When you serve your ideology by committing crimes against humanity you deserve prison, a lawsuit and prison.

All in all, *Novaya Gazeta*'s coverage of the conflict in Ukraine, as described by its editor and journalists, was actually consistent with the general liberal ideology underpinning the existence of the newspaper and the work of its editorial staff – an overriding belief in the values of liberal democracy and peace. In practice, this involved the condemnation/exposure of any authoritarian and ultra-right ideologies and practices as well as on-going attempts to hold the powerful to account by conducting thorough investigations, including on dangerous topics, and exposing any cases of corruption, injustice, and wrongdoings. However, while this general ideology appeared to be shared by all journalists I interviewed, the application of these principles in their day-to-day work, especially on a topic such as Ukraine, was not as straightforward. For most journalists, including their editor, Putin's understanding of patriotism, supported by the majority of the Russian population, did not coincide with their understanding of what it meant to love and serve one's country. The role they envisaged for their country on the world stage differed from the role Russia's president was consistently promoting. Yaroshevsky (2014, personal communication) summed up the prevailing sentiments:

He is ruling the state in a dictatorial manner. He is not on the side of democrats. People hate liberal values and anything to do with liberalism. His politics lack a human dimension. He is a person who plays the nationalist card and this is bad. This will not end well. This is what worries me. I am worried about the how, not the what. How are we going to come out of all this? I am sure that there will be a change but the question is when and what are we going to evidence – an even more extreme radicalisation or a softening? I can only guess – I don't know. But whatever I say of President Putin – it will be all bad.

However, there were a few journalists who offered more cautious evaluations or were not as quick in condemning Putin. Some refused to discuss Putin and his role. Zhilin (2014, personal communication), for example, said: "I have an opinion about him but it's my opinion … I can tell you that I don't like Mr Putin but that's all". Moreover, there were disagreements not only as to how far their newspaper should go in condemning Putin's approach and supporting/praising the Euromaidan movement in Ukraine, but also for some whether Crimea's annexation was a good or a bad thing for Russia and for Crimeans themselves.

A Living or a Way of Life – Common Challenges and Coping Strategies

These discussions and disagreements point to the wider question about the role the media should play in (the coverage of) wars and conflicts and more broadly whether that role should be different from the one they played in their mundane routine reporting (for the distinction between mundane/routine and exceptional reporting, see Bromley & Slavtcheva-Petkova, in press). This is why I probed journalists' beliefs and role perceptions further in my interviews with them by questioning them about the challenges they experienced and the role they saw themselves as playing in Russian society.

To start with, the journalists working for the three media organisations in my sample had experienced three main types of challenges: (1) business pressures, (2) threats and attacks, and (3) legal measures (Slavtcheva-Petkova, 2017). For *Novaya Gazeta* journalists, the first two types of challenges were the ones that most significantly affected their work, especially the various safety issues they faced.

Safety Issues – Threats, Attacks, and Harassment

Novaya Gazeta journalists had experienced by far the most brutal physical attacks and threats than any of their other colleagues. All journalists in my sample had either received threats and/or had been physically attacked or kidnapped. Yaroshevsky (2014, personal communication) said that Russia was one of the most dangerous countries for journalists in the world, quoting Reporters Without Borders press freedom ranking, according to which Russia was ranked 148th of 179 countries:

Journalists work in a difficult country. And in specific *Novaya Gazeta* works under even more difficult conditions. Six of our colleagues were murdered as you have seen from their portraits. Journalists' job is very dangerous because you pay the ultimate price one can pay for fulfilling one's professional duties. All six were murdered because they wrote materials that were very dangerous, which influential people did not like. That's why it's dangerous. There are no protective mechanisms in our country because we are in a state of opposition to the authorities and the state structures. Our editor-in-chief does not like it when we are labeled as an oppositional newspaper because he thinks we are a newspaper of common sense. We describe what we see and what we think ought to be said. But of course we are in opposition to the current regime.

(Yaroshevsky, 2014, personal communication)

Muratov (2014, personal communication) himself argued that the three most dangerous topics for his colleagues were investigations on corruption in the special services, the North Caucasus, and neo-Nazis. The six murders were indeed connected to these topics. Muratov (2014, personal communication) said that if people feared for their lives, they should not write about these topics. According to him, the most dangerous time for journalists was the period of preparation of the article for publication:

> They receive threats, they are intimidated, they try to bribe them – this happens regularly with our reporters who work on investigations, all the time, regularly, permanently. This is not Putin. He doesn't call people to ask them to threaten journalists. He doesn't call people asking them: Call Rumanin and threaten him. It's different kinds of mediators who deal with these threats, who offer bribes/money, threaten that their career will end. This is the general picture. If we are talking about the dangers journalists experience, they still experience dangers/threats but at least in the last four years we haven't had any casualties so it's better in that respect. But as far as the unfair judicial system is concerned, the attitude towards journalists, the threats they face – evidently not. I can read you some of the threats I have personally received: "Muratov, be careful, we are waiting for you! We will be there for you. Muratov, are you still alive and well? You will lose your beloved wife soon! We will come after your son. I am intercepting your phone".
>
> (Muratov, 2014, personal communication)

Whenever a journalist received a threat, they had to notify either Muratov or in his absence his deputy Sokolov. Both of them felt that it was their "duty" to protect their colleagues. All journalists I spoke to confirmed that this was what they always did. Sokolov oversaw the investigations' department, and he himself was robbed and brutally attached in 2013, resulting in a brain injury. Muratov said that the attack was definitely linked to his professional activities because the thieves stole important files from him. In some cases, Muratov had to evacuate journalists or even send them abroad. This had happened to Sokolov himself and to their correspondent in Sochi, Sergei Zolovkin, who was sent to a European country under the witness protection programme:

> Our aim is to evacuate them as soon as possible to avoid endangering their lives. When it's necessary, unfortunately, these cases have happened lately with our correspondents. A hired assassin shot at him [Zolovkin] but the police arrived and caught the hitman with the gun in his hand after firing the first shot. This is the first case when a killer was caught in action... He wrote a book about the experience called: "Not quite murdered".
>
> (Muratov, 2014, personal communication)

Dubov said that Zolovkin's assassin was a former employee of the security services. He claimed that it was not uncommon for him and his colleagues to receive threats, intimidations. and harassment, including by law enforcement officers. The most common types of threats were threatening emails, online comments, or text messages, but journalists had also experienced other forms of intimidation. Prusenkova once found a dead rat with a big knife under her doorstep with a note saying that she would be next, a donkey's ears in her post, and a swastika on her car. Most of the threats were linked to her work on neo-Nazis.

In addition to the physical attacks and the various threats, there had been other cases of abductions of journalists. Special correspondent Gordienko was abducted by local police in the North Caucasus (as she found out later) in 2008:

> I didn't know where I was. They didn't tell me. I showed them my press card but they didn't leave me and they kidnapped me. They thought that I was a terrible woman. They kept me for 24 hours. I spend a lot of time in the Caucasus. Russian law does not really work there. There is no legitimacy there, no rule of law. It's dangerous because local forces and local police consider themselves to be above the law.
>
> (Gordienko, 2014, personal communication, also
> quoted in Slavtcheva-Petkova, 2017)

Gordienko (2014, personal communication) said that the North Caucasus was definitely one of the most dangerous regions for reporters, although things had improved over the years. When working in the North Caucasus, she was frequently being followed or her phone was tapped. She was also used to receiving threatening emails. However, when asked whether she agreed with non-governmental organisations' claims that Russia was one of the most dangerous countries in the world for journalists, she said she did not agree because there were other much more dangerous places in Africa or in the Middle East. She admitted, however, that at times she had feared for her life, but she had actually felt much safer in the Caucasus than in Moscow because it was much easier for potential assailants to find her in Moscow. Gordienko said:

> People who deal with the North Caucasus have their own sources and friends and you know when you are there, you don't show yourself much. But when you are back and write articles, everyone can find your address and your address at work.
>
> (2014, personal communication)

Gordienko's (2014, personal communication) approach to dealing with threats was to notify the editor-in-chief and also to try to "solve" the problem herself because in her view, "the best way is to try to contact these people to find where the threats are coming for and to solve it eye to eye or find some connections in the Interior Ministry". When asked whether upon receiving her most recent threat she contacted the police, she said that although her editor advised her to do that, she did not do it because she did not have the time to do it, but, more importantly, she did not think that the police would help her. "They can actually do nothing about it and probably won't do anything anyway", Gordienko (2014, personal communication) said. She said that most of her colleagues adopted a similar approach – "they prefer to solve it by themselves". Similarly, when Dubov was threatened by a criminal group involved in the acquisition of football clubs, he did not contact the police:

> I don't trust the police. They are their friends, their informers so if I inform them, chances are they will in turn warn the criminals. The criminal world is closely connected to the business world so it's very difficult to tell who's a criminal, who's simply a businessman and who is whose friend or enemy. I don't want to further endanger my life.
> (Dubov, 2014, personal communication)

In addition to the threats he had received, Dubov (2014, personal communication) had also been offered bribes by

> different people who want to protect their status, people from the criminal world who prefer to negotiate with me by offering me information...The sums of money people are prepared to pay for a material not be published are huge – they can go up to a million dollars. Such sums have been offered to the newspaper on numerous occasions.

In his view, however, accepting bribes was completely unacceptable. Other journalists in my sample also mentioned that they had been offered bribes.

Normalising Danger and Precariousness

When describing the various threats they and their colleagues had received, journalists often underplayed their importance or presented them as "part of the job". Prosvirova (2014, personal communication) recalled a recent case when she received threats by a pro-Kremlin activist she had written about. She received "strange" phone calls for a month, and she was also being followed when going out:

> – I don't believe that it was something extraordinary. Here in Russia we just take it as it goes.
> – So are you saying that it's common practice?
> – I am not saying that it's common practice. Lots of people, my colleagues had worse things happening to them like real attacks near

their houses so I am not complaining. I know it's a part of my job. It's a common story... I stopped answering the phone and when I just hid myself somewhere, they stopped. It wasn't really scary. It's just that you are always nervous and you think: Oh, maybe this man who is sitting somewhere near me is following me.

(Prosvirova, 2014, personal communication)

She too did not inform the police because she did not trust them, but she followed precautions as advised by her editor who "can really help in this situation" (Prosvirova, 2014, personal communication).

Most of Prosvirova's colleagues also said they did not fear for their lives despite the dangers experienced. Yaroshevsky (2014, personal communication) summed up the prevailing sentiments:

Ever since Anna Politkovskaya's murder I have often been asked whether I fear for my life. I don't. I didn't then and I don't now. I am not a hero. I am a normal person. I've got children, grandchildren and I've got my responsibilities. I don't feel fear because it's not possible for me to live in such a state of mind. I can't imagine myself waking up, brushing my teeth and starting to fear. And then again at night. There are two solutions to this problem: 1. Change the newspaper or 2. Change my profession, and I don't have any plans to do either of these. I feared about my younger colleagues, especially the ladies. We had lots of young colleagues back then and I was worried that they will be crushed because it's scary - four shots in Moscow's city centre during daytime. But not a single person left the newspaper due to fear. Not one...What happens inside their heads, I don't know.

Similarly, Prusenkova (2014, personal communication) said that despite the fact that she had personally been harassed on numerous occasions she felt no fear. She said:

Like many of my colleagues, we are not suicidal; we are not crazy adrenaline maniacs. My murdered colleagues did something exact and painful for society. This was the only way. That's why maybe I see it as normal - you can be killed because you do something very important, very needed for all of us. *Novaya Gazeta* couldn't be just a job. It's a way of thinking, it's a way of life really.

(Prusenkova, 2014, personal communication, also quoted in
Slavtcheva-Petkova, 2017)

This perception of their job as a way of life, a lifelong commitment to the values their newspaper upheld had indeed been the main driving factor behind journalists' perseverance and resilience in the face of numerous challenges, including the very low pay they received and the declining prestige and trust in their profession and newspaper. Accepting dangers as normal is problematic, however, because it suggests that despite professing a commitment to the values of liberal democracy in general, some, if not most, journalists accepted the lack of adherence to these values as normal and did not really fight as strongly for their own rights and the rights of their profession as a whole as they did in relation to the topics they wrote about as journalists. They were all very strong defenders of the rule of law, but they did not trust the law-enforcement authorities in their country enough to rely on them to uphold the rule of law and protect them from dangers. This was precisely the point made by those few journalists who admitted to feeling fear. Dubov (2014, personal communication), for example, said that he felt "unprotected":

> When working on a given topic, you are trying to avoid danger as much as possible. Some people even avoid publishing stories on certain topics because the danger is quite clear and it's a fine line. I think it's safer nowadays. They may threaten you but murders are not that common. The attitude towards journalists has become a bit more civilized.
>
> (Dubov, 2014, personal communication)

Nonetheless, journalists' declarations of bravery did not necessarily preclude them from showing fear in their actions. As the conversation with Prosvirova (2014, personal communication) demonstrated, despite the fact she said she did not fear for her life, she was constantly looking over her shoulder and worrying whether her stalker was following her. Similarly, Prusenkova (2014, personal communication) admitted that she carried a self-defence device that made her feel "strong". Her personal strategy against feeling fear was to attempt to persuade herself that some events were down to "fate": "You become a little bit fatalistic. If it is bound to happen, it will happen. If not, it won't happen. I will try not to allow it to happen but it's not all in my hands" (Prusenkova, 2014, personal communication). This appears to be a coping strategy some journalists had adopted in the face of the on-going dangers they faced.

Financial Pressures

The safety issues were not the only challenges journalists had experienced. As already indicated, almost from the onset, the newspaper had also been in a precarious financial state, particularly exacerbated after Putin's return to the presidency. The newspaper was founded by a group of journalists, and the majority shares were in the hands of the paper's editorial staff – they owned "an inseparable pack of shares", as Prusenkova (2014, personal communication) put it. The other main shareholder (39%) was the

Russian oligarch Alexander Lebedev, who also owned the UK newspapers *The Independent* and *The London Evening Standard*. Former Soviet leader Mikhail Gorbachev owned the final 10% of the shares. Lebedev alone had allegedly invested $20 million in the newspaper, but in early 2015, he announced that he would stop "bankrolling" the paper because "of the expense and the strain under which it placed him". He explained to *The Times* (2015) that he wanted "some respite", "some time with the kids", and that he had been "left alone" by the authorities after withdrawing his financial support. Lebedev admitted to having suffered attempts on his life, having lost a significant amount of his wealth and having battled with depression.

Lebedev's announcement did not come as a surprise to *Novaya Gazeta* journalists because he had already notified them about his decision months earlier. Almost immediately after buying shares in the newspaper, Lebedev was embroiled in a corruption scandal involving the FSB. Lebedev himself was a former KGB agent. "It was a big scandal and he lost his business. It was a long story, a story of revenge on the side of the secret service", Prusenkova (2014, personal communication) explained. Yaroshevsky (2014, personal communication) said that the state "practically destroyed his business". He quoted *Forbes*, according to which Lebedev was one of the richest people in the world, but added that he was also a fighter for justice who "caused lots of troubles to a number of influential people" (Yaroshevsky, 2014, personal communication). Dubov (2014, personal communication) claimed that Lebedev had received "serious offers" to sell his pack of shares, and the harassment he was subjected to was "immense". "Before the appropriation of our shares, he was a billionaire, now he is a millionaire", Dubov (2014, personal communication) added. A few journalists used the word "strange" when describing Lebedev:

> Our owner is very strange. He didn't really envisage what risks he was undertaking. He ended the contract with us because he started experiencing problems with his business and in his personal life and this stopped his desire and willingness. He was a former KGB officer – maybe he was not expecting similar methods to be used against him. I think he wanted Russia to move closer to Europe, to the West, to England because he owns *The Evening Standard*. He underestimated the fact that Russian people are capable of conducting inappropriate deeds borne out of envy. Maybe it's different in Europe – we struggle with that. People in Russia are very suspicious towards anyone who is successful – they think there's something dodgy. He embarked on a few projects, which were unsuccessful. Similarly, they think that he couldn't just have come and given us some money without expecting something in return.
>
> (Dubov, 2014, personal communication)

Prusenkova (2014, personal communication) acknowledged that Lebedev "supported us at a time when we were on the ground. He saved us. He really saved us". She also said that he never interfered in their editorial policies. He had his own column in the newspaper in which he expressed his personal views. All journalists said that they had met Lebedev who had attended their social events such as anniversaries or Christmas/New Year's parties, but he had also convened a recent meeting to explain the difficulties he had been experiencing. Gorbachev was also a regular visitor at these events, but he was in ill health, so he had not visited the newspaper recently. As Gordienko (2014, personal communication) put it, "He's like the British Queen. Actually our so-called donors never decide".

Lebedev's withdrawal exacerbated the financial situation of the newspaper and led to an announcement by its editor that they might have to stop issuing the print edition. The financial difficulties of *Novaya Gazeta* have been a recurring story, but for the first time the newspaper announced that it might not have a print edition anymore. A key contributing factor was the lack of advertising. Prusenkova explained that the situation was very different during Medvedev's presidency. The first interview he gave as president was for *Novaya Gazeta*, and big business saw this "as a sign": "There are always signs and after this sign we had many, many commercials" (Prusenkova, 2014, personal communication). By contrast, when Putin was re-elected as president, he immediately convened a meeting with "big business representatives". "They were told that there were a few media they are not allowed to give any advertisements to. And we were at the important first place – always first place", Prusenkova (2014, personal communication) said. She gave an example of a drinks' company they had signed a one-year contract with for a huge sum of money. After the meeting with Putin, a representative from the company called the newspaper, asking them to withdraw any future advertisements but to keep the money they had pre-paid. According to Prusenkova (2014, personal communication), most companies were afraid of associating themselves with the newspaper, but another deterrent was the fact that advertisers preferred "a positive context" for their ads and *Novaya Gazeta* could not really provide such a positive context because they covered largely negative issues such as poverty, corruption, and scandals. She showed me the most recent edition of the newspaper in which only one ad was published. She said that the Internet edition was in a better financial state and it also subsidised the print edition.

How did these financial issues affect journalists? The most significant difficulty was the much lower pay they received in comparison with their colleagues at other media, especially those working for the state broadcasters. Moreover, due to the precarious financial state of their newspaper, they would often not receive their salaries or cash advances on time. The average salary was 5–10 times lower than that at publications such as *LifeNews* or *Izvestia* and in general lower than at most other newspapers, Prusenkova (2014, personal communication) said. As Zhilin (2014, personal communication) put it, "The level of our pay is a business mystery. I don't want to talk about prestige". However, Prusenkova (2014, personal communication) qualified her statement by saying: "The salaries here are not as high as in many other newspapers but that's in a way a compensation for the satisfaction we feel that we cannot feel in other places". Dubov (2014, personal communication) also said that salaries at *Novaya Gazeta* were "seriously lower than in other editions" and that even the editor-in-chief received in 10 months what other editors received in a month, but "people do not work here for the pay they get. They work here because of the pleasure and the satisfaction they get". Moreover, he added that there were opportunities for earning additional income such as writing articles for Western publications. Dubov said:

> I can write additional articles for English and American editions, for example – do a bit of work on the side. This is normal... Innocent texts – reports about neo-Nazis groups. It's not a problem. You can receive good pay especially if asked by a Western edition
> (2014, personal communication)

This sentiment was shared by all his colleagues in the interviews, but the informal conversations between them or with me revealed a slightly different picture. The pay the regional correspondents received was especially low, and one of them was telling a Moscow colleague how difficult it was for him and his family. He had gone shopping with his son the previous day and had been so careful not to exceed his budget that when his son grabbed a chocolate spread at the counter, he had to "break his heart...I realised I did not have enough money to pay for it. In fact, I did not have any money and if they don't pay me my cash advance today, I will remain penniless" (Slavtcheva-Petkova, 2017). A few other, also young journalists, were also interested in potentially studying or finding work opportunities abroad.

Other Challenges

In addition to their exacerbating financial woes, *Novaya Gazeta* had also faced a number of other challenges over the years. The newspaper had been embroiled in a few defamation cases – some of which with high-profile politicians. Dubov (2014, personal communication) cited a recent example of a legal case against one of his colleagues on "trumped-up charges". The Russian telecom regulator Roskomnadzor also issued two warnings within a 12-month period against *Novaya Gazeta* about alleged "extremist" coverage. The newspaper came under increased pressure from the state because of its critical coverage of Russia's role in Ukraine. The first warning served by Roskomnadzor was for an article by columnist and *Radio Echo of Moscow* host Yulia Latynina titled: "If we are not the West, then who are we?" The second one was for a book excerpt allegedly containing an expletive. Russian authorities were entitled to order the closure of a media outlet that had received two extremist warnings within a 12-month period.

Another challenge journalists experienced was professional espionage by a former employee in the advertising department who was transferring files for more than a year before they caught her. Prusenkova (2014, personal communication) said that they found "nanotechnology interception devices", and as a result they had enhanced their security. Her colleague (Anonymous, 2014, personal communication) recalled how they asked the young lady to leave the newspaper and they promised that they would not publicise the story if she stopped doing what she was doing at their newspaper. However, when they realised that she worked for another newspaper, they published an article about her and her activities. According to Gordienko (2014, personal communication), this young lady was hired by big businessmen the newspaper wrote about. Dubov (2014, personal communication) pointed out that "it's pointless for a spy to be infiltrated in our newspaper because we are very open … Our secrets come out every 2–3 days".

Finally, another measure frequently used against journalists was the denial of access to and accreditation for important events and/or press conferences, including the press conferences held by Putin. Prusenkova (2014, personal communication) said that they were rarely allowed to attend the president's press conferences. In the past two years, they were granted accreditation only on two occasions. A young female reporter even had the opportunity to ask a few questions about Russian oligarch Mikhail Khodorkovsky. Prusenkova (2014, personal communication) noted that her colleague might have been given this opportunity because "she is beautiful". Prusenkova (2014, personal communication) also said that Putin had never given an interview for their newspaper despite their attempts to request one. "Obama and Medvedev gave us interviews but Putin – no", she said. Muratov told me that the most recent request was for an interview on the situation in Ukraine. He showed me the response he had received from Putin's Press Secretary Dmitry Piskov – a letter he had stuck on his noticeboard. When requesting the interview, Muratov (2014, personal communication) pointed out that as a result of the propaganda he felt that there was a rift in Russian society ("раскол"), but in "his very polite reply" Piskov disagreed with his evaluation and said that due to Putin's significant commitments, he could not fulfil his request.

Novaya Gazeta's Role in Russian Society – Journalists' Perceptions

The role that *Novaya Gazeta* played in Russian society according to the journalists I interviewed was on two levels – the macro level (namely, in relation to the state, media, and political system in general) and the micro level (in relation to their readership and "ordinary" people). The key contentious issue on the macro level was: What is the newspaper's identity and mission? Is it an oppositional, a liberal, or an independent newspaper, and what wider purpose does it serve in Russian society? The editor-in-chief strongly objected to the use of the word "oppositional", but he also refused to assign labels to his newspaper. Another set of related questions was: Why does *Novaya Gazeta* still exist despite all the challenges and setbacks experienced during the years? Is it because the authorities need the newspaper as a window-dressing tool, or as Prusenkova (2014, personal communication) put it, so that they could demonstrate to the West that they had free media and valued the work of journalists, or is it simply because of the sheer resilience of its editorial staff in the face of so many adversities? Is the continued existence of *Novaya Gazeta* and other similar media organisations part of Putin's media strategy or is it just a case of him being unable or unwilling to fully destroy the newspaper?

Novaya Gazeta journalists did not provide unequivocal answers to these questions. According to the editor-in-chief, the newspaper was not oppositional because they did not "represent the opposition". Muratov said:

> We are an independent newspaper. The opposition wants to be in power. We do not have such aims. We want to continue working in the interests of society under every power. We are a newspaper, not a party or a sect.
>
> (2014, personal communication)

His deputy editor Yaroshevsky (2014, personal communication), however, argued that *Novaya Gazeta* was both oppositional and independent: "An oppositional newspaper is independent by default. An independent newspaper is a newspaper that is independent of the state. We are independent of the state. We earn our own living (which is not very high)". Gordienko (2014, personal communication) also labelled the newspaper as independent by defining independent as "independent from the state". She pointed out that "in the whole world there is no one 100% independent mass medium. I think that comparing with most other mass media in Russia, we are independent but of course not 100%".

Muratov (2014, personal communication) explained that *Novaya Gazeta* served "our society and people who are attracted to the European values and the values of democracy, who think that we do not have a good choice in Russian society – we have an autocracy and a dictatorship". In his view, their position was "philosophical", and it was endorsed only by a minority of the population because the majority had adopted a more pragmatic approach that did not include the "fight for justice" they had undertaken. *Novaya Gazeta*, therefore, served "the intelligencia, writers, artists, the young intellectuals, the old Moscow aristocracy" – a largely educated audience or what Yaroshevsky (2014, personal communication) labelled as "the progressive middle class". According to Muratov, 90% of their readers had a higher education degree and 23% were part of the ruling elite/decision-makers.

All journalists said that their newspaper was influential because if it was not, "we wouldn't have so many problems" (Anonymous, 2014, personal communication). Dubov (2014, personal communication) argued that *Novaya Gazeta* had "an important influence". He provided a few examples such as ministerial and police resignations, as a result of their publications:

> We have an important role to play – we do the job of the state authorities, we identify the problems and we find the criminals. The President is also interested in that – to know what bribes some of his people receive.
> (Dubov, 2014, personal communication)

He added that some people would not want to see their names appear in their newspaper. "We do not print out state newsletters. We tell human stories and write about serious stories. We have a very serious influence", Dubov (2014, personal communication) said.

When asked whether Putin had deliberately allowed the newspaper to exist and be critical so that the West could see that there were trends towards democratisation in Russia, Muratov (2014, personal communication) said:

> I know this question. I keep getting it regularly. They say: Citizen Muratov, can you please explain why they haven't closed you down? My answer is: Can you please tell me why are you asking ME this question? I am not the right person to answer this question. Legally speaking, I cannot be held responsible for their deeds. This question is not aimed at *Novaya Gazeta*. Do they want to use us as an ad, a window dressing in front of the West or not, I cannot tell you. What we do is our own business, not their business. It's not like the Deputy Prime Minister has come to me and said: We would like you Dmitry Andreeviech to be our window in front of the West so that they can say there is freedom of expression in Russia – you and *Ekho Moskvy*. Do you agree?

When I asked Muratov whether he felt he was a "thorn in Putin's side" – an expression used to describe the editor of *Ekho Moskvy* – Muratov (2014, personal communication) replied:

> This is an excellent question. Please write it down. Address it to Mr Piskov from Putin's administration. Please ask Mr Putin: Is

Novaya Gazeta a thorn in Mr Putin's side? My task is not to be a thorn in anyone's side. In fact, I don't care whether we are a thorn in anyone's side. Our function is to inform and this is what we do.

With a slight irritation in his voice, Muratov (2014, personal communication) also said that Western journalists "keep seeing a conspiracy plot":

– They explain that our peace is very precarious and if *Novaya Gazeta* exists, then Putin must have decided in favour of that. If the sun rises, then it's Putin's decision. If the river Volga flows into the Caspian Sea, then whose decision it is? Putin's. Why don't you ask me why Volga flows into the Caspian Sea? This is not so. Putin does not decide everything in the world. A lot of children were born without Putin's involvement. *Novaya Gazeta* exists without Putin's involvement. People die without Putin's involvement, people are happy without his involvement. In our state there is this perception of the President as a hero, the President as Batman. There is a difference between Batman depicted in the comic books and in reality. But our society, our people are like children, it's a childish nation. They need to be taken care of. Our President is our babysitter. This is what we are like. This is how we are built.
– But this is the legacy of communism perhaps?
– Yes, of course. You were born, then you went to a kindergarten, then to school, then to either a technical college or university and you would receive 130 rubbles there, you would go on a trade union holiday in Crimea or Sochi, you would receive a small, very uncomfortable home of your own. If you have enough money and good connections, you will also buy a car (not a very fast one) and at around the age of 65 your fine life will be over. Everything was pre-planned in the Soviet Union, it was like a journey, a voyage. But this journey was blown apart by the dissidents who led a partisan war against the state. And after that we realized that we like stability but democracy is about instability, because everything can be built from scratch only if the old system is destroyed. But destroying the old system meant new people will be in power. This system is insured against mistakes. The system will rectify itself. No one will rectify it. There is a self-protection option in its computer system. So if the computer is destroyed, there is no reaction because it is protected against making mistakes. Under absolute authority, there is no such self-protection. So nowadays people abhor what they have never experienced. For example, they resent the Europe they have never visited. They resent the democracy which they have never experienced and the free choice they have never had. The majority of people resent that which they

have never experienced. With this propaganda, soon enough people will start hating sex because it's very destabilizing. Our propaganda is capable of making people believe this.

(Muratov, 2014, personal communication)

All in all, as the editor-in-chief's words show regardless of what label he and his colleagues chose for their newspaper, their accounts of what role their newspaper played in Russian society were very similar. They all shared the same liberal values and they believed that those values were cherished by their readers – "very well-educated people who are perhaps not happy with the regime and are looking for an alternative, for a society where democracy rules, with free choice and no corruption" (Dubov, 2014, personal communication). They all condemned the current political regime in Russia, which in their view was not democratic. They did not put the blame for that on Putin alone, but they recognised that the majority of people in their society seemed to support Putin's political leadership and, as Muratov (2014, personal communication) put it, to reject democratic values and democracy as a whole – something they had never fully experienced.

So what did "ordinary Russians" think of *Novaya Gazeta*? This question did not have a straightforward answer according to the journalists working for the newspaper. On the one hand, a few of them such as Dubov (2014, personal communication) said that "ordinary Russians" did not like *Novaya Gazeta*. Yaroshevsky (2014, personal communication) said that there were individual cases when they received phone calls from people who called them "the fifth column", "CIA agents", "our President uses the term national traitor. Any critical citizen is called a national traitor because we don't want Russia to fight with anyone". Prosvirova (2014, personal communication) also said that the regular viewers of *Channel One* thought of *Novaya Gazeta* as the newspaper that creates "scandal, that is always against Russia and we don't like Russia. It's hard to explain that I have never met people who love Russia more than in this office". *Novaya Gazeta's* critical stance towards Putin and his policies often made the newspaper particularly unpopular among the soaring number of Putin's supporters. The conflict with Ukraine during which Putin's nationalistic discourse/agenda reached new heights contributed to these sentiments.

On the other hand, one of the key aspects of *Novaya Gazeta's* mission was to help "ordinary people", and the example with the kitten they took in is an illustration of that. A journalist who wanted to remain anonymous said that the newspaper received letters and personal visits from their readers every day, and they relied on journalists to help them. Dubov (2014, personal communication) also gave a few examples of human interest stories or charitable causes that they had supported and had made a difference to individual people's lives: a story about a policeman who was fighting cancer; another one about a remote school that needed funding, or the numerous articles about ill children who needed expensive treatment abroad. As Gordienko (2014, personal communication) put it, "The most useful things our newspaper presents ... were socially-oriented articles about ordinary people" that led to positive changes in these people's lives.

Finally, when asked "What are the most fundamental journalistic values for you?", journalists provided very similar answers to the ones they previously gave in response to the questions about *Novaya Gazeta's* role in society or indeed the coverage of Ukraine. For some, the main principle was "not to harm anyone" and to promote human rights and freedom – "freedom of speech, freedom of press, freedom of mind, freedom of meetings" (Prusenkova, 2014, personal communication). Most did not hide the fact that their personal values and beliefs influenced their work. As Yaroshevsky (2014, personal communication) said,

> Undoubtedly they do, because I have my own views and beliefs. For example, I know too well that because of me a lot of materials come out that condemn violence – between different countries, religions, that humiliates people due to different motives – national, racial. This is my position – of course it influences my work.

Gordienko (2014, personal communication) was the only one who said she believed in objectivity and the importance of balance – giving voice to the two sides in every conflict. Similarly, Zhilin (2014, personal communication) said: "It's the truth. I must present the facts that I think and nothing else". A journalist who wanted to remain anonymous also said that it was of fundamental importance to "find the truth" and to tackle stereotypes. Yaroshevsky's (2014, personal communication) position was that "we do not permit any propaganda, we hate wars". Truth and honesty were also important for Dubov and Prosvirova. Prosvirova (2014, personal communication) repeated what she was told by her editor: "If you know the information that could be useful for people, for your audience, you can't hide it".

Conclusion

Novaya Gazeta journalists saw their job not simply as a living but as a way of life underpinned by a shared ideology – a belief in the values of liberal democracy, justice, and the rule of law. All journalists I spoke to had made the deliberate choice of working for that particular newspaper precisely because they saw it as a platform for promulgating and defending these values. This was not an easy choice to sustain because they faced numerous challenges in their daily lives. Some had risked their lives for their profession, some had been brutally attacked or kidnapped, and most had received serious threats, including death threats. These journalists had never relied on receiving any support from the state and the authorities even when faced with grim dangers. For them, the main protection came from their editor-in-chief and his deputy.

The working atmosphere I observed coincided with the picture described by journalists themselves – there was a clear hierarchy operating in the newspaper, but all journalists felt a great degree of autonomy as well as strong support and guidance from their editor-in-chief, deputy editors, and section editors. As Zhilin (2014, personal communication) put it, there was "pluralism" in their newspaper. They all said they could attend the daily editorial meetings, and they also had the freedom to work on the stories they felt passionate about without following strict editorial guidelines. This is not to say that the editor-in-chief did not have his priorities and did not assign any topics – on the contrary. But there was no need for imposing strict editorial guidelines even on contentious issues such as Ukraine. After all, they were all driven by a belief in the value of freedom of expression, and their daily practices and routines showed that at least in *Novaya Gazeta*, freedom of expression was not a dream but a reality that sometimes came at a very hefty price – the portraits of their six murdered colleagues served as a permanent reminder of that.

5 Russia's "Last Independent Radio"

The History of *Radio Ekho Moskvy*

"I had never heard such ravings ... I was lying there in bed... and thinking: but this isn't news, this is serving the foreign policy interests of one state with regard to another, with regard to Russia ... You pour diarrhoea over me day and night" (BBC News, 2012). This is how President Vladimir Putin described *Radio Ekho Moskvy* to his editor-in-chief at a meeting with editors in 2012. Why did he feel this way towards *Ekho Moskvy?* This chapter traces the historical development of Russia's "last independent radio" (Nemtsova, 2015) - *Ekho Moskvy*. It follows a similar outline to chapter three and is organised around two main headings: (1) Founding of the Radio Station, Key Names, Constitutional Charter, and Early Years and (2) State Pressures and Challenges: the demise of Gusinsky's media empire, the role of Gazprom-media, and recent developments.

I start with a brief outline of when and how the radio station was founded and the key developments in the early history of *Ekho Moskvy*, including the constitutional charter set up by the journalists themselves. Then, I explore the role of some of the veteran figures, with a particular focus on the important role the Editor-in-Chief Alexei Venediktov plays. Putin himself has publicly recognised Venediktov's role. Starobin (2012) wrote that *Ekho Moskvy* was "a thorn in Putin's side that he has so far been unable, or unwilling, to extract". Finally, I provide an overview of how the situation has changed since Gazprom-Media appropriated the majority shares in the radio station. The radio station was also founded by journalists and has long been renowned for giving voice to critical views about Putin and the Kremlin. Since 2002, the main shareholder has been the state-owned company Gazprom-Media, but the more pronounced attempts to stifle critical coverage did not really start until 2012. However, most of these attempts have been unsuccessful so far because the editor-in-chief is still holding the fort due to a clever clause in the radio's constitutional charter that stipulates that the journalists in the radio station are the ones who elect their editor-in-chief. I have drawn upon a wide range of resources in this and the following chapter – fieldwork notes, interviews, official accounts on *Ekho Moskvy's* website, a book about the history of the radio station, recordings of broadcasts,

Table 5.1 Ekho Moskvy: Timeline

Year	Milestone
1990	First broadcast, initially for two hours a day
1991	"The first serious information baptism" – the coverage of the Soviet military intervention in Lithuania
1993	End of the "romantic" period
1994	Relocation to 11, Novy Arbat Street
	Start of round-the-clock broadcasting
	Media-Most (Gusinsky)'s appropriation of majority shares
1996	Inaugural Editor-in-Chief Sergey Korzun resigned
1998	Alexei Venediktov elected as editor-in-chief
2002	Gazprom-Media's appropriation of majority shares
2012	Putin accused Ekho Moskvy of pouring "diarrhoea" over him "day and night" (BBC News, 2012)
	Increased pressures
2014	Dismissal of the long-serving CEO Yuri Fedutinov and Presenter Alexander Plushev

news articles, and social media posts. The book about the history of *Ekho Moskvy* is not an academic or a historical account but rather a collection of on-air interviews and essays written by *Ekho Moskvy* journalists themselves and is therefore treated as a primary source of data (Table 5.1).

Founding of the Radio Station, Key Names, Constitutional Charter, and Early Years

Ekho Moskvy was founded in 1990. According to one of the founding fathers Sergey Korzun, it all started when the owner of the French radio station *Kiss FM* Georges Polinski visited the youth radio station *Yunost*. Three Yunost journalists were invited back to Paris. and Korzun (who later became the first editor-in-chief of *Ekho Moskvy*) was invited to be their interpreter. During the two weeks that he spent at *Kiss FM*, Korzun was given the opportunity to participate in a few programmes and to learn how to use the equipment – an experience he thoroughly enjoyed. His leaving gift was two dozen CDs, which then became "the first collection of quality music" for *Ekho Moskvy* (Korzun, 2015a, p. 105). Korzun knew Sergey Buntman – the long-serving first editor-in-chief and also one of the founding fathers – from the French Foreign Service at the state international broadcasting station *Radio Moscow* where both of them worked as news anchors/programme presenters in French. In April 1990, Buntman and Korzun also started working as news anchors on the new radio station *Nostalgie Москва*. A few months later, Korzun was summoned to an informal meeting with some of his colleagues from *Nostalgie*, and as he put it, "Korzun left the room as some kind of an editor-in-chief of a yet non-existent radio with no name, no studios, no staff and no equipment" (Korzun, 2015a, p. 105).

According to the official history published on *Ekho Moskvy's* website, the founders of the radio station got together in May 1990 at the Faculty of Journalism at Lomonosov Moscow State University to discuss the potential development of a "completely new" type of radio for the USSR – "a conversational radio station built on the principles of free journalism and a complete lack of propaganda and brainwashing" (*Radio Ekho Moskvy*, n.d.). The participants in that meeting were the Dean of the Faculty of Journalism Yassen Zassoursky, the head of the Department of Television and Radio Broadcasting George Kuznetsov, the heads of Association Radio Vladimir Buriak, Grigory Kliger, and Mihail Rosenblatt, Aleksandr Shcherbakov from *Ogonek* magazine, and Korzun himself. They agreed that Buriak, Kliger and Rosenblatt would be responsible for securing the radio frequency and the transmitter, Shcherbakov and Lev Gushtin would be responsible for "the nationwide love of the liberals", Zassoursky and Kuznetsov for the theory of journalism, and Korzun for any editorial and programming issues (Korzun, 2015a, p. 105). They also decided to invite the Moscow City Council of People's Deputies (now called Moscow City Duma) to join them as founders, which they agreed to do. After a period of deliberation, Shcherbakov came up with the name *Ekho Moskvy (Echo of Moscow)*. Other names considered were Молва (Rumour), Столица (Capital), Сталкер (Stalker). The name *Radio M*, coined by Korzun, was also initially used (*Radio Ekho Moskvy*, n.d.).

The founders of *Ekho Moskvy* were not professional journalists. Korzun invited Buntman to help him develop the conceptual framework for the new radio station at a time when Buntman himself considered leaving radio altogether. According to both Korzun and Buntman, it took some persuasion before Buntman agreed to become head of culture at *Ekho Moskvy*. Their first day on-air was on 22 August 1990. They started broadcasting at 6:57 p.m. with a news programme, which included an interview with a young Moscow reformer – Sergei Stankevich. The first song they played was "All my loving" by The Beatles.

The current editor-in-chief, Venediktov, was a teacher at the time. He had known Buntman and Korzun for 15 years prior to that after they met at a student party back in 1975. Korzun invited him to come and help them with the setting up of the radio station. Venediktov was not particularly interested in the beginning, so he turned up on the third day of broadcasts. His first "job" at *Ekho Moskvy* was to man the phone for two hours. Then he would occasionally interview experts on-air on educational issues. The radio only broadcast for two hours a day in these first few months – from 7 until 9 p.m. – which were then increased to three hours from 13 October 1990, and a few months later to four hours. Venediktov continued teaching and helped out in the evenings

(Venediktov, 2015). They would afterwards often go out for drinks. The first contributors were people like Venediktov – acquaintances, colleagues, or friends of Korzun – who had agreed to help out.

Another key figure was the long-standing CEO Yuri Fedutinov. Fedutinov also had a French connection – he studied at the same university as Korzun and Buntman. Like Buntman he was a teacher of French and worked as an anchor for the Foreign Service of state radio. Fedutinov (2015) explained that he was a very conservative person who was shaken up by the perestroika, so while he wanted to continue working in radio, he did not want to work as a journalist. Korzun's offer came at the right time for him because, as he put it, he was interested in "radio only as a business" (Fedutinov, 2015, p. 190)

The first more significant change in the initially established "routine" took place on 13 January 1991 during the Soviet military intervention in Lithuania. In March 1990, Lithuania declared independence from the Soviet Union, but in January 1991, the Soviet leader Mikhail Gorbachev demanded restoration of the constitution of the USSR and the revocation of all anti-constitutional laws. He also threatened with military intervention. After receiving intelligence from his friends in Vilnius, Korzun convened a 7 a.m. editorial meeting with Buntman and Venediktov. They decided that they could not wait for their regular broadcast at 7 p.m. because state radio was not covering the clashes. Thus, with the help of Rosenblatt, *Ekho Moskvy* broadcast from 10 a.m. until 11 p.m. that day, and it also continued the following morning.

I went into the studio – it was the first time for me to go on air. And when I put my hands on the radio console, I got two burns because the console had overheated – it was an old army console not designed to work for 24 hours and by that point it had already worked for 10 hours. I had to work for three hours and I still have the scars from the burns from the overheated console on which you could probably fry an omelette – it was that hot...And perhaps, this was the second birth of *Ekho Moskvy*, and perhaps, I realised then for the first time how much this was not a game but how much this was my job...not a job, but a hobby, coming to help friends produce some reports for free was not simply an escape from ordinary life but it was much more serious than that. Because for the first time then I saw people standing in the streets with their receivers and listening to *Ekho Moskvy*. People gathered around cars, and kept their doors open so they could listen to *Ekho Moskvy*. This was a start moment, which we did not understand at the time but it was the rebirth of *Ekho*. We were simply working. There were seven of us, maybe 10, and it was then that it all clicked for me, and I understood the historical significance of what we were doing. It was 20 January 1991.
(Venediktov, 2015, pp. 53–54)

This was a pivotal moment in the history of *Ekho Moskvy* according to the official history on its website: "The coverage of events in Lithuania was the first serious information baptism of the radio station, which after that became widely known amongst a narrow layer of Moscow intelligentsia" (*Radio Ekho Moskvy*, n.d.). Another pivotal moment was the coverage of the coup against Gorbachev later that year. In spite of the fact that the special services had stopped all broadcasting, *Ekho Moskvy* managed to stay on-air by using a telephone connection (Venediktov, 2015). According to the CNN (2001), *Ekho Moskvy* was the only independent radio station that managed to stay on-air during the coup.

The period 1992–1993 put an end to the romantic period in the history of *Ekho Moskvy* (n.d). What followed was a transition period towards a professional conversational radio. The official account on the website stated that "October 1993 put an end to the process of bidding farewell to illusions (and there were plenty of them). The radio did not just need people working for it, but technical equipment, facilities, transmission resources" (*Radio Ekho Moskvy*, n.d.). Korzun said that he even temporarily left his post as editor-in-chief in 1994 because he could not look his employees in the eyes since he could hardly pay any salaries due to the financial difficulties they were experiencing. He called this period "the darkest time – materially and morally" when they did not have the means to buy or rent a transmitter at the frequency they had won, and the negotiations with Gusinsky's Most company seemed to have come to a halt. *Ekho Moskvy* staff initially occupied one room, provided for them by Association Radio, which they used as an office in the morning and as a studio in the evening. Then in 1994, they moved to their current location at 11, Novy Arbat Street.

Venediktov's accounts of his meetings with Boris Yeltsin illustrated some of the main features of this first romantic period. Venediktov recalled in his account of the history of the radio station that he had met Yeltsin a few times. One of the most memorable meetings was after the 1993 coup. During the coup, Venediktov was in the White House. Yeltsin's rebellious vice president and self-proclaimed President Aleksandr Rutskoi borrowed his satellite phone to call the Air Force pilots to order them to bomb the Kremlin. Rutskoi's conversation was aired by *Ekho Moskvy*. "This happened on the air of *Ekho Moskvy* and we had on the one hand, Chubais {Yeltsin's Minister of Privatisation} and on the other hand, Rutskoi", Venediktov (2015) said. A few months later he was invited to a meeting with Yeltsin together with other reporters, but he himself was summoned to sit directly across from Yeltsin, which was unusual. Upon entering the room, Yeltsin angrily addressed Venediktov: "What a shame, Alexei, what a shame! Comrades, the planes should be launched, you have to go and bomb the Kremlin – you should be ashamed of yourself!" (Venediktov, 2015, p. 56). Venediktov (2015, p. 57) replied: "Boris Nikolaevich, shame or no shame – this is what my job is about. If you were to break through – you would be on air. Aleksandr Vladimirovich broke through – he was on air. Such is the nature of the job, do you understand?" Yeltsin then said: "Oh, well, you have a job. You're a good worker. So go work!"!{"Ну работой, работничек!"} (Venediktov, 2015, p. 56).

Venediktov had another memorable meeting with Yeltsin a few years later in 1997, which reveals the generally amateurish approach to journalism that characterised his first years in the profession. Yeltsin summoned journalists for a late meeting, but Venediktov had to urgently mark 60 contour maps about the Greco–Persian wars submitted for end-of-term assessment by his pupils. Venediktov took the maps with him to the Kremlin, and when he realised that the president would be late, he put the maps on the floor and starting marking them with a red pencil. His colleagues joined in and helped him. Yeltsin's assistant supplied them with red pencils.

> And at that moment Yeltsin enters! That was quite a sight: yes, fifth graders' contour maps lying on the floor in his reception area and journalists, gritting their teeth and marking them. He says: "What is this?" I say: "These are contour maps, Boris Nikolayevich. It's the end of term." He: "I do not understand. You are telling tales again – he said – get your stuff and let's go." We all went into his office and he turned to me: "You sit here and finish marking your maps, while I have a chat with these people"...Of course, he was an absolutely fantastic person.
>
> (Venediktov, 2015, p. 56)

In these early years, Venediktov also interviewed Putin. Putin was deputy chief of staff of the Presidential Executive Office and chief of the Main Control Directorate. Venediktov gave him a ring on his work number and asked him whether he would be willing to give him an interview about the Russian tanks sent to Armenia. Putin immediately agreed and was interviewed on-air two hours later. Venediktov said that whenever he had asked Putin for an interview since then, he had always replied: "I have already given you an interview...about the Armenian tanks" (Venediktov, 2015, p. 58).

In 1994, *Ekho Moskvy* started broadcasting round-the-clock. In the same year, the majority shares were appropriated by oligarch Vladimir Gusinsky's Most (later Media-Most) company. This was Korzun's idea, and he also proposed that they adopted a constitutional charter in which they clearly stipulated that the journalists themselves had the right to elect their editor-in-chief, and the board of directors' duty was just to approve their decision. Gusinsky agreed to this clause, which still remained in place at the time of submission of this manuscript. While they did not really have to defend their editorial policies from interference from Gusinsky himself, in later years this clause played a very important role in the radio station's struggle for editorial autonomy. Venediktov (2015) described Gusinsky as a man who "was constantly gushing with ideas that could sometimes be applied but more often than not were impossible to apply. But the most precious quality of our shareholder Vladimir Gusinsky was the fact that he never listened to *Ekho Moskvy*. He did not understand radio at all, he did not get into it. He was probably engaged with TV, newspapers and magazines but he was not interested in radio" (p. 56).

In 1996, Korzun decided that it was time for him to leave and devote himself to other projects. After much deliberation, he agreed to stay at *Ekho Moskvy*, not as editor-in-chief anymore, but as chairman of the editorial board. Venediktov (2015) explained that they decided against electing a new editor-in-chief. Instead, Buntman was appointed as head of programmes and Venediktov as head of the information service. Then in 1998, Venediktov was elected as editor-in-chief. He described their working relationship as "push-and-pull" – he was in charge of politics, and Buntman was in charge of all other programmes (Venediktov, 2015).

State Pressures and Challenges

Gazprom-Media and the Demise of Gusinsky's Media Empire

Putin's election as president in 2000 marked a new era for free media in Russia. The history of *Ekho Moskvy* itself serves as a powerful illustration of the pressures and challenges Russian journalists, their editors, and their owners have faced since. One of Putin's first battles was against the power of oligarchs (Chapter 1). Gusinsky was one of the first victims of his new policies. At the time of Putin's inauguration as president, Gusinsky was already experiencing some financial difficulties, which had led him to borrow money from the oil giant Gazprom. Moreover, his media had also gained a reputation for their critical stance, especially in their coverage of Russian military actions in Chechnya. Within weeks of Putin's inauguration, Gusinsky was imprisoned with embezzlement charges (Encyclopaedia Britannica, n.d.). Gazprom also started demanding repayment of their loans. Becker (2004) argued that the attack on Gusinsky's Media-Most empire "reeked of revenge for the editorial views expressed by Media-Most entities", and "few would argue that the government would have taken such an uncompromising approach had Media-Most supported Putin in the 2000 presidential elections and taken a less critical view of Russian military actions in Chechnya" (p. 151).

Gusinsky's legal battles went on for years and resulted in him losing control of his media holdings. He was eventually forced into exile. Gusinsky (UPI, 2000) argued that he signed an agreement with Russian Media Minister Mikhail Lesin who promised to drop the fraud charges against him in exchange for the transfer of his shares in the holding to Gazprom.

Lesin denied the allegations, but Gazprom-Media did indeed gain control of Gusinsky's media holdings. Thus, since 2002, Gazprom-Media has owned the majority shares (66.5%) in *Ekho Moskvy*. The remaining 33.5% are owned by a Russian company in which the shareholders are journalists, including *Ekho Moskvy* journalists. In all, 49% of the shares in that company were owned by Venediktov himself. At one point, the former director of Gazprom-Media and Chairman of the Board of Directors of *Ekho Moskvy*, Lesin, considered selling Gazprom's shares in *Ekho Moskvy*, but by law, if he decided to do that, he should have offered them to the minority shareholders first. According to Venediktov (2017), Lesin ordered an assessment on the value of the shares but then decided against selling them.

The shareholders elect the board of directors. Four of the representatives in the board of directors are from Gazprom-Media and one represents the journalists. Only the journalists themselves (to be more precise, those who are on payroll) have the right to elect their editor-in-chief in a secret ballot. Elections take place every five years, and the next elections are due in 2019. The board of directors have to then approve the newly elected editor-in-chief. As Venediktov has made it clear on numerous occasions, he alone is in charge of editorial policy. "It is not important who the shareholders are, at one point our shareholders were Garry Kasparov, Vladimir Gusinsky, Gazprom, but the editorial policy has never changed, not when Korzun was an editor-in-chief, never", Venediktov (2017a) said. Moreover, in a 2017 broadcast, he also explained that the CEO could only dismiss journalists if the editor-in-chief recommended the dismissal. Venediktov has two first deputy editors-in-chief – Sergey Buntman (from January until end of June each year) and Vladimir Varfolomeev (from July until the end of December each year).

The official history of *Ekho Moskvy* on their website did not deal with the period since Gazprom-Media appropriated the majority shares in the radio station and did not even mention Gazprom-Media's appropriation of shares. Similarly, in the book published on the history of the radio station, there is hardly any mention of the relationship between Gazprom-Media and the editorial staff, especially in the first decade. The editor-in-chief himself became much more vocal about the pressures experienced only after 2012. Why is that? The few available accounts on the topic suggested that up until 2012, Putin tolerated or even "protected" Venediktov, but his attitude changed after Venediktov refused to support his presidential candidacy (The Economist, 2012). The Economist (2012) described Venediktov and Putin's relationship as "an autocratic leader's to a wise fool, licensed to speak the truth. This made Mr Venediktov almost untouchable".

The editor-in-chief claimed in his interview on the history of the radio station that he stopped worrying about whether the authorities would close them down back in 2003. Up until that point, he admitted to constantly thinking about whether what they were doing would lead to their closure: "After that I stopped thinking about that because I realised that they can close us down due to reasons beyond our control... This creates heavy self-censorship" (Venediktov & Ryabtseva, 2015, p. 5). Venediktov said that Khodorkovsky's arrest and subsequent imprisonment made him reconsider his attitude: "I understood that if they could imprison such an affluent billionaire, extremely rich, closing down *Echo* would not be an issue for them – they could do it with one movement of their pinky finger" (Venediktov & Ryabtseva, 2015, p. 5).

In his view, Putin had not yet shut the radio station down because he used it as "an instrument". "He does not treat the press as an institution that should be kept, cherished, nurtured, watered and so on", Venediktov (Venediktov & Ryabtseva, 2015, p. 5) said. He added that Putin himself had told him this back in 2000. In another interview, he recalled how, during that meeting, Putin had explained to him that he categorised his critics into two categories: "enemies", namely those who fought him openly, and "betrayers", namely those who pretended to be his friends but "as soon as he grew weak stabbed him in his back" (Nemtsova, 2015). Venediktov was in the "enemies" category, Putin told him. "'True,' said Venediktov. 'I always played against Putin openly and honestly. That was probably why *Echo* has still survived'" (Nemtsova, 2015). In his view, the role his radio station played was to be "a valve for releasing oppositional steam", namely, a platform that would allow Putin to say: "In my country there is freedom of expression" (Venediktov & Ryabtseva, 2015, p. 5). Venediktov said that he knew for a fact that these were Putin's words. Another purpose his radio station served in Putin's eyes was to be an alternative source of information, "a useful instrument in the decision-making process" (Venediktov & Ryabtseva, 2015, p. 5). "We are some kind of a screwdriver – a small one but nevertheless an instrument", Venediktov (Venediktov & Ryabtseva, 2015, p. 5) said. In his view, it was also helpful that he had a personal relationship with Putin, which meant that the president knew that he had not waged a war on him per se. Unlike the editor-in-chief of *Novaya Gazeta* who when asked whether he had an informal relationship with Putin, he said: "I don't maintain personal relationships with men", Venediktov saw his personal relationship with Putin as important. Moreover, he also said that he considered Putin's spokesman Dmitry Piskov to be his friend, but that did not mean that they did not get into arguments – on the contrary.

However, Venediktov acknowledged that the external pressure on his radio had dramatically increased since 2012, and this had led to some internal frictions. At a meeting with editors in March 2012, Putin accused *Ekho Moskvy* of serving foreign interests. Putin told Venediktov how he had tuned into a programme about Russia's opposition to US missile defence plans in Europe and how he felt that the programme was extremely biased and served the interests of the USA.

Putin argued that where the missiles were situated was of fundamental importance. Putin said to Venediktov:

> What they are providing is not information. This is serving the foreign policy interests of one state with regard to another, with regard to Russia. I am telling you this as an expert who has worked on these issues for many years. These are very basic things one cannot be unaware of. I don't believe they don't know them and they do it with Russian taxpayers' money. To me, this is mind-boggling, how is it possible? In the US it wouldn't be possible at all, it wouldn't be allowed at all. I remember how the *Fox channel* covered the events in South Ossetia when two women – a young lady and her aunt spoke about these events. When they realised they were dealing with people who supported Russia's actions, well, you saw what happened. They started smirking, hissing, scorning, I don't want to say at the table what else they did. You understand that to serve the interests of Russia in relation to the US on a channel that belongs to a state company, is unimaginable, impossible in the US. And you are talking about freedom of speech, where is it, if that's not it?
>
> (Russia Insider, 2016)

At the end of their encounter, Putin explicitly asked Venediktov who he was going to vote for in the forthcoming presidential elections. Venediktov replied that he had not voted since 1996- the last Russian presidential election before Putin came to power – because he did not want his voting preferences to influence his editorial independence and to compromise his integrity. Putin then asked him whether he felt offended and Venediktov replied "Yes" but later clarified that he was joking. Putin's reaction was: "So I don't get offended when you pour diarrhoea over me day and night but you take offence at me – I just say two words and already you're offended" (BBC News, 2012). According to Venediktov, this episode was important because Putin "did not give an order to pursue him or *Ekho Moskvy*. But his public criticism was a green light to those keen to carve up the media market at a time of political uncertainty" (The Economist, 2012).

Post-2014 Pressures – Dismissals and Internal Frictions

While the external pressure on *Ekho Moskvy* increased since 2012, the year 2014 was particularly eventful. Two events contributed to the increased pressure on *Ekho Moskvy*. On the one hand, Grozev (2014) argued that *Ekho Moskvy's* coverage of the Olympic Games in Sochi was particularly irritating for the Kremlin. "Not only did *Echo* take a largely cynical line of questioning of the sound economics of the whole enterprise, but it dared publish an opinion piece by TV satirist Shenderovich, likening the Sochi Olympics to the 1936 Nazi Germany Olympics, and calling 15-year-old figure-skater Lipnitzkaya 'a prop for raising Putin's popularity'" (Grozev, 2014). Grozev (2014) wrote that the Kremlin "sent its sledge-hammer to deal with *Echo* on this one: *RIA Novosti's* chief Kiselyov, currently on the EU blacklist, went on a 15-minute televised tirade and called *Echo's* liberalism 'acts against the State'". On the other hand, the conflict with Ukraine led to an intensification of the Kremlin's efforts in curbing critical voices.

In an unprecedented move in February 2014, the board of directors dismissed the long-serving CEO, Fedutinov, who had been in charge of the radio station since 1992. The new CEO was Ekaterina Pavlova – a former deputy chairman and editor-in-chief at the Russian State Radio Broadcasting Company *Golos Rossii (The Voice of Russia)* and prior to that an editor-in-chief of the *Vesti* TV news bloc at Russian state TV. Pavlova was undoubtedly a pro-Kremlin journalist who also happened to be married to Alexei Pavlov – deputy chief of the Presidential Press and Information Office. Gazprom-Media did not offer an explanation as to why Fedutinov was dismissed. Venediktov and the *Ekho Moskvy* journalists strongly objected to the dismissal. Venediktov (BBC News, 2012) called the decision "unjust" and "totally political" "aimed at changing editorial policy". Venediktov himself was re-elected as editor-in-chief the following month, but there was a delay in his confirmation for the post by the board of directors.

Pavlova resigned in October 2014 and in December 2014, was replaced by Mikhail Demin – the former PR director of the Sochi Olympic Games Organizing Committee. Demin was dismissed in March 2015 and replaced by Pavlova who was still in post at the time of completion of this monograph. This "show" (as the editor-in-chief called it) was only the tip of the iceberg in the long-running attempts to influence editorial policy. When visiting *Ekho Moskvy*, I requested an interview with her or a short statement, but she refused to participate in the study. Deputy Editor-in-Chief Tatyana Felgengauer (2014, personal communication, also quoted in Slavtcheva-Petkova, 2017) explained:

> I know too well how hard it is for us to maintain our positions. There are constant attempts to control us. The example with the new CEO is a case in point. Nobody explained to us why this was necessary. The pressures are constantly there. That's the process of monopolisation and the attempts to fully control the mass media. It's not a very recent process but it's much more pronounced and visible. There is a definitive trend. In this situation everybody survives the way they can. In this situation we have been lucky. We have a really tough editor-in-chief. He really sort of protects us. And we have a very good constitutional charter so we are as secure as possible but I cannot predict how long this will be sustained for.

Presenter Alexander Plushev (2014, personal communication) had a more positive outlook on the situation. He said that the change in CEO or indeed the change in shareholders had not made a difference to his and his colleagues' work:

> - We – all the colleagues – I can speak about myself and I think I can speak on behalf of my colleagues – haven't felt any difference in terms of this. I don't know if more rain is pouring over our umbrella, more serious precipitations – I guess this might have been the case but it's only my speculations, not really interesting for others maybe.
> - So you think that because of your umbrella, you haven't felt any pressure or changes?
> - Probably, maybe there is no pressure – I really don't know. Ask Venediktov. I really enjoy working here. All the restrictions and limitations are more so to say in the artistic or creative area – they are questions of style.
> - Did you fear at any point that things might change?
> - Things can always change. Crimea is a perfect example of that. Nobody thought half a year ago that it would be part of Russia but now it is. Things can always change but the thing is that in the last 20 years that I've worked here the rumours about the difficult destiny/future of *Radio Ekho of Moskvy* appear all the time. And nothing serious happened. Even in the times when our sister channel *NTV* faced serious problems. The thing is our CEO has never been changed till the recent change.
>
> (Plushev, 2014, personal communication)

While Felgengauer and Plushev did not agree on the extent of pressures felt, both of them argued that the person who most acutely felt all the pressures and attempts at interference was their editor-in-chief whom Plushev also saw as their "umbrella" – their protector:

> We have a really well-organised system whereby all these {interference} contacts are guided to the editor-in-chief. What happens with them, quite frankly I don't know. If anybody ever tells me how I should do my job, I always say: Look, we have an editor-in-chief, please contact him. Anyone in this radio station will tell you the same thing. We are under an umbrella and the umbrella is Alexei Venediktov. What is happening with the umbrella – we don't know, no one tells us. I've worked here for 20 years and my 20-year experience has proven I can rely on him.
>
> (Plushev, 2014, personal communication, also quoted in Slavtcheva-Petkova, 2017)

The deputy editor-in-chief confirmed that Venediktov was "the personal protection of our radio station" (Felgengauer, 2014, personal communication, also quoted in Slavtcheva-Petkova, 2017). Venediktov tweeted regularly any plans discussed during editorial meetings (Plushev, 2014, personal communication), which some journalists found "annoying", but they accepted the rationale – it was yet another way of pre-empting censorship attempts, particularly on controversial issues. While Venediktov was not particularly vocal about the pressures experienced at the time of my fieldwork, a tweet he posted on the day I visited *Ekho Moskvy* was indicative of these pressures. The tweet showed a photo of a bended hand with the words "This is my day today". Venediktov cancelled his meeting with me a few minutes before it was due to take place due to "unexpected commitments". One of the tweets responding to his tweet said: "A monument to all journalists".

A few months after my conversation with Plushev, he was embroiled in one of the biggest scandals in the history of *Ekho Moskvy*, which illustrated the pressures the radio was subjected to – pressures Plushev had not previously experienced. He was dismissed by the CEO for posting what was perceived to be an offensive tweet about the death of the son of Putin's chief of staff. The editor-in-chief was not consulted, and he gave a few interviews explaining that he would fight the decision in court. In his view, this was the last straw in a succession of attacks his radio station has experienced, including a murder plot against him. Thus, Plushev's dismissal became the first and only dismissal so far of a journalist from the radio station directly by the CEO.

Plushev's tweet was in relation to the death of Kremlin chief of staff Sergei Ivanov's son Aleksandr who drowned in the United Arab Emirates. Ivanov's son avoided prosecution in 2005 after being involved in a hit-and-run accident, which resulted in the death of an elderly woman. Upon learning of his death, Plushev wrote on Twitter on November 5: "Do you consider the death of Ivanov's son, who ran down and killed an old woman and sued her son-in-law, as proof that God exists?" He later withdrew the tweet and apologised for it, but Lesin insisted that he should be dismissed from his job for "violating the principles of professional ethics" (*Radio Free Europe/Radio Liberty*, 2014a). Venediktov strongly objected to the dismissal. He said that Lesin and the CEO were not within their rights to dismiss Plushev or any other *Ekho Moskvy* journalist/anchor because, according to the station's constitutional charter, journalists could be fired only at the request of the editor-in-chief. Venediktov was adamant that Plushev should remain in post. As a result, Lesin threatened Venediktov that he might lose his own job for refusing to accept the dismissal. Lesin even convened an emergency meeting of the board of directors with the aim of deciding the fate of the editor-in-chief and the radio station's news coverage. However, the meeting was cancelled two days before it was due to take place on 21 November 2014.

Plushev's dismissal order was rescinded, but he was suspended from the air until mid-January (*Radio Free Europe/Radio Liberty*, 2014b). Lesin also held a meeting with *Ekho Moskvy* journalists, which gained notoriety in the public space for its confrontational nature. Shortly after the scandal – in January 2015- Lesin resigned from his position as director of the Gazprom-Media holding company. Lesin died on 5 November 2015 in Washington of blunt force trauma to the head.

Conclusion

The brief overview of the history of *Ekho Moskvy* shows that similarly to *Novaya Gazeta*, the radio station has a core team of editors and journalists who have worked together for years and who shared similar values and ideals. *Ekho Moskvy* started as an amateur radio in a room generously provided by a group of like-minded individuals from Association Radio. Similar to *Novaya Gazeta*, when starting off the project, the founding fathers had a rough idea of what kind of radio station they wanted to create, but their initial approach was more romantic than pragmatic – they lacked a clear conception of how to address the range of financial and technical issues that they would inevitably face if the radio station was to continue growing (which it did). Subsequently, they had to make important compromises along the way – most notably, allowing an oligarch and a state-owned company later on to appropriate the majority shares in the radio station. Even though the challenges experienced have not necessarily been that well documented, the available evidence clearly suggests that the radio station has faced numerous pressures, perhaps most acutely felt by the editor-in-chief.

The episode with Plushev's dismissal illustrates the powerful role the editor-in-chief plays, but it also demonstrates that it will be an understatement to present all challenges as coming directly from Putin and the Kremlin or indeed to claim that the president and his administration have assumed the role of a full-fledged media censor. The relationship between Putin and Venediktov and some of the very public encounters they have had over the years (well documented by news media and on YouTube) paint a much more complicated picture. On a very simplistic level, the outcome in Plushev's case can be seen as a victory for freedom of expression in Russia. However, the subsequent developments at *Ekho Moskvy* show that there is no victory without sacrifices. What followed was a period of frictions among staff and an attempt for editorial changes to be implemented. I further explore these developments and Venediktov's role in the next chapter.

The range of challenges experienced, the radio station's continued existence, and the very powerful role of its editor-in-chief suggest that Putin and the Kremlin's grip on Russian liberal media is not as tight as some Western media reports and commentators claim. However, it is undeniable that the challenges and pressures the radio faces have intensified since 2012 despite Putin's claim that *Ekho Moskvy's* programmes were testimony of the fact that there was freedom of speech in Russia or, in fact, a higher degree of freedom of expression than in the USA. If we consider the history of *Ekho Moskvy* as illustrative of Putin's general approach to liberal media, then the picture we get is somewhat blurred. The pressures *Ekho Moskvy* had faced over the years do not appear to have come about as a result of a clear and systematic strategy. The chaos and turbulence experienced at times looked like ad hoc attempts for regaining control. It is not clear who orchestrated these attempts – was it Putin himself, his cronies, or simply people who wanted to please him? Nonetheless, the intensification of these efforts over the past few years is undeniable, so it remains to be seen whether they would lead to the desired impact of toning down the critical coverage of Putin and his policies.

6 *Radio Ekho Moskvy* Today
Challenges, Practices, and Role Perceptions

"I love journalism, I love my morning show, I love my radio station ... The attempt on my life will not change it" (Roth, 2017). A month after being brutally stabbed in the neck by a listener while at work, *Ekho Moskvy*'s Deputy Editor-in-Chief Tatyana Felgengauer gave an interview to *The Washington Post* in which she voiced her determination to continue working and she even said that she should probably come up with jokes about her throat. The attempt on Felgengauer's life took place just as I was completing the two chapters on *Ekho Moskvy* in October 2017 as an acute reminder that the challenges journalists there faced were not just political and ideological, but also safety issues that endangered their lives. This chapter explores these challenges. It presents the findings from my fieldwork in Russia in May 2014, as well as subsequent developments up until the point of submission of the manuscript in December 2017. It is organised around four key headings: (1) Ethnographic Observations and the Coverage of Ukraine; (2) Common Challenges – threats, intimidation, and harassment, with a particular focus on the recent attempted murder of Felgengauer; (3) Soul-Searching or Navel-Gazing? Internal Battles and the Editor-in-Chief's Role; and (4) The Future – Journalists' Perceptions of the Role They Play in Russian Society.

I start by briefly sharing my ethnographic observations during my stay in Russia as well as the views of the journalists I interviewed on their radio station's coverage of Ukraine. I then move on to discussing some of the challenges journalists have experienced in addition to the ones already outlined in the previous chapter such as threats, intimidation, and harassment. Moreover, the intensified pressure *Ekho Moskvy* has been under since 2012, and in particular in 2014, led to an internal soul-searching (or was it navel-gazing) process that resulted in internal conflicts and the resignation of *Ekho Moskvy*'s founder and inaugural Editor-in-Chief Sergey Korzun. These frictions were to a great extent the result of personality clashes, but on a broader level, they revealed some profound disagreements in relation to the radio station's mission and role in Russian society.

Ethnographic Observations and the Coverage of Ukraine

My ethnographic observations at *Ekho Moskvy* were extremely limited because I did not have the same level of access there as I did at *Novaya Gazeta* or *Radio Free Europe/Radio Liberty*. Arranging a visit to the radio station proved very difficult. Using the official channels of communication as published on *Ekho Moskvy*'s website was a futile venture. Shortly before I was due to fly to Moscow, I tweeted Venediktov. He responded almost immediately and put me in touch with his assistant. The initial plan was for me to meet him and a few of his colleagues as recommended by him, but the plan fell through last minute because of the emergency meetings he had to hold on the day of my visit.

It was a very tricky time for *Ekho Moskvy*. The long-standing CEO was replaced shortly before my visit, and the new CEO was still finding her feet in the new post in the face of very vocal opposition from the editor-in-chief and his team. Venediktov pre-arranged all interviews for me. I did not have any choice on the matter as to whom to interview or what meetings to attend. He wanted me to meet two of his stars – Felgengauer and anchor Alexander Plushev. The meetings took place in Sergey Buntman's office. Buntman himself was abroad at the time. I was not given access to any of the meetings taking place at regular intervals during the day nor could I move freely in the building. There was always a member of staff who accompanied me even if I had to simply go from Buntman's office to the reception desk (situated very close by). My attempts at securing follow-up interviews with Felgengauer's assistance were not successful either. The tour of the premises that the team gave me was very short. The walls were covered with photos of VIP guests – mainly politicians, including US and Soviet/Russian presidents, secretaries of state, and so forth.

In spite of my limited access to potential interviewees and to the editorial meetings, the interviews I conducted were very useful indeed because Felgengauer and Plushev were undoubtedly two of the key figures at *Ekho Moskvy*. Both of them had been very loyal to Venediktov, but, more importantly, they had also been two of the very public/symbolic faces of the radio station. Felgengauer started working at *Ekho Moskvy* at the age of 16 while still at school. After 13 years of going through the hierarchy, she was appointed as deputy editor-in-chief. She is also the step-daughter of Pavel Felgengauer, a prominent *Novaya Gazeta* military journalist. Felgengauer's working day normally started at 8 a.m. On the days when she worked for the Information Service, she would first check all the news and events for the day, and then choose the topics and events that the radio station would focus on during the day. She was in charge of sending correspondents on assignment and deciding which sources to be contacted. She would also normally lead three editorial planning meetings during her shift. She was a coordinator of "all the services that work for our on-air transmissions" (Felgengauer, 2014, personal communication). Felgengauer was also a regular presenter with her own programmes.

Plushev is one of the veteran presenters at *Ekho Moskvy*. He joined *Ekho Moskvy* in February 1994 at the age of 21, initially as a news anchor. At the time when I interviewed him, he was extremely busy: he had two weekly talk shows on Friday and Saturday night, two shows on Wednesday – *Cover Page* and *With Your Own Eyes* – a news programme on Thursday, a weekly show about technologies and another one about *Ekho Moskvy*, called *Ekho Drom*. As he put it himself, his weekend was on Mondays and Tuesdays, but even then, he still had to prepare for his shows. I met him on a Tuesday and he said: "Today for example is also my 'weekend' but I came to record some promos for the air" (Plushev, 2014, personal communication).

Plushev's dismissal was not the only controversy surrounding his work. Just days before his dismissal, *Ekho Moskvy* received an official warning from the Russian telecom regulator Roskomnadzor that "information is contained in the given programme which justifies the practice of war crimes" (Venediktov, 2014). The programme was hosted by Plushev. His guests were two journalists who had eye-witnessed the fighting for Donetsk airport despite a ceasefire reached in September. It was not clear who violated the truce because both sides were blaming each other. The warning said: "In accordance with the law … information justifying practices of war and other crimes, aimed at full or partial annihilation of an ethnic or national group, is regarded as extremist activity". Venediktov strongly objected to the warning. He said in a tweet: "I don't understand this term 'information justifying war crimes'. Information can either be false or true" (Anishchuk, 2014). Roskomnadzor requested the transcript to be removed from the website and threatened to close down the website. If a media company receives two warnings within a 12-month period, the authorities have the right to shut it down. Venediktov said *Ekho Moskvy* would file a lawsuit against the watchdog, but nonetheless removed the transcript from the website.

The transcript is still available on *Euromaidan's Press* (2014) website. The controversial interview was with *Los Angeles Times* correspondent Sergey Loiko and with *Ekho Moskvy* and *TV Rain* journalist Timur Olevskii. They provided a very detailed account of what they saw at Donetsk Airport. They made some very specific claims, which implied that the "separatists" – the representatives of the so-called Donetsk People's Republic – were responsible for the fighting. They argued that the Ukrainian army did its best not to break the ceasefire. Olevskii said that he had lived for three days with the Ukrainian soldiers, and he was impressed by how intelligent and motivated they were. He mentioned that they all spoke Russian because they had not studied Ukrainian:

T. OLEVSKII: They talk in Russian – this is very important. Several of them say that they have never used any other language than Russian in their whole life and never studied Ukrainian. And despite that one of them even told me that he hates Russian. So I say: how is this possible?

A. PLUSHEV: A portion of them are ethnic Russians.

T. OLEVSKII: Absolutely. They're not only Russian, they're also not integrated in the Ukrainian speaking culture. They're defending their homeland; for them it's a moment of principles. Overall it's a collection of people that feel that they need to go until the border and free Ukraine from what's going on in DPR {Donetsk People's Republic}. And of course they're all saying that they're fighting a war with Russia, every single man there. And what's surprising… I don't know, I don't want to draw populist parallels, but for me it really seemed like I saw what happens when you take good, kind people and bring them to a point where they won't take it anymore.

(*Euromaidan Press*, 2014)

The journalists discussed the negative actions of the "separatists" at length, and they even described one of the battles in which allegedly one group of separatists had fought against another one. In response to a listener who said: "Army that's killing their own people cannot be heroes", Loiko (*Euromaidan Press*, 2014) said:

Alex, I spent the last half a year at the Ukrainian War. I don't know which army is killing their own people, because the army that's there, that has their own people there, isn't destroying them. And the army that's killing them – that's not the Ukrainian army.

Loiko added that he had seen with his own eyes,

as a mini-Stalingrad is breaking the back of, I don't know if it's fascism or not, but marauderism, orcism, this meaningless, pointless terrorism – that's for sure. I don't have any doubt that these DNR, LNR {Luhansk People's Republic} are both artificial imaginary semi-fascist organizations, the point of which is not to do something for the Ukrainian people, not to create something for the Ukrainian people, not to give happiness to the Ukrainian people, but to create an endless zone of terror, to turn all of Ukraine into the airport. Who needs this – is not for me to say.

(*Euromaidan Press*, 2014)

Olevskii's views were even more explicit:

> We have Donetsk and Luhansk, where the situation is totally different and there I saw groups that at first would rob the people, then would hide behind them from shelling and would keep saying that they're defending the people. But there too, they would say that this is a war against Fascism. So here the question comes up. There they're saying that a war against fascism is happening there. The DNR is saying that they're fighting against Fascism, against the junta. The Ukrainian army is saying, this is Great Patriotic War and brings up analogies with WW2 where they too battled fascism. But this is a relatively important story, because they now see Russia as that nation, fascist Germany in a different time. They're seeing Russia as the aggressor, and it's very important for us to understand, this is for forever.
>
> The children of their children will be remembering this. This, is the idea: that in the end Ukraine is feeling and with good justification that it's fighting not with DNR, but that it's fighting with Russia. This is the tragic part of this story.
>
> (*Euromaidan Press*, 2014)

Plushev (2014, personal communication) himself did not express his personal views in that specific programme, but in his interview with me, it became clear that he too had very strong views on the situation in Ukraine. While he acknowledged that it is "a very complicated situation", he said that the conflict could have been resolved in a more peaceful way if it was not for Russia's intervention, most notably the annexation of Crimea, which had hindered the peaceful resolution of the conflict:

> The problem is that the more peaceful demonstration was oppressed in a military way. And then after that many opposite sides used the situation, including Russia who joined and annexed Crimea. Crimea has always been pro-Russian ... The current lack of stability in South-East Ukraine can also be explained by the Russian activities because it is a fact that there are Russian military forces there. We can actually discuss the topic of whether these forces were sent by the government or not but we will never reach consensus on this issue. But it's an absolute fact that the Russian citizens are there. To conclude my overview of the situation, I don't agree with the viewpoint that Ukraine is not efficient as an independent state. But there are forces that are interested in making this state not efficient.
>
> (Plushev, 2014, personal communication)

When asked "How does your radio station cover the situation in Ukraine?", Plushev (2014, personal communication) replied: "This question reminds me of the question The Beatles were asked: What do you think of America? On the basis of what I told you, we are trying to be objective and to give voice to all the sides". He explained this meant that in their news bulletins, they would give voice to the Russian officials, the Ukrainian officials, the proponents of federalisation ("we call them separatists", he explained), and they would also try to avoid evaluations in the news. However, he admitted that their commentaries were subjective. As he (Plushev, 2014, personal communication) put it, "commentators are also subjective – otherwise they will lose their jobs". Plushev (2014, personal communication) said that he had a programme specifically dedicated to giving voice to "a whole variety of viewpoints, including the most extremist ones as well as banal ones".

Plushev's views were also shared by Felgengauer. She compared the situation in Ukraine to the French Revolution:

> It's very complicated, very tough and it is a situation we will observe for a long time. A really tough process begins there and it is absolutely normal when the revolution occurs, there are regions of the country that are not prepared for that or didn't want it at all. And they don't know how to react in this situation. And therefore we have all these movements in Donetsk and in other regions. But if we check the history, it was the same with the French Revolution or with any other. And it is also normal that there are states that want to use the situation in their favour. I just feel very sorry that this state is my one in this situation.
>
> (Felgengauer, 2014, personal communication)

Felgengauer (2014, personal communication) said that *Ekho Moskvy* covered the situation in Ukraine "professionally as always". The deputy editor-in-chief added:

> We give voice to all points of view and represent the situation objectively with all the propaganda and now counter-propaganda pouring from the state channels that we are facing, we just try really hard to dissect and find the real information that is happening.
>
> (Felgengauer, 2014, personal communication)

Common Challenges

Ekho Moskvy's critical stance towards President Vladimir Putin and the Kremlin and their deliberate attempts to give voice to controversial or indeed "extremist" voices meant that in addition to the state pressures the journalists had experienced, some of them had also faced safety threats.

Unlike *Novaya Gazeta*, *Ekho Moskvy* did not specialise in investigations, but their liberal ethos had also made them crusaders in the fight against illiberal beliefs and practices such as the neo-Nazi movement in Russia or the situation in Chechnya. Venediktov himself had received numerous death threats and lived "under a constant threat of assassination", leading to a doubling in the number of bodyguards responsible for his protection (Nemtsova, 2015). Venediktov said in an interview:

> Might not save me, but I feel a bit more confident … Chechen leader Ramzan Kadyrov considers me an enemy of Islam and friend of Charlie Hebdo; Kadyrov promised there would be somebody to punish me, and a month and a half later some people killed [political opposition leader] Boris Nemtsov, whom Kadyrov had threatened, too, in the same fashion.
> (Nemtsova, 2015)

The threats intensified and proliferated after the Chechen leader gave a press conference in 2016 in which he said that Putin's opponents should be tried as "enemies of the people" because they were "traitors" and a "fifth column" (Balmforth, 2016). Kadyrov's words were followed up by a picture posted online of him "with a slavering dog named Tarzan straining on a leash", accompanied by a threatening message. The Instagram photo was posted by Chechen Parliament Speaker Magomed Daudov. The message was very long and very strongly worded. Here is an extract from it: "This again is Tarzan … Our old friend. … Tarzan just hates dogs of foreign stripes … Especially American ones … European breeds are also annoying". The post included an implicit reference to *Ekho Moskvy*. In it, Daudov singled out prominent Russian liberal opposition politicians, activists, and journalists, including Venediktov. Prior to posting the message, Daudov publicly called for the closure of *Ekho Moskvy* and *TV Rain*. This provoked *Ekho Moskvy*'s presenter Matvei Ganapolsky to write an open letter to Putin:

> Vladimir Vladimirovich Putin! Dmitry Anatoleevich Medvedev! Vladimir Vladimirovich, I don't know what your relationship with Venediktov is. But I have worked at *Ekho Moskvy* for 26 years. And my friends work here. My friends have children. Vladimir Vladimirovich, we are facing a direct threat to the life and safety of the employees of the TV channel *Dozhd* (which I highly value and consider to be an outstanding medium) and of the radio station that has existed since 1990 – before you actively entered politics. Vladimir Vladimirovich, why are you silent? Don't you see that this is an appeal for some proper Chechens to kill somebody from *Ekho Moskvy* radio station or from *Dozhd*, while holding your portrait in front of them? … Why is your administration silent? Why are you being silent when the speaker of a parliament of a territory

entrusted to you openly threatens the media? Do you want a *Charlie Hebdo*? Do you want this? Probably not. But maybe you do. And if you don't – then why aren't you reacting? … Why aren't you reacting to the direct threats to the security of citizens of the Russian Federation, journalists of the Russian Federation? I am asking, react. Or you will have a *Charlie Hebdo*.

(Ganapolsky, 2016)

Putin did not respond directly to the letter but soon after it was published, his chief of staff said: "As for the actions of the leader of the Chechen republic, it raises no questions in the president's administration" (*Moscow Times*, 2016).

The extent to which incitement to hatred is tolerated in Russia became evident once again at the time of completion of this manuscript. Felgengauer was brutally attacked just two weeks after Russian state *TV Rossia-24* aired a news broadcast accusing *Ekho Moskvy* and Felgengauer herself of siding with Western oppositional forces and receiving funding from Western non-governmental organisations (NGOs) with the aim of fostering pro-Western propaganda ahead of Russia's 2018 presidential election. According to *Rossia-24*, *Ekho Moskvy* had received more than three million rubles in 2016 from "foreign counterparts" such as the *BBC* and *CNN*. The report also showed photos of a meeting that Felgengauer, Plushev, and another *Ekho Moskvy* journalist had attended with representatives from Reporters Without Borders and the German Robert Bosch Foundation. It also showed footage in which Felgengauer was claiming that there was a crisis in journalism in Russia. "Essentially, these are genuine foreign agents who aren't even hiding what they're doing", the anchor said. The accusations came months after *Ekho Moskvy* announced that it had fully complied with the Russian media regulator's order to "reject all foreign funding" by 15 February 2017. The report was condemned by the Russian Union of Journalists and Media Workers for inciting hatred towards their colleagues. The Union argued that the report "could have provoked an unstable person into attacking Tanya" (Walker, 2017).

On 23 October 2017, Felgengauer was stabbed in the throat by a 48-year-old man who broke into *Ekho Moskvy* studios after spraying pepper in the face of a security guard. Felgengauer underwent a surgery after the stabbing and was initially in a medically induced coma. Her attacker was a mentally ill man with dual Israeli–Russian citizenship, who claimed that Felgengauer had made telepathic contact with him and had been following him in his mind. A week after the attack when answering a question about it, Putin said: "That was just a sick man … What does freedom of speech have to do with this?" He also reminded that Ekho Moskvy was state-funded (*Associated Press*, 2017). Another *Ekho Moskvy* journalist was forced to flee the country earlier in the year after a series of intimidations such as an attempted arson attack on her car and a canister of faeces thrown over her in central Moscow (Walker, 2017).

Venediktov and other *Ekho Moskvy* journalists linked the attack to *Rossia-24*'s report because they claimed that this and similar reports generally created an atmosphere of hatred, which had also contributed to opposition leader Boris Nemtsov's murder. Felgengauer's colleague Ksenia Larina wrote: "Solovyov {*Rossia-24* journalist} really wanted this, the beast. Who, he said, will shut their [critical journalists] filthy mouths? Volunteers were found" (Lenta.ru, 2017). Venediktov also referred to Solovyov's words when discussing the attack against Felgengauer.

At the time when I interviewed Felgengauer, she said that while she agreed with Western NGOs' claim that Russia was one of the dangerous countries in the world for journalists, she had not personally experienced any dangers. "I have never had any fears", Felgengauer (2014, personal communication) said. In her view, the most dangerous topics for journalists were the Caucusus and corruption, and journalists were "in danger" when covering these topics. She acknowledged that she had received "lots of insults on our website, phone-ins on air or letters but I don't think it's a really serious issue to discuss" (Felgengauer, 2014, personal communication). Felgengauer gave a few examples of journalists she knew who had faced "real" dangers. For instance, Aksana Panova from the ura.ru website had been banned from practising her profession for exposing corruption and negligence among powerful local figures in the Yekaterinburg region in the Urals. "It was a really serious issue because she was arrested, there was a court case against her, her child was taken away from her. This is a really serious issue", Felgengauer (2014, personal communication) said. In her view, practising journalism in the regions was much more dangerous than in Russia – a sentiment shared by a few of her colleagues from *Novaya Gazeta* as well.

Similarly to *Novaya Gazeta* journalists, their *Ekho Moskvy* colleagues consistently underplayed the seriousness of the threats they received. In spite of the fact that Plushev had been persecuted by a youth neo-Nazi group – most probably Nashi– when asked whether he had personally experienced any dangers, he said: "Slightly. I know lots of colleagues who have actually faced some kind of danger – they have experienced serious problems". He said that he was not entirely sure whether he was persecuted because of his radio work or because of his blog, but he had a very strong reason to suspect that Nashi activists were harassing him. His persecutors knew where he lived, they harassed him on the phone, and they also tried to damage his car a couple of times:

> The most hilarious thing they did was gluing a toilet brush to the roof of my car. And the glue was very good so I couldn't really do anything about it. So of course I spent money on that and the police

couldn't do anything and the prosecution stopped as immediately and as spontaneously as it started. I called the police although it was absolutely useless because they demanded endless explanations and didn't do anything about it. They used the broken bureaucratic procedures – in that way the process was prolonged due to the bureaucratic procedures. I couldn't claim on my car insurance and it was not very effective. But it stopped after a while. I didn't do anything else.

(Plushev, 2014, personal communication)

He also recalled receiving an insulting note, which was of "anti-Jewish character. *Ekho Moskvy* was somehow connected with the Jews in their mentality … It was some kind of insult and a threat: Go back to Israel or something like that" (Plushev, 2014, personal communication). Despite the threats, the radio presenter said that he had never really feared for his life because "fearing would be silly because we receive many similar messages every day – on Twitter or by SMS" (Plushev, 2014, personal communication).

Similarly, his colleague Vitaly Ruvinsky (2015) said that he was used to receiving threating letters every day in

which they personally promise me that they would physically destroy me, including by describing the process in detail. I am almost used to observing how in front of my eyes sane decent people (often virtual, but after all alive!) go crazy, choke with hatred, and infect everyone they can reach with it. But I am also used to the fact that people constantly and genuinely thank us, they call us a breath of freedom, a beacon of light and last hope.

(p. 162)

Underplaying the threats, rarely involving the authorities, and relying mainly on their editor-in-chief were also the approaches adopted by *Novaya Gazeta* journalists. The rule at *Ekho Moskvy* was also that all serious threats or attempts at interference should be directed to the editor-in-chief.

Soul-Searching or Navel-Gazing? Internal Battles and the Editor-in-Chief's Role

This view of Venediktov as the umbrella – the protective shield from the various pressures and challenges the radio station had been subjected to – was not just shared by Felgengauer and Plushev but by some of their colleagues as well in the book about the history of *Ekho Moskvy*. Ryzhkov explained that all important decisions were taken in

Venediktov's office. His door was always ajar whenever he was in his office. Ganapolsky (2015) said:

> I feel that I will be protected here … and this gives me strength. It is extremely important that you feel informally protected at work. I know this is what it's like at *Novaya Gazeta*. If they touch somebody, the whole collective will rise up.
>
> (p. 63)

Dimarsky (2015) recalled how in 1998, while on a trip to Paris with Venediktov, they had to stop at a few ATMs so that Venediktov could withdraw cash from multiple bank cards. "In Moscow – he explained to me – the ATMs do not work, we have to pay people their salaries, that's why I am going to withdraw cash now" (Dimarsky, 2015, p. 98).

Venediktov was not a saint, however, and many of his colleagues acknowledged that he was not an easy person to work for. His temper was notorious. Vorobieva (2015) said:

> Everyone has their own "Echo". And everyone, probably, has their own Venediktov. For me he opened a big radio world, gave me the universe on a plate. He has sworn many, many times. And he will probably swear at least as much. Sometimes when Venediktov makes his appearance in the radio station, this reminds me of the movie "The Devil Wears Prada" when Miranda Priestley goes through the editorial office. We often joke at the expense of the editor-in-chief. But when the red phone starts ringing in the information service (it is thought that AAB is the only one who has this number), the managing editor loses a couple of thousands of nerve cells. I do not know if we are a sect or a family, or worse. I think that in fact *Echo of Moscow* is more a way of life.
>
> (p. 60)

Orekh (2015) summed up the prevailing sentiments:

> The best praise from Alexey is when he passes calmly by you and says "Hello". But heaven forbid that you mess up. A helmet and a bulletproof vest as well as earplugs are your main gadgets at such moments. The truth is that if he could kill us every time when he threatened to do it, the air would have been silent for a long time now and Arbat corridors would be like a desert.
>
> (p. 128)

Former Duma Deputee and *Ekho Moskvy* Anchor Vladimir Ryzhkov (2015) described Venediktov as "an emotional person, impulsive, explosive.

If he is in a bad mood, he can shout at his employees but that quickly passes. If he is a good mood, then all is well at the radio station" (p. 166). The editor-in-chief was normally in an excellent mood whenever one of his favourite guests such as Mikhail Gorbachev visited the radio station. According to Ryzhkov (2015), Gorbachev was always well received, and every time he came to *Ekho Moskvy*, Venediktov arranged a small feast for him in his office with alcohol and a spread with his favourite "old Soviet-style butterbrots" (p. 166).

Larina and Ganapolsky discussed on-air Venediktov's managerial approach:

M. GANAPOLSKY: *Ekho Moskvy* consists of two parts. It consists of its collective who feel themselves as free citizens – they freely say what they think.

K. LARINA: Even to the editor-in-chief.

M. GANAPOLSKY: Yes. I would say so, I consider it my duty to do so. *Ekho Moskvy* is not for sale … "free radio for free people".

K. LARINA: This is Korzun.

M. GANAPOLSKY: Korzun. So free people, free radio but there is one more thing. Venik is not a bastard {"Веник – не сука", the word "Веник" is used in a derogatory way to refer to Venediktov, but its literal meaning is "broom"}.

K. LARINA: I did not hear that.

M. GANAPOLSKY: I'll explain it to you. I correctly named things by their own names … Venik is not a bastard. To his radio station he is like Putin, he has learnt a lot from Putin or maybe Putin has learned from him … Putin does not betray his own people so in this sense Putin is not a bitch/a bastard … Ksenia? Ksenia! Why are you laughing? Listen to what I've got to say. Nowadays the first duty of a manager is the ability to protect his collective/team. This is the thin politics of negotiations, conversations, drinking vodka with someone, chats, telephone calls, persuasion, this is very … this is a life skill, do you understand me? The ability to protect one's collective/team. I will remind you that when he gets a phone call and the shouting begins and so on, he summons people to him. I remember the first time this happened to me and he told me – so I received a phone call. Do you know what he told me? A simple phrase. Try changing something in your broadcasts.

K. LARINA: I'll say more. I know that in many cases he doesn't even tell us, doesn't summon us. At some point later in time he would tell you that he had received a phone call about you 10 years ago.

M. GANAPOLSKY: So when you are on air, you know you are behind a stone wall.

K. LARINA: Yes.

M. GANAPOLSKY: And then you present your programme without looking over your shoulder.

(Ganapolsky, 2015, p. 72)

All in all, decision making at *Ekho Moskvy* seemed to be even more centred on/around the personality of the editor-in-chief than it was at *Novaya Gazeta*. Venediktov admitted himself that he had "moulded" the radio station on his "taste and interests", and that he exercised authority over his programmes:

L. RYABTSEVA: Everyone says that *Echo* – this is you.
A. VENEDIKTOV: They say that, because I have been here for 17 years. People who understand it, understand that this is all down to my personal taste and subjective judgement, every journalist, every programme, every new guest that we invite to our programmes – important, unimportant, whether to take part or not, it is always my decision. It is a question of responsibility and I'm used to assuming responsibility.

(Venediktov & Ryabtseva, 2015, p. 9)

Nonetheless, Golubev (2015) said that most, if not all, journalists at *Ekho Moskvy* could pretty much work on any topic and in any department. In his view, the key to success was the effective management system.

Absolute dictatorship and authoritarism prevail in the radio station, which as experience shows are very effective despite the love of freedom of its staff. Alexei Alexeevich is feared and respected because he alone has the right to punish or encourage (most often encourage), execute or pardon (mostly pardon).

(Golubev, 2015, pp. 75–76)

Despite Venediktov's generally authoritarian management approach, Golubev (2015) argued that journalists had a high degree of autonomy. He said that *Ekho Moskvy* had been accused of being "the 'Echo' of the State Department, Gazprom, the Kremlin or Washington", but in his view, all his colleagues were united in their desire to be honest:

For five years of work, no one has ever even hinted at me, that one or another question would be worth highlighting in a special way. The leadership team gives me the opportunity to say everything that I see and hear ... In this sense, one of the slogans of *Ekho* – "We say everything that we know" – is completely justified.

(Golubev, 2015, p. 79)

Golubev (2015) also made an interesting point about the values that journalists shared (or in some cases did not share). He said that everyone had their personal values, and they often started heated arguments because although in theory they all shared liberal values, in practice "the ideals of tolerance in our editorial office crash into a complete fiasco"

(Golubev, 2015, p. 79). He said that if a black person (he used the "n" word) or a gay activist turned up, then *Ekho* would be the most tolerant place you could end up in, but "all tolerance evaporated instantaneously" when they discussed the Orthodox Church. As he put it, "everything is ridiculed" in the presence of believers (Golubev, 2015, p. 79).

Another bone of contention in recent years had been the situation in Ukraine. According to Golubev, the split in society was reflected in their editorial office as well. Venediktov took issue with the fact that some of his colleagues understood journalism as a form of social activism:

> I understand it, but I do not share it, and therefore it will not be practiced here while I am here. I just think that it's a different profession. Maybe more noble, maybe now they need to spread alternative information, anti-Putin, I do not know what … I just think: well, if you want to change your profession, change your profession, that's not an issue.
>
> (Venediktov & Ryabtseva, 2015, p. 8)

Venediktov said that he knew that adopting a stance was allowed at other publications and this was probably what their listeners expected from them too, but in his view, this was a profession he was not "interested in" (Venediktov & Ryabtseva, 2015, p. 8). The harder line that Venediktov seemed to have adopted in recent years in relation to discouraging activism and insisting upon more thorough fact-checking, especially after he was publicly reprimanded by Putin, was met with some resistance among his staff.

This split in *Ekho Moskvy* as a result of differences in values and personality clashes came to the fore in May 2015 when the radio station's founder and inaugural Editor-in-Chief Korzun left the radio station. He explained that "Venediktov's radio" was no longer "his radio". In a *LiveJournal* blog post called "*Ekho Moskvy* 1990–2015 RIP", Korzun (2015b) said that he longer worked for *Ekho Moskvy* because the *Ekho Moskvy*, born in 1990, was dead or to be more precise, its "body is still working, but its brain is already dead". His decision was prompted by two publications on *Ekho Moskvy*'s website by Venediktov's 23-year-old personal assistant and journalist Lesya Ryabtseva. In the first post, Ryabtseva (2015a) accused Russia's opposition leaders of being "spineless jerks who deceive themselves". In the second one, she used "vulgar" words to describe some of her colleagues. She said that "at work we are surrounded by jackasses who don't understand anything and don't know anything" (Ryabtseva, 2015b). Korzun said that he felt that these posts were published with Venediktov's blessing, and they were offensive for his colleagues and for their target audience of intelligent, liberal-minded people.

"Unprofessional, arrogant, malicious and simply offensive judgements have migrated from the comment section to the posts themselves, and open trolling from the side of some of the anchors towards some of the guests has made it into the programmes on air", Korzun (2015b) said. Korzun felt so strongly about his decision that he did not even allow *Ekho Moskvy* to reprint his blog post on their website. Other commentators and experts followed suit.

Venediktov himself said that he did not really understand why Korzun had decided to quit. He defended his decision not to take any measures against Ryabtseva by saying that by allowing her to express her opinion, he was actually defending *Ekho*'s core values. In an interview he said: "This is not a choice between Ryabtseva or anybody else and *Echo of Moscow* but a choice of our basic principles: *Echo* gives voice to everybody, including those who represent the majority and also including radicals ... It's me who suffered most of all from Ryabtseva's comments" (Nemtsova, 2015).

Ryabtseva said that she did not understand why Korzun left either. She explained in an interview that she had a very good relationship with Venediktov, but the rumours that she was her mistress were untrue but were sustained by him. Ryabtseva argued that the public image Venediktov put forward of himself as an eccentric alcoholic was carefully crafted by him and had little to do with what he was really like as a person. "He plays a fool whom no one expects to be attacked by. But internally he is very composed and always ready to attack", Ryabtseva (Sokolova, 2015) said. She argued that Venediktov had a clear strategy as to how to act in every situation and even had a black list of enemies that he would struck out one by one, including half of his staff. Ryabtseva said she was "Venediktov's favourite project" (Sokolova, 2015) and that she would also maintain her personal relationship with Venediktov even if she left *Ekho Moskvy* (which she did shortly after the scandal in December 2015). Ryabtseva also claimed that she, Felgengauer, and another colleague – Katya Kobzeva – were Venediktov's favourite "trio".

> We are his most valuable staff, a new generation. Venediktov understands that a new wave is needed, an atmosphere of freshness. And so he chose three girls who always have access to the body. Every one of us can go to this office, propose a new project, etc.
>
> (Sokolova, 2015)

When questioned about her own rudeness on air and in her posts, Ryabtseva said that this was her image "coordinated with the editor-in-chief. The editor is pleased with me, and I do not report to anyone else" (Sokolova, 2015):

> Why do liberals, who speak about freedom of speech, freedom of opinion, prohibit me from writing and speaking? What a domestic

tyranny?! That is, if it is profitable for him, then he is a liberal-democrat, and if he doesn't like something, then the immediate reaction is "How dare you, bastard?" This is hypocrisy.

(Sokolova, 2015)

The final point Ryabtseva made in this interview was that the frictions were the result of a generational gap – the older generation did not share the values of the new generation and did not understand the need for change. In her view, journalism was about asking questions, and it did not necessarily entail a level of expertise in any area. Ryabtseva herself had been accused on a number of occasions of inaccuracy or incompetence in her journalistic work, but she dismissed these accusations:

Mitya {Aleshkovskiy – a photojournalist and her co-presenter} believed that a journalist should be an expert and I must understand the issues surrounding philanthropy. And I believe, like Venediktov, that a journalist should ask questions. I do not have to understand all the intricacies of the problem! I have questions that are the same as those of my listeners … He {Venediktov} understands that a change of generations is necessary, that the swamp is stagnant. New people are needed, young people who understand what the 21st century is – the age of technology, information, the Internet, social networks, promotion. It's a completely different brain! We are set up differently. Venediktov's generation does not understand this.

Ryabtseva said that she had taught Venediktov how to use social media and that she now regretted it. She said she wanted to work on her own project and to build up a new medium that would outperform *Ekho Moskvy* in a few years.

The Future – Journalists' Perceptions of the Role They Play in Russian Society

The history of *Ekho Moskvy* and the outline of the range of current challenges, practices, and controversies show that there was general consensus among the radio station's founders, current editor-in-chief, and journalists about the role *Ekho Moskvy* should play in Russian society. A key mission for the radio station was to promote and uphold liberal values and to provide a platform for anti-Kremlin and generally critical voices of the authorities – both national and regional. However, beyond a general commitment to democracy and its values, journalists' perceptions of what liberalism actually entailed in practice differed. A major bone of contention in recent years has been the extent to which the radio station should be provocative in its programmes, namely, the extent to which it should provide a platform for rude commentators or for extremist views as well as fundamentally what journalism's mission in society should be. *Ekho Moskvy*'s role was further compounded by the fact that the majority shares in the radio station were indeed in the hands of a state-owned company – a fact that they had been reminded of much more often in recent years than ever before, including by Putin himself. When asked whether *Ekho Moskvy* and Venediktov himself were "a thorn in Putin's side", Plushev (2014, personal communication) replied:

– You can ask Putin whether he has anything in his backside. We should take into account that on this thorn there is the word Gazprom out there.
– What is the significance of that?
– I don't know. If only I knew ... Let's think logically. It would be weird not to destruct the thorn that is disturbing you but at the same time this thorn has the name of Gazprom and Gazprom is absolutely people who are close to Putin. In this situation what I don't like is when my colleagues – due to their simplicity or the general situation – make this situation appear either black or white. I love the English word complicated. This fully applies to this situation. Because what you are now asking is: why isn't Putin closing down *Radio Echo Moskvy?*
– Some people say that this is due to the fact that he needs you and *Novaya Gazeta* to demonstrate to the West that there are trends towards democratization in the country.
– It may be so but my own impression is that in the last couple of years Putin doesn't need to guard any appearances before the West because he doesn't pay any attention to such details as criticisms about freedom or no freedom.

Accusations of treachery and betrayal of the national interests have often been fired at *Ekho Moskvy* not just by Putin and Kadyrov but by some of their listeners. Felgengauer (2014, personal communication) said:

The average Russian does not like *Radio Echo of Moscow*. They constantly blame us: claiming that we are the Echo of the US State Department ("Эхо Госдепа"), that we are not patriots, that we have sold ourselves to the Americans, that we are against Russia and our government so things like that. On the other hand, the other side of the population we hear say that we have sold ourselves to Kremlin and we work for Putin and we praise the authorities. All that criticism means that we work professionally, nobody likes us.

(Felgengauer, 2014, personal communication)

Felgengauer's understanding of professionalism, or as she called it "real journalism", was that she should not be influenced by her own personal views, she should always be objective, and she should not allow herself to make any evaluations:

> The news and the interviews are absolutely untouchable. As far as my morning show is concerned, there we do have discussions and I do express my political views but it is sort of an exception … For me the most important thing is to give voice to all participants in a situation – to present all points of view. I consider our listeners intelligent enough to get all the necessary information and to reach their own conclusions. And not to lie – never!
>
> (Felgengauer, 2014, personal communication)

Plushev echoed her words. In his view, the journalistic principles that drove his work were "quite universal and simple – informing of what is really happening, talking objectively and truly, and representing different viewpoints", but he also acknowledged that regardless of how hard he tried to remain objective when working for the news, "one is limited by one's possibilities. One cannot control oneself fully" (Plushev, 2014, personal communication). Similarly to his deputy editor-in-chief, he expressed his opinion in his own programmes, and he also admitted that the way in which he asked his questions could also indicate what his opinion was:

> I actually use my political position for the show. The show comes before my political position. But to make a hot discussion with the guests, I can accept the political position, which is not actually mine but it serves a good purpose for the purposes of discussion. Work is more important for me and in any case I have my own blog where I can express my personal position.
>
> (Plushev, 2014, personal communication)

Both of them admitted that they held very strong political views. Unsurprisingly, both of them did not think highly of Putin. Plushev (2014, personal communication) said that he had never voted for Putin, but he acknowledged that Russia's political life is "complicated" and "it's very difficult to vote for someone else just because the political competition is destroyed. That's why if you ask me who would be the political leader I would vote for, I would have real problems". The presenter said that his mother was concerned about him and had advised him "not to mess up with Putin too much" (Plushev, 2014, personal communication). Felgengauer's (2014, personal communication) views on Putin were stronger: "He is not just leading the country in the incorrect direction but he is getting us nowhere. And every year it's getting worse and worse in that respect so I cannot tell you anything good about President Putin". In a 2015 interview, Venediktov (Nemtsova, 2015) also said:

> I told Putin that he burned to death all competition, all alternative opinions in all spheres – now everything, including aggressive lies and propaganda about Ukraine is the consequence. The competition's been destroyed when it comes to decisions on the economy, in the political field, in opposition and in ideology – as a result obscurantism took over in all decisions.

Venediktov felt very strongly against Russia's increasing isolationism and the prospects of Stalinisation of his country.

Felgengauer admitted she had good informal relationships with a few prominent opposition politicians and her personal cycle of friends included journalists from other liberal media. Her step-father was a prominent *Novaya Gazeta* journalist and during my interview with her, she received a phone call from "a pal" from *TV Dozhd*. "We have informal relations, we can go out together but it is not shown on air. I have known Alexei Navalny for a long time. It's a very complicated story because for me he is not a politician but a very old friend so it's very difficult to divide the two but I try to", Felgengauer (2014, personal communication) said.

Conclusion

All in all, despite the range of challenges and pressures *Ekho Moskvy* had experienced in its 27-year history, including the recent internal frictions and disagreements, *Ekho Moskvy* journalists appeared to be united in their ideological endorsement of the values of liberalism. Nonetheless, their understanding of liberalism and its limits especially with regards to freedom of expression differed. Similarly to their *Novaya Gazeta* colleagues, *Ekho Moskvy* journalists saw their job not as a living but as a way of life, and they genuinely loved their job. As Plushev (2014, personal communication) put it, "I have the best job in the world – I don't do anything. I just talk and that's it. People recognise me by my voice and it's very pleasant". Felgengauer (2015) said that *Ekho Moskvy* was "some kind of incurable disease, possibly, a rare form of mental disorder. In my case, even slight Stockholm syndrome. Not everyone can work here but if you get used to *Ekho*, you've got a new crazy family" (p. 197). She also said that she agreed with Venediktov's words that they were "at war" (Felgengauer, 2015, p. 198). For many journalists, their working day did not end when their shift ended. Their editor-in-chief and some of his colleagues were very active participants in Russia's social and political life. They went out for dinners and meetings with (opposition) politicians, Western NGO representatives, and colleagues from other liberal media.

They were certainly not motivated by the financial remuneration that they received because as both Felgengauer and Plushev acknowledged, the pay they received was lower than that of most of their colleagues, especially at other state media. "Our salaries are low and especially here we have 20% below the market salary – we work for the idea", Felgengauer (2014, personal communication) said. Plushev (2014, personal communication) said that whenever he felt that his salary "was not enough", he wrote articles about technology for magazines or Internet editions or he took part in parties or conferences organised by technology companies. He did not consider these additional activities to be a conflict of interests. "Conflict of interests and independence of the work of my colleagues is judged by our attitude on air", Plushev (2014, personal communication) said.

Both Felgengauer and Plushev were optimistic about the future of their radio station. He said:

> We are one of the very few mass media that really manage to do their job because what a lot of mass media do, including the federal channels, they don't really do the activity I call working. They can do propaganda, entertainment, distracting attention, filling air time but it's not journalism in the real sense of the word. But we do that well – journalism – and I really hope that there will be more media sources that do that. It's really hard to work with almost no competition. We are one of the few stations with this profile.
>
> (Plushev, 2014, personal communication)

Felgengauer (2014, personal communication) shared a very similar view:

> Now everyone says that journalism has no real future. I don't agree with that as long as you do your work fairly and you work well, it will all work out for us. I became a deputy editor-in-chief not that long ago and I would like to maintain and keep this position.

Shortly after *Ekho Moskvy*'s 27th anniversary, Venediktov said in an interview that the radio was swimming in "hydrochloric acid" (Popova, 2017), and these trends had only intensified in recent years. "We see how the media close down one by one, cuts are made, so we continue to swim in hydrochloric acid. But we learned to survive in it. For this we have spacesuits and various other adaptations", he (Popova, 2017) concluded. This strategy of resistance and daily firefighting in the face of numerous challenges had indeed underpinned *Ekho Moskvy*'s existence and success. Some of the compromises made along the way had not been particularly popular among both staff and listeners, but they appear to have allowed the radio station to maintain its relatively critical stance and to continue attracting listeners. In that sense, *Ekho Moskvy*'s experience can serve as a lesson for media organisations in similar situations around the world.

7 From behind the Iron Curtain

Brief History of *Radio Free Europe/Radio Liberty*

"Would there be earth without the sun?" (Urban, 1997, p. 148). This was former Polish President and Nobel laureate Lech Walesa's evaluation of the role of *Radio Free Europe/Radio Liberty* (*RFE/RL*) during the Cold War. While the radios do not any longer broadcast in Central and Eastern Europe, *Radio Liberty*'s mission in Russia and in some of the former Soviet republics is not yet accomplished. This chapter traces the historical development of *RFE/RL* with a focus on *RL* (I will refer to it as *RL* or with its Russian name – *Radio Svoboda*) (see Table 7.1). It is organised under three subheadings: (1) Founding, Mission, and Funding, (2) *Radio Svoboda* during the Cold War, and (3) *Radio Svoboda* after the Cold War. The chapter starts with an outline of the reasons why *RFE* and *RL* were founded (they were two separate entities until 1976). Then, in the second part, I examine *Radio Svoboda*'s development and the important role it played during the Cold War. The broadcaster boasts itself on playing "a significant role in the collapse of communism and the rise of democracies in post-communist Europe" (*RFE/RL*, n.d.). Finally, in the third section, I switch the focus to post–Cold War developments again, with a particular focus on Russia. In spite of the fact that *Radio Svoboda* now has an official office in the centre of Moscow, half of the journalists covering Russia, including the director of the Russian Service, are not actually based in Moscow but in Prague – the radio's headquarters. This chapter does not offer a comprehensive history of *RFE/RL*, but it focusses on key events and developments mainly in the history of *Radio Svoboda* as a means of setting the context in which journalists currently work and in an attempt to better account for the role the radio station plays in present-day Russia.

Founding, Mission, and Funding

RFE and *RL* were established in the beginning of the Cold War, with the aim of transmitting "uncensored news and information to audiences behind the Iron Curtain" (*RFE/RL*, n.d.). Initially, they were two separate entities. According to the official history on *RFE/RL*'s website, George F. Kennan from the US Department of State and Frank G. Wisner from

Table 7.1 *Radio Free Europe/Radio Liberty Russian Service*: Timeline

Year	Milestone
1953	First *RL broadcast*
1971	End of CIA involvement
1976	*RFE* and *RL* merger
1991	Yeltsin officially recognised *RFE/RL* with a decree
1995	Headquarters' relocation from Munich to Prague
2012	End of AM waves license
2014	*Current Time* brand launched
2016	*RL* moves to online-only broadcasts
2017	*RL* designated as a "foreign agent" by the Ministry of Justice

the Office of Policy Coordination, later the US Central Intelligence Agency (CIA), came up with the idea in an attempt "to utilize the talents of post–World War II Soviet and East European émigrés in support of American foreign policy" (*RFE/RL*, n.d.). Kennan was a proponent of the so-called policy of "containment", namely, not so much attempting "to liberate Eastern Europe from Soviet domination" but "a strategy of preventing the spread of the Soviet empire beyond its East European boundaries" by

> creating complications for the Soviets within their own sphere of influence, since the more Moscow was preoccupied with keeping the restive peoples of Eastern Europe in check, the less likely it would be to cast a hungry eye on Western Europe.
>
> (Puddington, 2000, p. 8)

RFE was founded in 1950 and initially broadcast to Bulgaria, Czechoslovakia, Hungary, Poland, and Romania. Its first broadcasts started on 4 July 1950. *Radio Svoboda* started broadcasting in the Soviet Union on 1 March 1953, initially under the name *Radio Liberation* (Освобождение), which was changed to *RL* (Свобода) in 1959. The broadcasts in the first few weeks were only in Russian, but other languages were soon added. *Radio Svoboda* also began broadcasts to Estonia, Latvia, and Lithuania in 1975.

Here is an excerpt from *Radio Svoboda*'s opening broadcast, which clearly illustrates the foundation mission of the radio:

> Fellow countrymen! For a long time the Soviet regime has concealed from you the very fact of the emigration's existence. Only rarely is it mentioned in the press, and then it is tied to some scandalous case of a well-known person deciding not to return home, or some other event unpleasant for the Soviets such as the trial of Kravchenko (a famous defector). The rest of the time nothing good or bad is said about us. We have been covered with a gravestone of silence, but

we have not died. We are well aware why the Soviets have decided not even to rail against us in written or verbal attacks. That would mean constantly reminding the people about the existence of an anti-Bolshevik Russia which did not find a place in the motherland, about a Russia which took arms against Bolshevism and to this day has not ceased its struggle, and awaits its hour. Every intelligent person in the Soviet Union is sure in the depths of his soul that the Bolshevik tyranny in Russia, which is so monstrously abnormal and defies reason and humanitarian principles, cannot endure forever. Only that certainly gives us the energy to bear the hardships that have befallen us. You suffer from unheard oppression and physical torture, and we suffer the bitterness of exile and dispersal throughout the world.

(Sosin, 1999, p. 15)

This first broadcast contained a very strong political message. It did not simply condemn the Soviet political regime but it also made it clear that the radio was opposed to the restoration of absolute monarchy or indeed to any form of new dictatorship that might replace Bolshevism:

We are for full freedom of conscience and religious preaching. We are not only for the liquidation of the exploitation of man by man, but also for the liquidation of the exploitation of man by the Party and the state...The happy life about which our enslavers shout is unthinkable until the elimination of the system of terror, force, and all forms of slave labor, until the monstrous concentration camps are removed – that shame and horror of our times, until the kolkhozes are broken up and the peasants are offered the right to choose their own form of agriculture.

(Sosin, 1999, p. 16)

The opening statement showed that the main role *Radio Svoboda* envisaged to play was an ideological one. This was not a conventional Western radio station. This was a radio station with a clear ideological mission – the overthrow of the repressive Bolshevik regime and ultimately the establishment of democracy in the Soviet Union, or as they put it, the right of all nationalities situated on the territory of the Soviet Union "to freely choose their fate on the basis of democratic self-expression" (Sosin, 1999, p. 16). The message at the end of this opening address was unequivocal:

Our task is to tell you about what you never will hear in the Soviet Union, to provide you with truthful information, and to help liberate you from that web with which Soviet propaganda is enveloping your souls...But one thing cannot be taken away – the possibility of thinking freely!

(Sosin, 1999, p. 18)

While the militant/combative and strongly oppositional tone adopted in the opening broadcast was not surprising, it did not last as long as anticipated. In his book about *Radio Svoboda*, Gene Sosin (1999), who worked for the radio since its inception for 33 years (in fact, even in the period when they were preparing to start broadcasting), wrote that the word "liberation" was dropped in favour of the word "liberty" in large part in recognition of the fact that the policy of "'rolling back Communism' proclaimed by the Eisenhower administration was empty rhetoric" (p. 18). The Soviet suppression of the Hungarian revolution played a big role in that process (Sosin, 1999). Nonetheless, Sosin (1999) argued that while the opening broadcast made *Radio Svoboda*'s priorities clear, the mission of the radio was not to incite any specific form of action against the Soviet regime. He said that they realised very early on that

> the Radio would be effective only to the extent that it did not promise more than it could deliver and we must take into consideration the complex psychology of average Soviet citizens, who had many gripes against the regime but at the same time were proud of their homeland's victory over the Nazi invaders and suspicious of voices from the capitalist world abroad.
>
> (Sosin, 1999, pp. 18–19)

The main difficulty for *Radio Svoboda* was to find a clear identity that would allow it to fulfil its main mission by also attracting substantial support for its ethos from inside Russia. Puddington (2000) argued that finding "an overarching broadcast theme, or message" was much more difficult for *Radio Svoboda* than for *RFE* because "communism had not been imposed on Russia by outsiders; it was a home-grown affair" (p. 154). Moreover, due to Russia's isolationism and Stalin's victory over Hitler, there were no real oppositional sentiments in Russia at the time. As Puddington (2000) put it, "they were not likely to respond favourably to an appeal based on the evil nature of their leaders, the superiority of the American economy, or to lectures among the immorality of imperial aggression against smaller neighbours" (p. 154).

The difficulty of finding a clear identity was further compelled by the fact that *Radio Svoboda's* staff were initially granted a great degree of autonomy in deciding on editorial policy and direction. This liberal approach backfired almost as soon as it was adopted because it led to a period of tumult – a lack of coordination and internal frictions and conflicts. Sosin (1999) argued that there had been an on-going tension at *Radio Svoboda* between the Russian emigrants and the non-Russian employees of the radio station because, in his view, the Russian had "their own political agenda" and prejudices. Puddington (2000) wrote that the internal strife began even before *Radio Svoboda* started broadcasting. He said that the private entity that managed *RL* – American Committee for the Liberation of the Peoples of Russia (AMCOMLIB) – "had set itself the goal of forging unity" among the Soviet exile organisations, but instead of unity, their "efforts" led to "a series of acrimonious faction fights, pitting Russian exiles against other Russian exiles, Russian exiles against non-Russian exiles, and Russians and non-Russians alike against Amcomlib's American management" (pp. 153–154). Urban (1997) summed up the main underlying reason for these frictions:

> Radio Liberty's identification with the interests and feelings of the Russian nation drew fire from American intellectuals and journalists much more readily than Radio Free Europe did for *its* identification with Poles, Czechs, and Hungarians. Russian national sentiment was suspect in the eyes of these American critics because Russian history was suspect. Steeped as they thought Russian history was in the spirit of autocracy and orthodoxy, with few democratic episodes to make it palatable to the modern Western mind, numerous members of the American intellectual establishment looked upon the Russian legacy as something Radio Liberty should scrupulously avoid embracing. Whatever the rights and wrongs of that judgement, it did have an impact and made it exceptionally difficult for Radio Liberty to perform its mission as a Russian "home service".
>
> (Urban, 1997, pp. 3–4)

In addition to these internal frictions, *RL* experienced significant technical issues due to the low number of shortwave receivers they had in the Soviet Union. A further complication was the difficult search for suitable writers and editors. The internal conflicts led to a reconsideration of the policy of autonomy and ultimately to much stricter US control and direction. Sosin occupied different posts at *Radio Svoboda*, including director of broadcasting. He recalled that the main principle of his work and the work of his predecessor had been to "shape the future broadcasts into effective weapons of psychological warfare", which targeted "'the loyal Soviet citizen,'" "not merely those who were already enemies of the regime" (Sosin, 1999, pp. 6–8). The concept of "psychological warfare" was particularly pertinent in the post-war period. One key difference between *Radio Svoboda* and radios such as the *Voice of America* and the *BBC* was that it was conceived to be a local radio, not a radio that focussed on life outside of the Soviet Union (Sosin, 1999). Urban (1997) explained that there were "two kinds of broadcasting in the national languages of Eastern Europe and the former Soviet Union" (p. ix). The first group included radios such as the *BBC*, the *Voice of America,* and *Deutsche Welle,* whose aim was to "pursue national diplomacy by other means, and their brief was to 'project' their nations" (p. ix). The second group included *RFE* and *RL*, whose purpose was to identify "fully with the interests, culture, history, and religion of the nations under Soviet or Soviet-inspired rule" by articulating "the kind of opinions that free media would have done had a free press, radio, and television existed" (Urban, 1997, pp. ix–x). The latter group was "in effect national 'home' services speaking from abroad" (Urban, 1997, p. x). Urban himself was a long-serving member of staff and even director of RFE, so not all commentators would agree with his account.

Sosin (1999) also argued that if there was one word that best characterised *Radio Svoboda*'s initial programming, it was the word glasnost – "filling in the 'blank spots' of censorship" (p. 22). However, there was not much glasnost as far as *RL*'s financial affairs were concerned, and, in fact, the radio broke its promise to be truthful almost immediately after professing a commitment to truthfulness by disguising the real source of its funding. Initially, both RFE and RL were funded by the US Congress through the CIA, but RFE also received private donations. However, this fact was kept secret for years. The funds for RL were disbursed to a private entity in the state of Delawere, which was renamed a few times – from the American Committee for Freedom of the Peoples of the USSR, to the American Committee for the Liberation of the Peoples of Russia (AMCOMLIB), to the American Committee for Liberation from Bolshevism, to the American Committee for Liberation to Radio Liberty Committee. As Sosin (1999) pointed out, "the façade of a private company was supposed to establish greater credibility for the Radio as an independent voice rather than as an official arm of the US communications network that included *Voice of America*" (p. 2). He recalled how after passing his security check, he was summoned to the office of the president of AMCOMLIB where he was told that "Amcomlib and the radio station under its control were indeed 'assets' of the CIA, which received funds from annual appropriations of the US Congress, secretly disbursed with the knowledge of only a few senators and representatives on the Hill" (Sosin, 1999, p. 28). He was asked to sign a document pledging not to reveal this secret. Sosin (1999) himself admitted to openly lying about the funding arrangements for two decades, but he said that "the deception was justified if it protected us from Soviet efforts to undermine our mission" (p. 28).

The year 1971 was a particularly turbulent year in the history of RFE/RL after Senator Clifford Case from the Republican Party publicly revealed that RFE and RL were funded by the CIA. Another senator – James William Fulbright – from the Democratic Party argued that the radios should be terminated, and as a result, President Richard Nixon appointed a commission of inquiry. The inquiry concluded that it was in the long-term interests of the USA for the radios to continue existing. All CIA involvement ended in 1971, and RFE and RL had since been funded by the US Congress through the Board for International Broadcasting (BIB), and after 1995, the Broadcasting Board of Governors (BBG). Subsequently, the two corporations were merged into RFE/RL in 1976.

Radio Svoboda during the Cold War

The official history of *RFE/RL* acknowledged that in the first years of the Cold War, *RFE* and *RL* adopted "more confrontational editorial policies than other Western broadcasters" but with the caveat that the broadcasts "did not promote uprisings and, after 1953, emphasized evolutionary system change" (*RFE/RL*, n.d.). The more humble approach was in recognition of the fact that it was unlikely that the overthrow of communism would be a smooth and rapid process. The official label used for style of reporting adopted by *RFE/RL* has been "surrogate" broadcasting – "an unbiased, professional substitute for the free media that the countries behind the Iron Curtain lacked", with an emphasis "on local news not covered in state-controlled domestic media, as well as religion, science, sports, Western music, and locally banned literature and music" (*RFE/RL*, n.d.). Dissidents, opposition activists, and prominent intellectuals as well as religious leaders were frequently given a platform for expression. One of *RL*'s most prominent contributors, for example, was Father Alexander Schmemann – an Orthodox priest whom Solzhenitsyn, famously referred to as "my priest". The radios' headquarters were in Munich in West Germany, and they had transmitters in Germany, Spain, Portugal, and Taiwan (until the early 1970s). In spite of the fact that they had the same source of funding and shared both a similar ideology and the same building, there was no close collaboration between *RL* and *RFE*. In fact, Puddington (2000) argued that *RFE* officials considered *RL* to be inferior to *RFE*, especially in terms of their professionalism. Also, the perception had always been that *RL* was much more tightly controlled by the CIA – an allegation refuted by *RL* staff. Urban (1997) recalled that the merger between the two radios was not well received by either of them, and was in fact met with "detriment and dissatisfaction" (p. 76). As Urban (1997) put it, staff were not happy with the fact that "the distinction between the Soviet aggressor – addressed by Radio Liberty, and the victims of aggression – addressed by Radio Free Europe, was being blurred" (p. 76). Moreover, the process was accompanied by cuts and a general "loss of purpose and direction" (Urban, 1997, p. 76).

Numerous types of attacks such as jamming, espionage, and violence were launched at *RFE/RL* during communism:

> Regimes launched technical, espionage, diplomatic, and propaganda offensives intended to discredit the broadcasts. Stalin personally ordered the establishment of local and long-distance jamming facilities to try to block broadcasts. The radios utilized high power and multiple frequencies to overcome jamming. The Soviet KGB and Warsaw Pact intelligence services penetrated the stations, jailed sources and even resorted to violence in attempts to intimidate *RFE*

and *RL* staff. For example, Bulgarian Service correspondent Georgi Markov was murdered in London in 1978, evidently by Bulgarian intelligence.

(*RFE/RL*, n.d.)

In 1981, the headquarters in Munich were bombed. The bomb injured six people and caused significant damage to the building. According to *RFE/RL*'s history, the bomb was planted and paid for by the Romanian security services. *RL* and *RFE* employees were not allowed to travel to their home countries because it was too dangerous for them since the perception of them was as traitors and CIA agents.

Sosin (1999) also recalled that the Komitet Gosudarstvennoy Bezo-pasnosti (KGB) actively interfered in the work of *Radio Svoboda* "in an effort to terrorize and discourage its employees, including in all probability the murder of two members of the Munich staff during the 1950s" (p. xiv). *RL* had faced "many crises" during its history:

> The Radio was infiltrated with "plants" in the person of alleged defectors, who later returned to the Soviet Union and branded the Radio as a haven for Nazi collaborators and CIA agents. There was some truth to those accusations, because early recruits from among the emigres in Western Europe included former Soviet citizens who had fought on the German side.
>
> (Sosin, 1999, p. xiv)

Puddington (2000) also claimed that spies were infiltrated in every language section, both at *RFE* and at *RL*. A KGB agent worked in the Russian section for 20 years and was even a candidate for the chief editor's post. However, while the spies provided the communist countries' security agencies with files of information about the radios, their role was not to influence broadcast content. Puddington (2000) argued that despite all the spying activity going on, the spies' role was inconsequential because "the radios' message remained unchanged" (p. 226). Urban (1997) disagreed with this account of the role of the KGB. He argued that the KGB was very effective in "inventing and then in fanning the flames of the conflict" between the warring factions at *Radio Svoboda* (p. 4).

Another form of assault on *RL* was jamming, which started 10 minutes after the first broadcast began in the Soviet Union and ended on 29 November 1998 on Gorbachev's orders in line with his policy of glasnost (Sosin, 1999). There were even speculations that communist countries spent more money on jamming than *RL* and *RFE* spent on broadcasting. One way in which the *RL* team tackled jamming was by trying to penetrate it by playing a distinctive "sharp" musical signal – Alexander Grechaninov's "The Hymn of Free Russia". The words were from a poem by

Konstantin Balmont celebrating the short-lived democratic revolution of February 1917. The opening words were: "Long live Russia, a free country" (Sosin, 1999, p. 23).

In spite of all the difficulties experienced and the initial internal battles at *RL*, the radios' powerful role during the Cold War seems almost undeniable. Puddington (2000) argued that *RFE* "was arguably the most influential politically oriented international radio station in history" (p. ix), and by the 1970s, *RL* "ranked as one of the most influential radio stations in the world" (p. 155). Similarly, Sosin (1999) wrote that "from a weak voice in 1953, the Radio {*RL*} became the most powerful medium of communications to penetrate the Iron Curtain, influencing millions of Russians, Ukrainians, and other ethnic groups in the major populated areas of the Soviet Union" (p. xiv). In Puddington's (2000) view, the two stations were "unique in the annals of international broadcasting" and to the history of diplomacy because, unlike other ideological stations, their purpose was not to promote the American way of life but to bring communism down via "surrogate" reporting (Puddington, 2000, p. ix). Thus, in spite of the fact that they were broadcasting from outside the countries of transmission, the focus had always been on internal affairs.

Sosin (1999) wrote:

> It was little short of a miracle that a group of Americans, mostly inexperienced in the art of international communications, managed to combine their talents and energy with a similarly untrained group of embittered victims of Soviet tyranny bent on revenge against the power that had wronged them and their families. During years of dramatic changes within and outside the Soviet Union, this improbable alliance built a permanent bridge that linked the outside world with millions of listeners who grew to depend on the Radio's broadcasts as the voice of their secret thoughts, frustrations, and hopes. Soviet leaders from Gorbachev and Yeltsin on down, including a KGB general, have acknowledged the impact of the Radio. Of particular significance were the endorsements of Andrei Sakharov, Aleksandr Solzhenitsyn, and other prominent opponents of the dictatorship. They risked their freedom and sometimes their lives to reach public opinion abroad and, primarily via *Radio Liberty*, to deliver to their own people *samizdat* ("self-published," uncensored documents) articulating their demands for civil and human rights that the regime denied its citizens.
>
> (Sosin, 1999, pp. xv–xvi)

According to *RFE/RL's* (n.d.) website, they provided "a 'megaphone'" through which independent figures – denied normal access to local media – could reach millions of their countrymen with uncensored writings. Former Polish President and Nobel laureate Lech Walesa was quoted as saying that the radio's role in Poland's struggle for freedom "cannot even be described. Would there be earth without the sun?" (*RFE/RL*, n.d.). Both Puddington and Sosin did not deny the fact that *RFE/RL* were ideological instruments, and they worked very closely with the US authorities. However, as Puddington (2000) pointed out, the US "doctrine" towards the Soviet Union and the communist world as a whole evolved through a few different stages of development – "liberation, gradualism, détente" – and as a result of that, *RFE*'s and *RL*'s missions also evolved while their ideological underpinning remained stable:

> *RFE* continued to fulfill its original mission as an instrument of anti-Communist diplomacy. *Radio Free Europe*, along with its sister organization, *Radio Liberty*, stood as the most visible institutions of official American anticommunism, and were arguably the most suc-cessful Cold War vehicles established by the American government.
>
> (Puddington, 2000, p. 5)

The practical application of this anti-communism doctrine in the daily broadcasts was not as straightforward, and as Puddington (2000) ar-gued, "broadcast tone remained a perennial problem" (p. 169). An internal review of adherence to policy guidelines during the 1960s criticised the use of "a strident and propagandistic vocabulary" (Puddington, 2000, p. 169). During the 1970s, *RL* adopted a policy of broadcasting samizdat documents – non-conformist essays or reports by people who lived in the Soviet Union but were unhappy with certain aspects of life there. *RL* was inundated with samizdat documents, each of which was carefully checked and verified before being broadcast. In that period, *RL* also managed to attract more staff. Puddington (2000) argued that *RL* paid well, and it was "able to woo the best and brightest of the new emigration away from the *BBC*, where compen-sation was comparative low" (p. 172). Both Puddington (2000) and Sosin (1999) acknowledged that *RL* changed its propagandistic tone to a more moderate one, whereby the main objective was no longer to achieve the overthrow of communism but to "give expression to and encourage those trends...which can lead to democratization, social jus-tice, and national self-determination" (*Radio Liberty* Policy Manual, 1976, as quoted in Puddington, 2000, p. 173).

The 1976 policy manual also included guidance on what the target au-dience should be – "real or potential decision making elements", "think-ing members of the Communist Party and Komsomol", "the scientific, technological, and creative intelligentsia", or "skilled workers and their supervisors" (*Radio Liberty* Policy Manual, 1976, as quoted in Pudding-ton, 2000, p. 173). The policy guidance included even specific advice on how Lenin and his policies should be discussed in a more moderate way than before, but Puddington (2000) argued that it was not clear to what extent *RL* staff – all of whom were firm believers in the negative role of communism – did actually put these policies into practice. He referred to this second stage in the history of *RL* as "the era of détente" (Puddington, 2000, p. 174).

Ronald Reagan's election as president of the USA and the deterioration of the relationship between the USA and the USSR led to a new era in the history of *RL* in the 1980s, labelled by Puddington (2000) as "its period of greatest influence", which also brought about "a degree of strife and controversy unprecedented in the station's history" (p. 174). Puddington (2000) wrote than no US President had been as committed to the mission of *RFE/RL* as Reagan was because his presidency was underpinned by an ideological belief in the "global war of ideas" and the power of "public diplomacy" (p. 253). While under previous US presidents, the future of *RFE* and *RL* had been threatened, under Reagan, they were not worried about their finances, redundancies, or potential relocation of their headquarters because they received more money than before. However, Reagan's "disdain for détente" also meant that the new appointments made at *RFE/RL* were of staff who shared his "hatred of communism" and would encourage "sharp, hard-hitting commentaries – restrained polemics that would zero in on Communist failure, Communist hypocrisy, and Communist immorality" (Puddington, 2000, p. 254).

While *RL* was becoming more popular and more influential than ever, it went through yet another period of internal frictions and clashes in the late 1970s–early 1980s. Prominent intellectuals and dissidents took issue with the radio's stringent editorial guidelines. In 1977, Vladimir Bukovsky claimed that policy guidelines were similar to the censorship imposed by the Soviet authorities. Solzhenitsyn himself accused *RL* of self-censorship and wrote that "*RL* broadcasts 'have degenerated to such an extent that, if they continue the way they are going, it would be better to do away with them altogether'" (Puddington, 2000, p. 274). There were two warring factions at *RL* – the "Westernizers", namely, the new hires who were "often Jewish, suspicious of Russian nationalism, critics of Solzhenitsyn, and strong advocated of democratic change in the Soviet Union", and the "Slavophiles", namely, "members of the older generation, ethnically Russian, advocates of an 'authentically Russian' programming orientation, devoted to Solzhenitsyn, fervently anti-Communist but inclined towards skepticism about Western democracy" (Puddington, 2000, p. 274). Accusations of anti-Semitism were not uncommon at the time of these frictions, and the battles also transcended into the public space. The US Senate Foreign Relations Committee sent a representative to Munich who wrote a report claiming that there was no evidence of anti-Semitic broadcasts, but there was evidence of anti-Western broadcasts. The General Accounting Office also published a report enumerating various policy violations by *RL*. In 1986, human rights activist Ludmilla Alexeyeva published a report for Helsinki Watch in which she argued that the Russian language services of *RL* were "tolerating broadcasts that featured expressions of extreme Russian nationalism and a hostility to pluralism and democracy" (Puddington, 2000, p. 280). The internal battles also led to management changes.

Nonetheless, despite facing such internal challenges, RL also experienced a period of upheaval during the 1980s, best demonstrated by the coverage of the Chernobyl nuclear disaster in Ukraine. One of the four reactors at the Chernobyl complex exploded on 26 April 1986, killing 31 people and spreading radiation throughout Eastern Europe. Puddington (2000) argued that the disaster was seen "as the first important test of glasnost" – the policy announced by Gorbachev – and it was "the ideal story for *Radio Free Europe* and *Radio Liberty*" (p. 285). He praised *RFE/RL's* coverage of the disaster. The radios devoted hours of coverage. They included political and expert analysis, but also a lot of practical advice for their listeners, including decontamination and protection strategies. In Puddington's (2000) view, "this would be one of *RFE-RL's* finest hours" (p. 286) that resulted in a dramatic increase in the number of listeners. The Kremlin initially tried to defend itself by launching a counter-attack on *RL*, but Gorbachev eventually changed his approach and put an end to jamming as well as "fortified his resolve to reduce censorship, promote openness, and bring the Soviet Union into the modern era where the rapid transmission of accurate information was critical to economic success" (Puddington, 2000, p. 286).

Radio Svoboda after the Cold War

The end of jamming, Gorbachev's perestroika and glasnost policies, and the subsequent end of the Cold War were a mixed blessing for *RL*. On the one hand, the broadcasts of *RL* could now easily reach its audiences, but, on the other hand, the potential liberalisation of Russian media meant that *RL* had to yet again reconsider its identity and mission. As Puddington (2000) put it, *RL* "was burdened by the notion that it was something less than normal news radio, an attitude that had been inculcated by years of serving as the target of Soviet propaganda" (p. 287). The changed political landscape also led to a change in leadership at *RL*. The new service director was Vladimir Matusevitch, who was chief editor during the previous period of internal frictions but was then sent to London. Matusevitch initiated a few programming and production changes, and during his tenure, it "also scored some hard news coups" and its "ratings soared, as did its influence" (Puddington, 2000, p. 288). One of the stories that *RL* broadcast that gained prominence was an interview with Boris Yeltsin in which he accused the KGB of having threatened to kill him (Puddington, 2000).

While the Russian language service of *RL* had always attracted the most funding and attention, the minority language services were significantly strengthened during this period. They played an important role in the Soviet republics' battles for national independence. Puddington (2000) wrote that "in most cases, *Radio Liberty* served as the media of choice for the partisans of independence; indeed, in some cases, *RL*, or in the case of the Baltic states, *RFE*, effectively functioned as an instrument of the independence forces" (p. 292). The stations provided extensive coverage of independence politicians and demonstrations, and in Puddington's view (2000), despite its professed commitment to unbiased coverage, the coverage was tilted towards independence due to "the heavy reliance on sources from within the republics" (p. 292). While the glasnost era presented numerous opportunities for the minority language services, it was also a very challenging time for them because they were generally very understaffed and were yet coming to grips with the professionalisation of journalism and the technological advances.

One marked change during this period was the fact that Kremlin and KGB officials started giving interviews to *RL*. The Soviet press also published the first positive articles about *Radio Svoboda* after years of attacking the radio. *RL* developed a network of correspondents and/or stringers in the Soviet Union who covered the 1991 coup extensively. Both Yeltsin and Gorbachev praised *RL* for its coverage of the coup. Yeltsin (1991, as quoted in Parta, 2007) said that during the coup, *RL* was one of the very few channels which sent news to the rest of the world and to Russia because "now almost every family in Russia listens to *Radio Liberty*" (p. xv). An audience survey actually showed that about 30% of Muscovites had listened to *RL* during the coup, and the figure was higher among the elites (43%). Puddington (2000) also praised *RL* for its coverage of the coup and quoted Mikhail Gorbachev's and Boris Yeltsin's testimonials:

Gorbachev had relied on *RL* and other foreign broadcast stations during the critical days of August; Yeltsin, of course, had relied on *RL* to maintain contact with the Russian people. Meanwhile a revolution had swept away both communism, one of the most repressive political systems invented by man, and the Soviet Union, an empire that had endured for decades by force of arms but split apart almost without resort to violence. To Paul Goble, Radio Liberty's greatest achievement was in discouraging the use of force during the final, convulsive years of the empire. "I think we helped make the revolution, and I think we helped make it peaceful," he recalled several years later. "If it hadn't been for Radio Liberty, I'm sure there would have been more killing. Whatever we can be taxed for, the fact remains that there are a lot of people who are not dead because of this radio station".

(Puddington, 2000, p. 306)

The important role RL played in the coverage of the coup and more generally in "the course of the democratic processes in Russia" was officially recognised by Yeltsin who issued a decree on 27 August 1991, permitting RL to open a permanent bureau in Moscow and to obtain official accreditation as well as to be provided "with the necessary channels of communications". Mark Pomar, the executive director of the Board for International Broadcasting, said at the time: "This makes us a legitimate news service within the country" (Rosenstiel, 1991). The decree also required the mayor of Moscow to assign office space for $RFE/RL's$ bureau. Sosin (1999) argued that Yeltsin's decree was unprecedented. The bureau opened in January 1992 in central Moscow, close to Mayakovsky square.

Yeltsin was not the only politician who officially recognised the role of RFE/RL. The end of the Cold War brought about a brief period of "recognition and acclaim" in their homelands for RFE and RL journalists throughout the region, who could freely go back to their countries where they would often be greeted as heroes (Puddington, 2000, p. 307). However, this period of acclaim was short-lived because the end of the Cold War also gave rise to the perennial question for RFE and RL about the radios' mission and identity. RFE and RL were Cold War creations, so should they continue existing after the Cold War was over? The answer to this question was not unequivocal. At the end of 1991, a total of 11 "distinguished Americans" were tasked with assessing the past and the future roles of RFE/RL (Sosin, 1999, p. 225). After a six-month investigation, the task force concluded that $RFE/RL's$ mission was not complete because it had an important role to play in the years to come, but it had evolved from a surrogate to an alternative mission (Sosin, 1999). A key task for RFE/RL in the post–Cold War era was to assist local media in their efforts to change their practices so they can better serve their societies in their transitions from communism to democracy. This was likely to be a much more difficult and lengthy process than initially envisaged. The 1992 annual report recognised that RL "is helping in important ways to compensate for the weaknesses of today's media" (Sosin, 1999, p. 226). RL's mission was to "provide a moderate, alternative non-partisan perspective on domestic and regional affair, and a counterweight to voices of extremism" (Sosin, 1999, p. 225). One of the controversial issues in the post–Cold War period had also been the extent to which RL should work towards promoting US foreign policy or whether it should simply aim to be a non-partisan medium free to criticise the USA and its policies.

The task force's positive report did not really put an end to the ongoing discussion about the future of RFE/RL in the changing societies of Central and Eastern Europe. In 1993, the new Clinton administration decided to eliminate "much of the operation, placing what remained of the radios under the oversight of the United States Information Agency"

(Puddington, 2000, p. 308). *RFE/RL* also moved their headquarters from Munich to Prague in 1995 not least because Czech President Vaclav Havel offered them rent-free premises in central Prague. Havel himself strongly believed in the power of *RFE/RL* and insisted that the radios should continue existing. He was quoted as saying: "We need your professionalism and your ability to see events from a broad perspective" – a sentiment shared by other former dissidents and officials in Central and Eastern Europe (*RFE/RL*, n.d.). The move to Prague was undoubtedly an essential phase in the process of downsizing. Many of the Munich-based staff either retired or left *RFE/RL*. While initially *RFE/RL* was very active in the region by establishing local bureaus and training local journalists, it eventually "fulfilled its mission" (*RFE/RL*, n.d.) and closed its services in Hungary (1993), Poland (1997), the Czech Republic (2002), Estonia, Latvia, Lithuania, Slovakia, Bulgaria (2004), and Romania (2008). These countries all became NATO and EU member states, so the continued broadcasting of *RFE/RL* on their territories was not really justified, given the radios' mission. However, not only did *RL* not close its operations in Russia and the former Soviet Union, but it also reinstated broadcasts in Avar, Chechen, and Circassian in the North Caucasus in 2002, and in October 2014, in cooperation with the *Voice of America*, it launched Russian-language programming "for the global Russian audience under the '*Current Time*' brand" (*RFE/RL*, n.d.). Moreover, *RFE/RL* also launched new services in former Yugoslavia and the Middle East.

Radio Svoboda's honeymoon period in Russia was rather short-lived, not only because of the identity issues the radio faced in the post–Cold War period, but also because of President Vladimir Putin's administration's attempts to silence the radio's voice via a range of legal and administrative measures. The first clear signal – that despite its fancy office in central Moscow, *RFE/RL* was unlikely to be allowed to freely operate in the country – came as early as 2002 when Putin annulled Yeltsin's decree. The Kremlin's explanation was that Putin's decision was "purely technical" and would not affect the work of *RL*. According to the Kremlin, this was "simply an attempt to treat *Radio Free Europe/Radio Liberty* as it does all foreign news organizations" (Myers, 2002). At the time when Putin annulled Yeltsin's decree, *RL* had an AM waves broadcast license. While it never had an FM waves license, in 2005, *RL* boasted of having 30 local affiliate radio stations that broadcast its content on FM waves. However, in the next decade or so, all local affiliates stopped broadcasting *Radio Svoboda's* content due to the political pressure they faced. *Radio Svoboda* suffered a very serious blow in November 2012 when it lost its AM license due to the coming into force of an amendment to the Federal Law on Mass Media, which made it illegal for an entity that directly or indirectly has more than 50% foreign ownership to hold a radio broadcasting license. BBG Governor Michael Lynton strongly condemned the tightened regulatory framework. He said that Putin "has taken steps that sharply curtail freedom of expression" during his first 100 days as president after he was re-elected to the post (Stine, 2012). *Radio Svoboda's* management was strongly criticised for its weak response to these developments and for the fact that it made a number of staff redundant (according to unconfirmed reports as many as 40 employees were laid off). The majority of them openly protested against the decision and the general direction *RL* was taking.

Conclusion

Radio Svoboda's history is a reflection of the history of the Cold War and the post–Cold War period as well. It is a story of turbulent relationships between the US Congress, the CIA, the editorial staff, the émigré community, Soviet audiences and the Soviet authorities, and the KGB. It shows the strained relationship between the communist Soviet bloc and the capitalist US-led West with the various trials, tribulations, and insecurities along the way. While the work of *RFE/ RL* was clearly motivated by an anti-communist ideology during the Cold War, it still went through a few different phases, especially in Russia – from strong anti-communist propaganda, to a muted acceptance that communism was likely to last for much longer than expected, to a triumphant victory (albeit a short-lived one) of liberal and democratic values. The future of *Radio Svoboda* has never been certain nor has its identity and mission ever been entirely fixed and clear-cut. The history of *Radio Svoboda* tells the story of a perpetual strife towards a clear mission and identity – professional, political, cultural, and ideological. As Urban (1997) put it:

> Despite valiant efforts to overcome it by successive teams of executives, the conceptual confusion at the heart of Radio Liberty's mandate jeopardized its execution to the end of the Cold War. The United States did, of course, want to weaken the Soviet empire, but it did so slowly, hesitantly, away from the public gaze, and with a characteristically guilty conscience. That the Radio nevertheless performed as well as it did was owing to the dedication of some of its directors...and the flexible interpretation of their brief...The multiplicity of purposes it was called upon to serve was a true reflection of the changing moods of members of the American political class and of their wavering resolve about whether – and to what extent and in what way – they wanted to see the power and influence of the Soviet system and the Soviet Union globally eliminated.
>
> (Urban, 1997, p. 6)

It is undeniable, however, that *RFE/RL* played a very important role during the Cold War – as numerous political leaders and ordinary listeners in the former Soviet Union and in Central and Eastern Europe have recognised. Puddington (2000) succinctly summed up the role of the radios:

> Through RFE-RL and the other foreign broadcast entities, the Communists were never able to gain a media monopoly, and were thus deprived of the more potent tools of totalitarian control. It is unfortunate that most histories of the Cold War deal with RFE and RL as footnotes, or as CIA-manipulated propaganda instruments. For in fact the radios proved one of the most successful institutions of America's Cold War effort, and made an important contribution to the peaceful nature of communism's demise...In the war of ideas between communism and democracy – and this, after all, was the central conflict of the Cold War – the freedom radios proved to be one of democracy's most powerful weapons.
>
> (Puddington, 2000, p. 313)

8 Radio Free Europe/Radio Liberty Today

Challenges, Practices, and Role Perceptions

What is the role of *Radio Svoboda* in the post–Cold War era? Is it still a weapon in the psychological warfare between Russia and the USA, which seems to have intensified in recent years? Does the radio station have a clear identity in the Putin era? What role do journalists believe that they should be playing in their society? I turn to these questions in this chapter, which gives voice to the editors and journalists working for *Radio Svoboda*. It presents the findings from my fieldwork in Russia in May 2014, as well as subsequent developments up until the point of submission of the manuscript in December 2017. It is organised around three key headings: (1) Ethnographic Observations and the Coverage of Ukraine, (2) Common Challenges – Safety Issues, Legal and Administrative Measures, and (3) From the Voice of Freedom to the Voice of the Enemy? I start by providing an empirical account of the daily routine journalists follow, including the virtual editorial meetings with their colleagues in Prague. The discussions about the coverage of the situation in Ukraine as well as a detailed account of the decision-making process are outlined. Then, in the second part, the focus shifts to some wider issues – the diminishing role the radio plays in Russian society, recent challenges and changes that the editorial staff have experienced, and a few new laws that jeopardise the future of *Radio Svoboda* in Russia. Finally, the chapter concludes by presenting journalists' views on the role they see themselves as playing in Russian society.

A recurring theme is their fear that especially in light of President Vladimir Putin's soaring popularity and the conflict in Ukraine, they are increasingly seen as representing the interests of "the enemy". As a result of that, they are losing listeners and their credibility is diminishing. It is almost paradoxical that at a time when they are allowed to broadcast from the centre of Moscow, they suffer from an identity crisis they have never experienced during the "dark ages" of communism when they were operating in secret. Moreover, despite the professed pursuit of "uncensored news", the daily routines and considerations journalists at *RL* make are inevitably affected by the ideological role the radio station is meant to be playing in Russian society. When discussing the editorial decision-making process, a few journalists kept referring to the BBG – the independent US federal agency that oversees and governs the broadcasts of all US civilian international media, including *RL*. The board appears to have been particularly proactive in Russia. A prominent member of the board was in Moscow at the time when I visited *RL*. Even the science correspondent in the radio station mentioned that when selecting stories about scientific inventions, for example, he often considered whether they would be of interest to an American as opposed to a Russian audience.

Ethnographic Observations and the Coverage of Ukraine

The physical space occupied by *Radio Svoboda* in Moscow looked markedly different from the spaces occupied by *Novaya Gazeta* and *Ekho Moskvy*. Their offices and studios were located in a modern, impressive, and spacious building. Most journalists worked in a huge open space area. The chief editor of the Moscow bureau of *Radio Svoboda* Leonid Velekhov had his own office, but his colleagues from *Radio Svoboda* and the *Voice of America* worked in the open space area. In spite of the constant talk of downsizing and the redundancy issues experienced by *Radio Svoboda*, just by looking at the premises it was clear that money was not such a big issue for *RL* as it was for *Novaya Gazeta* and *Ekho Moskvy*. The journalists I interviewed confirmed this implicitly when asked about the pay they received and the pressures they experienced. Financial issues were not mentioned by any *Radio Svoboda* journalists, and the pay they received was much higher than that of their colleagues at other liberal media. Although none of the journalists and editors I interviewed wanted to remain anonymous, I will not reveal their identities when discussing pay. Suffice it to say, that the salaries they mentioned were at least two times higher than those of their colleagues at *Novaya Gazeta*, and in some cases considerably higher than that.

Velekhov (2014, personal communication) explained that they had 25 permanent members of staff in Moscow and 20 in Prague, but in addition to that, they had a lot of freelancers around the world; so a total of 70–80 journalists worked for *Radio Svoboda*. The Director of the Russian Service Irina Lagunina and her deputy Andrey Shary were based in Prague, whereas Velekhov and the head of the Information Service Eugenia Nazarets were based in Moscow. All four of them still worked at *Radio Svoboda* at the time of submission of this monograph, but Lagunina was replaced by Shary and Velekhov was replaced by Nazarets.

The Prague and the Moscow staff usually held a virtual meeting in the morning (or just before noon). The meeting I observed lasted 23 minutes, and it involved a small group of senior editors – Lagunina, Shary, and Ukrainian correspondent Andrey Sharogradski from Prague, and Velekhov, the chief of the video team Arslan Saidov, and the two editors on duty responsible for the website on the day of the meeting and on the following day. Shary was clearly dominating the meeting, while Velekhov himself did not say much at all. Ukraine dominated the discussion, but the conversation was very practical – it revolved mainly around the coverage of a roundtable taking place on the issue later that day, which *Radio Svoboda* would participate in and broadcast. The atmosphere of the meeting was much more businesslike and to the point with no banter or joking, so in that sense the meeting was very different from the one I observed at *Novaya Gazeta*.

Velekhov explained that there was an on-going discussion between the Moscow and the Prague bureau over email and by phone. The Prague staff were mainly political journalists who would make frequent phone calls to sources in Russia and offer stories on different topics. "They are living in Prague but their mind is in Russia, of course", Velekhov (2014, personal communication) explained. When I asked him why it was still necessary for *Radio Svoboda* to have so many journalists based in Prague, he said: "This is a historical tradition. The main headquarters are abroad. It was so during the Soviet times. I think it's a tradition, which is convenient for the chiefs, for the big bosses in Washington" (Velekhov, 2014, personal communication). Velekhov himself was not a long-standing member of staff at *Radio Svoboda*. He only joined the radio station in October 2013. Velekhov had a PhD in Latin American culture and folklore, and he worked in academia during communism. He then became a political journalist in the beginning of the 1990s – first at "one of the first independent newspapers" *Nezavisimaia Gazeta* and then at Gusinsky's *Today* newspaper and *Itogi* magazine. "It was practically closed, changed completely when Putin decided to finish with *NTV*, with Gusinsky, with Media-Most, and it was a very sad time for Russian independent media", Velekhov (2014, personal communication) recalled. After Putin put an end to Gusinsky's media empire, Velekhov worked for 11 years as an anchor and a vice editor-in-chief at *Sovershenno Sekretno* – a newspaper and TV channel.

Ukraine clearly dominated the coverage of *Radio Svoboda* during my visit to Moscow. Velekhov explained that 60%–70% of their total coverage was about Ukraine and the relationship between Russia and Ukraine in the same way in which the Chechen war was a "hot topic" for *Radio Svoboda* a few years ago. They used a network of stringers and some of their own Moscow-based or Prague-based journalists who were sent to Ukraine. In addition to that, they used various other sources, including personal acquaintances, social media, and online videos. In Velekhov's (2014, personal communication) view, the situation in Ukraine was "very difficult, really bad" and it was not clear what solution could be reached, but he did not feel that it was difficult for *Radio Svoboda* to cover Ukraine because "we are speaking the truth".

The word "truth" was used by most *Radio Svoboda* journalists I spoke to. When asked to elaborate, the Moscow bureau chief editor explained that this meant looking "at the situation as it is without any kind of propaganda, without any sympathy for the Russians, the Ukrainians, the Americans or so on. And as it's said in Bulgakov's The Master and Margarita, the easiest thing in the world is to tell the truth" (Velekhov, 2014, personal communication). However, he recognised that in the case with Ukraine, "the full picture doesn't exist now" (Velekhov, 2014, personal communication). Special correspondent and science observer Sergey Dobrynin said that the first stages of the conflict were particularly challenging because there was a lack of factual information, so the media had to rely on social networks and local media full of fake or propagandistic content. "It's very difficult to find the real truth", he (Dobrynin, 2014, personal communication) said. However, once they sent a few correspondents to Ukraine and started talking to experts as well, it became easier for them to make sense of what was going on. "Otherwise, it's just a shower of gossips. But little by little I don't think it's a shower of gossips anymore", Dobrynin (2014, personal communication) added.

Editor at large, Mark Krotov was one of the Moscow-based journalists who were sent to Ukraine in early 2014. He explained that he "wanted to go there" and that "we did one of the best reports from there" (Krotov, 2014, personal communication). He also used the word "truth" to describe *Radio Svoboda*'s coverage. He said:

– Our radio station is different from Russian official media. We say the truth, they say lies. That's the difference.
– What is the truth?
– The truth is that there is no fascism, which Russian media says often. There is no pressure over Russian-speaking people there, for example. There is a visible presence of Russian influence, I mean military – militants. All myths that are created by Russian propaganda – one part of our work is to destroy, to destruct these myths. We even have every day an article called "disinformation of the day". Practically every day there are enough myths that we have to destroy.

(Krotov, 2014, personal communication)

Krotov's definition of the "truth" was somehow limited to mainly exposing what he perceived to be the lies disseminated by the Kremlin and by Russian state media. Krotov's personal views of Putin were also very strong:

He is a bloody dictator. We will be happy when he dies. Fortunately we are younger than him so we have a chance. That's personal – I'm joking, you understand. What can I think? He ruined our hopes for a better country. I was born in 1977. In 1991 we had a lot of hopes as you did in Bulgaria. But then things went wrong...There is no politics in Russia, no politicians as well. We don't have elections, we don't have freedom of speech.

(Krotov, 2014, personal communication)

When I asked Krotov whether his political views influenced his work, he said: "Maybe they make me do my work better. Of course, it will be hard to imagine pro-Putin men working here" (Krotov, 2014, personal communication). He admitted that one of the arguments they recently had at *Radio Svoboda* was what terminology to use with regards to the men fighting in Eastern Ukraine – whether to call them separatists, militants, and so forth, and whether to use the word referendum at all. He said that overall the editorial policies they had were liberal, and although as a result of "this American bureaucracy" they received "a lot of papers about what you can what you cannot write ... nobody really cares. You should follow your conscience and everything will be OK" (Krotov, 2014, personal communication). Dobrynin (2014, personal communication) also said that they had to follow certain editorial policies, which were mainly related to the use of language, for example, not using words such as "отечественний" because they were considered "low language" and "close to the yellow press". However, he acknowledged that "we are quite democratic", and he said that he was sure that if he did not agree with these style policies, he could just write an email and say so. All journalists I spoke to said that the representatives of the BBG did not interfere in their editorial policies. All discussions were held between them and the editorial staff in Prague. Velekhov (2014, personal communication) also said that he had not experienced any attempts at interference. The presence of the BBG was visible. Journalists pointed to the desk of the chairman of the BBG, Jeff Shell, who was in Moscow at the time of my visit, and according to journalists themselves they often saw him there.

When discussing the coverage of Ukraine, most of the journalists I spoke to also acknowledged that they were personally affected or moved by what was going on. Social media editor and Moscow correspondent Olya Kurachyova (2014, personal communication) said that her attitude was "rather human than political. I just worry about people and it doesn't matter what side they present. I just worry about their lives and their health because people are dying". Nazarets said that she had personal arguments with some of her friends and relatives who thought that "Putin is right in the Ukrainian situation":

> I dislike Putin because he's very arrogant, impolite and rude sometimes and aggressive in his speech, in his manner. But I understand that he just plays a role. He just gives the people, society what they want...We know that 80% of Russians according to psychological researchers say: "Putin is right in the Ukrainian situation. We have to have Crimea. And I think he just does what the country, most people want from him...Russia needs time to understand that Putin is not good for Russia but I think it will be a long, long time...When I try to explain to them, I always give them a simple example from their life. I just ask them to imagine: If your grandma has a flat

or a car, and you are sure she will give it to you after her death, but she decides not to do it but to give it to another person, not even a relative, you can't kill or maybe fight with this person to take this car or this flat.

(Nazarets, 2014, personal communication)

In Nazarets's (2014, personal communication) view, the Crimean situation was identical and there was only one right way of solving the issue – the use of laws and the relevant legal procedures, not "illegal methods like referendum, a strange referendum, occupation and annexation".

Dobrynin (2014, personal communication) acknowledged, however, that the anti-Putin propaganda was also very strong. He said that his cousin was a member of the Euromaidan movement, and he was "a victim of the opposite type of propaganda. He says things like: We have to kill them all, all those people who are rebels because they are all Russians" (Dobrynin, 2014, personal communication). What made the situation particularly difficult for Dobrynin's family was that his aunt (his cousin's mother) was pro-Russian. Dobrynin's family situation was indicative of the split in Ukrainian society journalists at other liberal media were referring to, or, in fact, the schism in Russian society as *Novaya Gazeta's* editor-in-chief labelled it. Dobrynin's account was also indicative of the role he believed *Radio Svoboda* should play in the coverage of the conflict:

The country is really very much separated. And this problem existed a long time ago. The only way for them to survive in the country and to contain peace is to find a way to understand each other. And both sides don't seem to be willing to do that actually. Of course, the rebels don't try to do it but also the Kiev side, these educated, young guys, even their representatives are not trying hard to understand the other side. They are saying that they are all poor and stupid people and let's forget about them. That's a big problem, that's really the biggest problem. So I really hope that first of all Russia will not interfere in the situation, not in a military way. Of course, they will still watch Russian TV and this is a big intervention but we can do nothing about it. At least I hope Russia will not put any armed forces and then I really hope that they will start to negotiate probably with Russian and Western efforts also.

(Dobrynin, 2014, personal communication)

All in all, despite professing a commitment to the truth, the definition of the truth that *Radio Svoboda's* editorial staff provided was very narrow. It revolved around exposing what they perceived to be the lies emanating mainly from Russia. For *RL* journalists, the role Russia and Putin played in the conflict was negative and unlawful. Unlike their colleagues at *Novaya Gazeta* and *Ekho Moskvy*, who seemed to have disagree-ments on the issue and who discussed the role of the USA and Europe at much greater length, *Radio Svoboda* journalists appeared to be singing from the same hymn sheet. Krotov (2014, personal communication) said that Russia was "an actor in this conflict. We know the exact names of the Russian agents in Ukraine". By contrast, he did not feel that the USA had such a stake in the conflict apart from investing in civil society there prior to the protests. He concluded by saying: "Of course Ukraine should decide what to do next, they should rule themselves – nor America not Russia should interfere in a way to make it possible for people to say that this is a one-to-one game" (Krotov, 2014, personal communi-cation). Dobrynin (2014, personal communication), however, acknowl-edged that some of the Western powers such as the UK and Germany were not purely driven by values, but also by economic considerations in their decisions as to when and what sanctions to impose on Russia.

Common Challenges –Safety Issues, Legal, and Administrative Measures

While spared most of the business and harassment pressures, *Svoboda* journalists had been at the receiving end of legal and administrative measures and had also faced some safety issues.

Safety Issues

All *Radio Svoboda* journalists I spoke to had received threating mes-sages, but similarly to their colleagues at *Novaya Gazeta* and *Ekho Moskvy*, they underplayed the importance of these threats and did not notify the police. The chief editor himself said that he did "nothing, really nothing" when receiving a threatening letter. "I know that you have to contact the police but you know that the police we have here is noth-ing similar to Great Britain or to American police. We don't believe so much that the police can help" (Velekhov, 2014, personal communica-tion). Velekhov (2014, personal communication) did not even discuss the threats with his colleagues. He said that he used to do that in the 1990s but had since stopped because, with the advent of the Internet, "a lot of people receive something similar". He acknowledged, however, that not all of his colleagues reacted to the threats with the same calmness with which he approached them:

> It depends on the person. Some persons are very afraid, some are very angry. But well. I think that when somebody wants to make something bad to you, he will not send letters. He will do it but will not send letters, emails, and so on.
>
> (Velekhov, 2014, personal communication)

His successor Eugenia Nazarets (2014, personal communication) shared a very similar view: "It's just blah blah – it's only words". However, she admitted she took safety issues into consideration. For example, when they bought a new flat in Moscow, her husband wanted to publish their address on social media to show it to their relatives, but she asked him not to do it: "Somebody can track it and it's dangerous for me, and I know it's very very possible in Russia to be at risk" (Nazarets, 2014, personal communication). Nazarets recalled how during a meeting of Putin's party in Yekaterinburg as soon as party members realised she worked for *RL*, they started pushing her out. "I wasn't hurt but it was dangerous. I just decided not to fight with them and stepped out", Nazarets (2014, personal communication, also quoted in Slavtcheva-Petkova, 2017) said. She was also used to receiving anti-Semitic threats because of her surname, which is Ukrainian, but some people "take it as Jewish". "Sometimes people say: 'Go out to Israel', 'Russia for Russians' and something like this. *Radio Liberty* is the home of Jews and something like this" (Nazarets, 2014, personal communication).

The anti-Semitic abuse against *Radio Svoboda* staff was nothing new indeed, but Nazarets said that she had never received death threats. It was usually "advice" to "have your brains washed" (Nazarets, 2014, personal communication). Krotov (2014, personal communication) said that he knew that some of his colleagues received death threats ("We will kill you") "much more than me". His approach was to resend all threats to his boss in Prague. He was the only one who referred to editorial policy on this issue. In his view, Lagunina had asked them to resend the threats to her maybe because she wanted to "present these letters to her bosses to show how afraid we are here" (Krotov, 2014, personal communication). Krotov's decision to follow the editorial policy did not seem to be motivated by fear because, like his colleagues, he said that he never notified the police since: "These threats are obviously only words. When the threat is real, they don't send you an email before" (Krotov, 2014, personal communication). In his view, it was not really dangerous for journalists in Moscow because there had not been that many cases in the past few years of beaten journalists, but this was not the case in the Caucasus and in Chechnya in specific.

Similarly to their colleagues at *Novaya Gazeta* and *Ekho Moskvy*, *Radio Svoboda* journalists distinguished between "real dangers" (Dobrynin, 2014, personal communication) and the threats they received. In Dobrynin's (2014, personal communication) view, although he had received unpleasant comments, he did not feel that he had experienced "real danger". His coverage of Sochi after the Olympic Games attracted offensive comments

> that I am a drug addict, prostitute or representing the US government...But I was ready to receive such things. We all receive such

comments from time to time. But it's not a danger actually. Just an example that it might turn into danger.

(Dobrynin, 2014, personal communication)

However, despite the fact that he downplayed the importance of the threats he received, he admitted that when he was in Sochi, he did not show his press card because he did not want people to know that he worked for *RL* because *RL* was "considered to be Russia-phobic and then probably I might be in danger" (Dobrynin, 2014, personal communication). He said that Russia was a dangerous country for journalists because there had been lots of examples of people harassed, detained, or killed for their professional work, but it was not as dangerous as China or Mexico. Dobrynin recalled how a friend of his who worked for *TV Rain* was stopped at the border on his way to Crimea and was then thrown into a ditch and interrogated. "It was quite scary...quite strict, a very hard interrogation", Dobrynin (2014, personal communication) said. The people who interrogated the journalist claimed that they were from the Russian special services but they did not have any ID to prove that this was indeed the case. The journalist was eventually sent back to Kiev. When evaluating the political situation in Russia, Dobrynin (2014, personal communication) said that "the local picture is very bad", and he was not satisfied "with everything our President is doing but at the same time so far I don't see any preferable alternatives".

In Kurachyova's (2014, personal communication) view, Russia was a dangerous country not just for "independent journalists" but even more so for activists and non-governmental organisations (NGOs) because "you just cannot feel safe. You just don't have the feeling that the government is going to help you, to care about you. You can only rely on the civil society – your friends, your colleagues, people you know". She said that as an LGBT activist, she had feared for her life, especially when participating in organised actions. "Some aggressive people come and just throw, try to attack activists with eggs, water, paint", she said (Kurachyova, 2014, personal communication).

Legal and Administrative Measures

Putin's presidency brought an end to *Radio Svoboda's* favourable treatment by his predecessors. As already indicated, in 2002, Putin annulled Yeltsin's decree that explicitly recognised the role of *RL* and allowed it to freely broadcast in the country. Then *Radio Svoboda* suffered yet another serious blow in November 2012 when it lost its AM license due to the coming into force of an amendment to the Federal Law on Mass Media, which made it illegal for an entity that directly or indirectly had more than 50% foreign ownership to hold a radio broadcasting license. At the time when I interviewed *Radio Svoboda* journalists, the radio station was still broadcasting on shortwaves and online. Editor at large Mark Krotov (2014, personal communication) said, "It's practically impossible to catch these radio waves in Moscow but it's a bit better in the countryside where there are no buildings". However, it stopped its broadcasts on shortwave on 25 June 2016 and moved to online-only transmissions.

Its ability to officially exist in Russia had been further compromised after the passing of a few new laws/amendments to existing laws. The first one barred foreign investors from owning more than 20% in Russia's media outlets. It was passed in 2014 and came into force in 2016, but media organisations had to comply with it by 1 February 2017. The second one was passed by the Russian Duma in 2015, and it included provisions for the banning of "undesirable" foreign/international organisations defined as any organisation that "presents a threat to the defensive capabilities or security of the state, to the public order, or to the health of the population" (Luhn, 2015). A few NGOs such as the National Endowment for Democracy and George Soros's Open Society Foundations were subsequently banned as a result of this new act. The third piece of legislation was an amendment to an existing law that Putin signed in November 2017 that required foreign media to be listed as "foreign agents". The amendment was passed in retaliation to the US government's request for *RT (Russia Today)* to register as a foreign agent under the Foreign Agents Registration Act. *RL* reported that it had received a warning from the Ministry of Justice of the Russian Federation that they might face potential restrictions, although the letter did not specify what these restrictions would be. On 5 December 2017, the Ministry of Justice officially designated *RFE/RL* as a foreign agent, together with six other organisations, including the *Voice of America*. This law was very similar to the one that led to the banning of a few NGOs. According to its provisions, "foreign agents" must include in any information they publish or broadcast to Russian audiences a mention of their "foreign agent" designation. They must also be officially included in a government register and should "submit regular reports on their sources of funding, on their objectives, on how they spend their money, and who their managers are" (Osborn, 2017). *RFE/RL* President Thomas Kent (*RFE/RL*, 2017) was quoted as saying that it was too early to speculate on the potential effects of this amendment, but they remained "committed to continuing our journalistic work, in the interests of providing accurate and objective news to our Russian-speaking audiences". In Velekhov's (2014, personal communication) view, the attacks on *RFE/RL* were not a result of the fact that Putin considered the radio to be a threat to him but they were part of his wider campaign "against all kinds of opposite views". Velekhov (2014, personal communication) said:

> I don't think that he is afraid of *Radio Svoboda*, or *Dozhd TV* channel but he wants to have this media sphere as during Soviet times when everybody was agreeing with the general line. And everybody

and each media was supporting this general line and personally Mr Putin. And I don't think, I repeat, that he is afraid and sees any threat. No.

At the time when I conducted my interviews, the future of *RFE/RL* in Russia was as uncertain as it was in 2017 because the passing of the bill restricting foreign ownership to 20% was imminent. Journalists offered different interpretations as to what might happen to their radio station, and some were more concerned than others. Journalists were unclear how the legislation would affect them or whether they would be allowed to broadcast legally from Russia. Velekhov (2014, personal communication) said:

> I don't know what will happen. I hope that this won't happen. This relation is changing but it's changing in a bad way... We are not very clear, very sure in our future, thinking about our future because you know that a lot of Internet sites, independent news sites of opposition sites like granny.ru, like *Yezhednevny Zhurnal* disappeared. It was closed in one hour, in ten minutes... Everything might happen. Let's see, but we are optimists.

Nazarets (2014, personal communication) told me how her mother had asked her whether she would have to leave the country.

> I replied that I want and must use all the possibilities to stay in Russia for two reasons – because of my relatives and because Russian journalists are good in Russia – what can I do in another country? This doesn't make sense.
> Nazarets (2014, personal communication)

She added that the situation had "become more difficult" (Nazarets, 2014, personal communication). The younger journalists I interviewed were not as worried as their older colleagues. Kurachyova (2014, personal communication) said she was worried but "not so much". Dobrynin did not think that the law would affect them because his status was no different from any other foreign correspondent in Russia who had an official accreditation from the Russian Ministry of External Affairs.

Krotov (2014, personal communication, also quoted in Slavtcheva-Petkova, 2017) also acknowledged that *RFE/RL* was not a Russian media outlet, but he was considerably more concerned about the future:

> – We are not Russian media. We are a branch of American media. That's why this law is not about us. That's why we cannot get waves. Now the question is different – can we at least have an office in Moscow and will our website be blocked? That's what we are worried about now. If Putin goes further, if he tries to gain control over all Ukraine or other Soviet

republics, if he begins a real war, then who knows what will happen to us. Of course, if the situation deteriorates, I don't think we will have a possibility to work here in the centre of Moscow.
– What's the alternative?
– Broadcasting from Prague, anonymously from our homes.
– Do you worry about these things?
– Yes, of course.

Krotov's view of the future of Russia was not very positive. He described the current relationship between Russia and the West as "hate, war, Cold War" (Krotov, 2014, personal communication). He said that the Cold War was "coming back" and he was worried what effect the sanctions imposed on Russia would have.

> Maybe in half an hour everybody will not be allowed and we will have to arrange some exit visas. Everybody is very frightened about that. International payment systems will probably go away from Russia – Visa, MasterCard. It's only the beginning of this. If Putin decided to restore the Soviet Union, now we are only in the beginning of this.
>
> Krotov (2014, personal communication)

However, in his view, one difference between the situation during communism and the post–Cold War period was that they had more information so they could make arrangements for their families if something were to happen:

> In the Soviet Union we didn't know anything – we had no information. But now the situation, thank God, is different...We can always leave the country now...I love my country. I want to fight for it, not to leave, but if I get no choice....
>
> (Krotov, 2014, personal communication)

From the Voice of Freedom to the Voice of the Enemy?

Krotov's professed love for his country is a useful reminder of the fact that *Radio Svoboda* journalists are not simply employees of a US Congress-funded media entity but they are also citizens of their own country. What is journalists' own understanding then of the mission their radio station should and does play in Russian society and of their own role as journalists? Velekhov acknowledged the important and "very special role" *Radio Svoboda* played in Soviet history as an instrument for democratisation. He said that he was told that during communism the radio was as popular as the most widely read newspaper in Russia, whereas the 1990s proved a very challenging period because other "independent" media appeared on the market.

The '90s were a very difficult time for *Svoboda* to look for a new place, for a new role in Russian society. But the most important thing is that *Svoboda* could find this place. Of course, thanks to the situation, which has changed because when Putin came to Kremlin a lot of things changed and a lot of independent media disappeared. And now we have a situation, for example, when we have *Svoboda, Ekho Moskvy, Novaya Gazeta* and maybe nothing more.

(Velekhov, 2014, personal communication)

Kurachyova (2014, personal communication) also shared the view that the decreasing media freedom meant that *RL* was now playing a more important role. The Moscow bureau chief argued that the radio had a very good online rating (occupying 44th place in the top 55) and "a very wide audience now". In his view, the radio had his mission, namely, propagating democratic Western values, but this did not involve acting as a propaganda tool for the US president or US foreign policy. "We are American media. In our line, in our media policies, we are independent", Velekhov (2014, personal communication) said. Kurachyova (2014, personal communication) also said that she had never felt any censorship in her work but she did not know what would happen if they decided to criticise the US government.

Velekhov (2014, personal communication) acknowledged that lots of Russians think that "America, the United States are the great enemy of Russia, a very bad and dangerous enemy", but in his view his radio did not have a duty to "speak with" these people or indeed try to "explain something to them". As he put it, they could just "switch off" (Velekhov, 2014, personal communication). Krotov (2014, personal communication) said that in his view, "ordinary Russians" thought that "we are the agents of enemy and our only dream is to ruin Russia". In Kurachyova's (2014, personal communication) and Dobrynin's (2014, personal communication) view, "ordinary Russians" "don't know anything about *Radio Liberty*" because they would mainly watch state TV, and *RL* did not really market itself. However, Kurachyova (2014, personal communication) acknowledged that there were some people like her great-great grandma who thought that it was "a voice of the enemy", while the liberal part of society considered it as "just a source of information they can use". Their audience was the people who wanted to know "the other point of view, not only the point of view of the Kremlin and the personal point of view of Mr Putin" but the people who wanted to know "what is happening in the world, why not all the people and the Western world agree with Putin's line, for example" (Velekhov, 2014, personal communication). This audience consisted mainly of educated and politically oriented people (Nazarets, 2014, personal communication).

While most of his colleagues shared Velekhov's view of Putin, their accounts of the radio's mission and current role were much more nuanced. Other staff at *Radio Svoboda* acknowledged the identity difficulties and mentioned that the radio had recently undergone a process of "rebranding", although they were not very clear on what the process actually entailed apart from staff changes at the top and the recent meetings they had have with "directors" from Washington. Dobrynin (2014, personal communication) said that the overriding commitment to liberal values and democracy had remained unchanged.

On a normative level, all *Radio Svoboda* journalists I spoke to professed a commitment to balance and objectivity. Nazarets (2014, personal communication) said that her main motivation to start working at *RL* was the "high standard of journalism" and the lack of censorship. What this meant in practice was "no black list" of topics and sources.

> I take my job as a doctor. I don't feel myself like I am fighter for democracy or something like that. No, I am just a journalist. I have to be careful with information. I have to practice my job.
>
> Nazarets (2014, personal communication)

Similarly, Velekhov (2014, personal communication) said that the guiding principle in his work was

> to tell the truth as you understand it, not to lie to yourself, not to think that your audience is more stupid than you or that you have to teach your audience...To tell to your audience as if they are people like you, as if they are your friends.

For Krotov, Dobrynin, and Kurachyova (2014, personal communication), objectivity was most fundamental to their work. However, Dobrynin (2014, personal communication) acknowledged that "when you live in the media world, it's really hard to be objective because sometimes there are not enough facts just to be objective, there are not enough facts but opinions, and opinions are always biased".

In spite of professing a normative commitment to quality journalism, *RL* journalists recognised that the quality of their work was sometimes compromised by the lack of access to authoritative sources and their focus on providing the alternative point of view. Nazarets (2014, personal communication) said that they had never experienced any censorship and they were "independent from our bosses...from the USA" but their job depended on Russian life. As she put it,

> We sometimes can't do something as journalists because we are *Radio Liberty* journalists. Are we independent? Maybe yes. But our possibility to do more is limited by Russian life, Russian authorities, Russian laws and attitude and the attitude between *Radio Liberty* and the Russian authorities.
>
> (Nazarets, 2014, personal communication)

Some of the practical restrictions included not gaining accreditation for press conferences or not securing sources from Putin's party and the authorities for their interviews because they did not want to take part in *RL*'s broadcasts. Velekhov (2014, personal communication) said that the situation was very different during the 1990s when politicians were "very open". He said that the situation "has changed completely" since then and "they need only these kind of media who will transmit what they are saying, their point of view and nothing more" (Velekhov, 2014, personal communication). Nazarets (2014, personal communication) said that because *RL* presented a point of view different to the official one, "many people and even official organisations in Russia take us not as enemies but something which Russia doesn't need at all". Some of the remarks she often heard were: "'I don't want to talk to you because you are *Radio Liberty*. You should go abroad because Russia doesn't need a person like you'" (Nazarets, 2014, personal communication).

Has the lack of access to official authoritative sources and the liberal pro-Western ethos of *RL* inevitably led to a degree of bias in its reporting? Kurachyova (2014, personal communication) said that it was not easy for journalists to stay objective in the current situation in Russia and that she felt that her readers and listeners could sometimes "feel my vision of these things". "It's about normal lifestyle and absurd lifestyle. So it's not so bad that you cannot stay absolutely uninvolved", she (Kurachyova, 2014, personal communication) added. According to Dobrynin (2014, personal communication), "it's very hard to stay objective even if you are trying hard" because of the general context they lived in and the fact that there were not many liberal media in Russia. "When you take this niche, when you take the spot, little by little you grow in a way more radical in this part of the spectrum", he (Dobrynin, 2014, personal communication) said.

> Sometimes we overreact when we have to cover what's going on with the civil rights, with local politics, etc. People who are very sensitive to these kinds of things they also overreact and this is how we get to be Russia-phobic. The general political situation and social situation in Russia implies that people take different sides more and more. The break is growing little by little and whether you are on one side or on the other side, the other side will consider you to be their enemy. That's why I am trying to be objective.
>
> (Dobrynin, 2014, personal communication)

Dobrynin (2014, personal communication) gave two examples to illustrate his point. First, he said that *RL*'s reporting of Ukraine was biased in favour of the Euromaidan movement because the coverage focussed on its activities and sources. Second, when he himself went to Sochi after the Olympic games, he said that "everything looked fine", there were new roads built, it was cleaner, and people generally looked happier, but his mission was to "find people who were not happy" (Dobrynin, 2014, personal communication). He added that finding such people was "hard work", but he succeeded and his article was mostly an outline of the problems these people identified. "My mother was disappointed with me. She told me: 'This time you were biased.' She may be right", Dobrynin (2014, personal communication) said. His bias was not borne out of the fact that he was urged by his editors to focus on the negative aspects but it was a result of his news values – the belief that a positive story was not a good journalistic story. Dobrynin (2014, personal communication) also said that although they were broadcasting for a Russian audience, he would often focus on topics he knew would be of interest to the Americans.

Targeting a Russian audience with US interests in mind seemed to be the approach generally adopted at *RL*. Nazarets (2014, personal communication) said that *RL* looked at Russia "through American glasses". She added:

> It's an important thing you need to keep in mind when reading *Radio Liberty*'s website or listening to *Radio Liberty*. It's American media but well-informed and reliable but they always tell about things and events which are important for America not for Russia. For Russia, for example, the price of living is important and good weather, bad infrastructure... But *Radio Liberty* prefers to talk about politics and macroeconomics. This is what I heard about *Radio Liberty* from other people.
>
> (Nazarets, 2014, personal communication)

Nazarets (2014, personal communication) said that while she agreed with this approach in general, in her work she tried to turn attention to Russian society a bit more. When trying to explain to journalism students what *RL* was all about, she always presented it as giving "another point of view", which in practice meant that sometimes they did not even mention the official point of view.

In spite of all the limitations, *RL* journalists were adamant that their radio was playing an important role in Russian society because there were "people who need some independent and free information" in this climate of "less and less independent information and more and more state propaganda every day" (Kurachyova, 2014, personal communication). As Krotov (2014, personal communication) put it, "We know that what we are doing is telling the truth even if we are funded by America and even if Americans don't tell the truth all the time". In Dobrynin's (2014, personal communication) view, *RL* was growing and "little by little" it was becoming "the biggest independent liberal medium in Russia" because they have stuck to their mission of telling "people things which they wouldn't be able to find out from other sources".

Conclusion

To sum up, similarly to their colleagues at *Novaya Gazeta* and *Ekho Moskvy*, *Radio Svoboda* journalists shared a commitment to liberal values and democracy. They expressed their sadness at Russia's current plight, which most of them blamed on Putin, although some acknowledged that it would be too simplistic to blame it all on him alone. The bureau chief said:

> I am very sad about what is happening in my country right now. I am very sad that Russia wants to go back to the Soviet times, to these totalitarian times but at the same time I think that this is impossible. I want to be an optimist. I want to believe that things will change. I don't know by what manner. But I hope that this period is not forever.
>
> (Velekhov, 2014, personal communication)

RL journalists personally experienced some of these challenges in their work. The future of the radio in Russia was uncertain after the passing of a few pieces of legislation that threatened its legal existence in the country. Journalists were concerned about these developments and what they might entail for them on a professional and on a personal level.

In addition to that, the radio had undergone a process of rebranding in search of a renewed identity and mission in the post-Soviet Union era. On the one hand, the deteriorating political freedoms and the decline in freedom of expression had presented new opportunities for *Radio Svoboda* to play a more visible role in Russian society. On the other hand, the radio lost all its transmission frequencies and had been struggling to compete against a growing number of information websites. Moreover, as Krotov (2014, personal communication) acknowledged, the fact that the radio was funded by the USA was more of "a problem" in the post-Soviet era than before. "In the Soviet Union it was not a problem for anybody that *Radio Svoboda* is American. Everyone listened and trusted us because there was absolutely no other independent media", he (Krotov, 2014, personal communication) said.

In the post-Soviet period, in the eyes of many Russians, *RL* was nothing more than a voice of the enemy, and the coverage of the conflict in Ukraine was a particular challenge in that respect. Attracting a wider audience with the promise of objectivity at a time when Russia faced significant sanctions from the West, and Putin's popularity was soaring at home was a significant challenge. *RL* journalists were stuck between a rock and a hard place because there were too many competing and conflicting demands that affected their work: from the rebranding effort initiated by their US funders linked to their increased marginalisation in Russia as a result of all the legal and administrative measures adopted against them to the deteriorating relationship between Russia and the USA and Putin's enhanced efforts in promoting nationalism. It is unclear what the future holds for *RFE/RL*, but for the time being journalists persevered in their daily efforts to present an alternative point of view to the one put forward by the Kremlin.

Conclusion
Russia's Liberal Media – Handcuffed but Free

I started this academic project because I was personally intrigued by the articles I read in Western media about Anna Politkovskaya's murder and the role of *Novaya Gazeta* in Russia, and I was surprised that there was hardly any academic research into the state of liberal media in President Vladimir Putin's Russia. From a personal point of view, I wanted to find out whether the dire picture described in Western media was an exaggeration of the actual situation on the ground. I am from a former communist country myself, and it was also interesting for me to observe a different type of post–Cold War journey in none less than the leading country in the former communist bloc. During the three years in which I intermittently worked on the project, I realised that Western media's accounts of the plight of liberal media in Russia were not exaggerated. On the contrary, the situation was much worse. Liberal journalists in Putin's Russia experience numerous challenges – from abductions such as the one I witnessed on my first day of fieldwork at *Novaya Gazeta*, to physical attacks such as the one *Ekho Moskvy*'s deputy editor-in-chief was subjected to at the time of completion of this manuscript, to restrictive legislation such as the most recent law signed by Putin that led to the designation of *Radio Svoboda* as a foreign agent.

From an academic point of view, I focussed on four main research questions: (1) What kind of constraints, controls, and restrictions do Russian liberal journalists face and how do they tackle these challenges? Are the "breadth, depth, and mechanisms" (Becker, 2014, p. 202) of control very different from the ones used during Soviet times? (2) What role do liberal media play in the mediatisation of the conflict in Ukraine and to what extent have they provided an alternative framing to the conflict to the one offered by Putin and state-aligned media? (3) What role do liberal journalists believe they (should) play in post-Soviet Putin's Russia? Finally, what do all these trends tell us about the Russian media system and the potential for development of democracy in the country? I summarise the main findings of my study in this chapter and I also outline the major limitations and venues for future research.

Breadth, Depth, and Mechanisms of Media Control in Putin's Russia

My study shows that the breadth, depth, and mechanisms of media control in Putin's Russia are different from the ones used during the Soviet era. Liberal media do not face any direct censorship from the state, and the Kremlin's approach to media management is not driven by a strong overriding ideology. It is also questionable whether the pressures liberal journalists face are the result of a clear long-term strategy adopted by Putin or an ad hoc reactive approach.

Liberal journalists faced three main types of pressures (for a full outline, see Slavtcheva-Petkova, 2017):

1   Business and financial pressures such as ownership-related and market-related pressures.

These types of pressures were mainly experienced by *Novaya Gazeta* and *Ekho Moskvy* because *RL* was funded by the US Congress. *Novaya Gazeta* had been in a precarious financial state for years. Its main shareholder Alexander Lebedev was subjected to targeted attacks by the state, including money laundering and embezzlement charges, which nearly cost him his business and led him to announce that he would no longer fund the newspaper due to the pressure and the strain he had been put under. Moreover, *Novaya Gazeta*'s print edition stopped attracting advertising after Putin allegedly convened a meeting with big businesses in Russia and explicitly discouraged them from advertising in the newspaper. In a similar way, *Ekho Moskvy*'s former owner – oligarch Vladimir Gusinsky – was put under so much pressure by the Kremlin that he lost his media empire – Media-Most – which fell into the hands of state-owned Gazprom-Media. Gazprom-Media then became the majority shareholder in *Ekho Moskvy*. Journalists at both *Novaya Gazeta* and *Ekho Moskvy* received significantly lower pay than their colleagues at other media, especially state media. The situation was worse for *Novaya Gazeta* journalists who would often not receive their salaries on time due to the financial struggles.

While this is not a study into the marketisation of Russian media, it becomes clear from my findings that there are two fundamental changes in comparison with Soviet times. First, private ownership is allowed in post-Soviet Russia and the regulatory rules are not as stringent for newspapers as they are for broadcasters. Second, competition is not governed by market forces alone. The state plays a very strong role, and as a result of that, private media have to compete both with market forces and other (mainly political) forces. Politicians, private businesses, and the media are intertwined in a complex relationship – a trend evident in Central and Eastern

Europe as well, but the state is indeed the main actor in Russia, and its grip on media has significantly tightened over the past few years (Vartanova, 2012).

2   Safety issues such as threats, physical attacks, and murders.

All journalists in my sample had either received threats and/or had been physically attacked or kidnapped. *Novaya Gazeta* journalists had experienced the most brutal attacks. Six of their colleagues were murdered. Their portraits, hung above the table around which they met every day to plan their work, were a constant reminder of how dangerous journalism could be in contemporary Russia. The most dangerous topics for Russian journalists according to the editor-in-chief of *Novaya Gazeta* were corruption in the special services, the North Caucusus, and neo-Nazism. The normalisation of danger I observed among liberal journalists was worrying. Most of them accepted the numerous threats they received as normal and did not report them to the authorities. They tended to underplay their importance by differentiating between the threats they received or had experienced and "real" threats such as murders and physical attacks. While it will be misleading to claim that all threats emanated from Putin and the Kremlin, the political environment and the general culture of impunity and lawlessness were key contributing factors.

The types of dangers experienced by journalists in post-Soviet Russia are different from the ones experienced in Soviet times, but based on the evidence that I have, it is hard to say whether journalism is a more dangerous profession in contemporary Russia. The number of murders, abductions, and physical attacks is significantly higher than before, but we should not forget how dangerous criticism of the authorities was for journalists during the Soviet era, especially before Gorbachev put his glasnost policy in place.

3   Legal and administrative measures.

The three media outlets in my sample had been at the receiving end of a range of legal and administrative measures – warnings by the media regulator, trumped-up charges, defamation and other lawsuits, and foreign ownership restrictions. *Radio Svoboda* had been most hardly hit by these measures. The radio had experienced the most significant decline of the three media organisations in my sample. From a station with 30 local affiliates in 2005, which was broadcasting on FM, AM, and shortwaves, *Svoboda* had now become an online-only medium with no radio frequencies. Furthermore, the most recent restrictive law that was passed in November 2017 led to the official designation of *Radio Svoboda* as a "foreign agent" by the Ministry of Justice in retaliation for the USA's treatment of *RT*. It remains to be seen whether this new piece of legislation would actually force the radio to close down its official operations in Russia, but there is a real danger that this might indeed happen.

By comparison, during communism *Radio Svoboda* was not officially allowed to broadcast from Russia but it was doing that for decades from its headquarters in Munich. Its role in Russian society appears to have significantly diminished since Putin's coming into power, and this limbo state the radio had found itself in had done more damage to its credibility than the open war the Russian state launched on it during communism.

The Mediatisation of the Conflict in Ukraine

The coverage of the conflict in Ukraine was a priority topic for journalists from *Novaya Gazeta, Ekho Moskvy* and *Radio Svoboda*. However, their accounts of how the conflict should be covered differed. A key bone of contention was whether the coverage should be objective/impartial/unbiased or "alternative", namely, focussing on the viewpoints, facts, and perspectives that state media chose to ignore or misrepresent. All three media outlets recognised that it was important for them to rely on their own correspondents rather than social media or other reports from external sources. The disagreements journalists had were linked to two wider issues: the role Russia played/should play on the world stage and their own duties as journalists. Most journalists I interviewed recognised that the situation in Ukraine was complicated but some hastened to condemn Putin's policy as infringing the sovereignty of Ukraine, while others offered more nuanced interpretations by acknowledging the pro-Russian sentiments in some parts of Ukraine.

In their coverage of Ukraine, journalists were not just led by their professional values and duties, but also by their national identities and patriotism. Thus, *Novaya Gazeta*'s editor-in-chief and *Radio* Svoboda's editor at large Mark Krotov both said: "I love my country" when justifying their approach to the coverage of Ukraine. In both cases, they claimed that their love for their country justified their critical coverage of Putin and his policies because in their view he was bringing Russia into disrepute on the international scene by also jeopardising Russia's peace and stability. However, most journalists also recognised that the practical application of their love for their country in their reporting differed from the prevailing popular interpretation of what one's love for one's country should entail in relation to the conflict in Ukraine. Liberal journalists recognised that Putin's popularity was soaring and while the majority of Russians were rallying behind the flag and supporting their President's actions, they considered *Radio Svoboda, Novaya Gazeta,* and *Ekho Moskvy* as US/Western agents, "enemies" of Russian authorities and Russian people, and national traitors. A few journalists themselves were concerned that their coverage of the Euromaidan movement was too favourable, thus undermining their credibility even more in the eyes of the Russian public.

While my study does not include content analysis of the actual articles/news broadcasts about Ukraine, the ethnographic work and the interviews with journalists as well as the warnings received by the Russian media regulator suggest that the type of coverage provided by these three media outlets was different from the coverage provided by state-aligned media in Russia. Liberal journalists attempted to give voice to a wider range of sources and voices, including the Euromaidan movement and its supporters. However, it seems that the majority of Russians did not appreciate that, and the attacks on these liberal media by the state as well as the dangers that journalists experienced had intensified. The disagreements between some journalists about the extent to which their own views should be reflected in the coverage as well as whether the coverage should be balanced or biased revealed a wider lack of consensus about the general role journalists should play in society.

Liberal Journalists' Role in Post-Soviet Putin's Russia

All journalists I interviewed were driven by liberal values, the underlying belief in democracy and the rule of law, and the need for all authorities to be accountable for their actions. They all made a deliberate choice to work for these three media organisations precisely because of this shared ethos. However, the application of these liberal values in their journalistic work was not uniform across and within the three media outlets, and there were considerable individual differences as well. The book demonstrated that developments in Russian media and society should indeed not be interpreted through Western lenses and with existing (predominantly normative) Western media theories and concepts. Journalists' operationalisation of their values, principles, and role in society fundamentally differed from the dominant paradigm in the West. Even for US-funded *Radio Svoboda* journalists, the conflict between their mission imposed by the USA and their day-to-day experience was clearly evident.

Most journalists professed a normative commitment to journalistic professionalism, balance and objectivity, and an adherence to ethical standards. They also recognised that their objectivity was compromised both by the range of pressures and challenges they had been experiencing and the endemic self-censorship at state media, which further enhanced the need for them to present the alternative (i.e. anti-Putin/Kremlin) point of view. Surely, no reporting can be defined as impartial and objective if it places undue focus on one side in an argument.

The more fundamental question is, however: Can these liberal journalists both provide balanced coverage and be strong advocates of democratic liberal values in a context such as the Russian one? The evidence in my book suggests that this is not feasible. But is it desirable? Is it something they should strive towards? Should their reporting be as balanced and impartial as possible or should they be strong advocates for political change in Russia? This is a question that some of these journalists have grappled with for years. For the senior editorial staff, especially at a newspaper such as *Novaya Gazeta*, being detached watchdogs was not an option because their verdict on present-day Russia and their vision of their country were fundamentally different from the ones promoted by Putin and state media. The fundamental and irreconcilable difference between Putin and *Novaya Gazeta's* editorial staff was the opposing vision they held for Russia's future and its role on the world stage. According to Muratov (2014, personal communication):

> Putin is a person who dreams about the happiness of his country. He loves Russia deeply, in a fantastic way. But he envisages Russia as a country in which power and rule do not change. I don't envisage Russia as an authoritarian country – I see it as a democratic country. Putin thinks that patriotism is about fighting. I think patriotism is when people like living in their country and are not scared of each other. These are fundamental differences. Moreover, I think that our country has fought a lot. A few million people have died in combat – during the First World War a hundred years ago, during Stalin's repressions who no one apologised for – they don't even pay repression pensions. Tens of millions of people died during the Second World War for our great nation. In fact, one of our observers recently read that Russia had lost 360 million people in the wars in the last century, which is 2.5 times the population of Russia at the moment. We all know that lots of people die in wars. Our country burnt in wars.

For people like Muratov and Venediktov, journalists could not simply be detached watchdogs because they should play an active political role in Russian society (Koltsova, 2006; Mickiewicz, 1999; Oates, 2006, 2013). A similar view was shared at *Radio Svoboda* where their main role was seen as promulgating democratic values and providing alternative narratives. Nonetheless, liberal journalists were under no illusions that their attempts at promoting democratic values and highlighting the wrongdoings of those in power would be well received and appreciated by the majority of Russians. If Oates (2006) was right in claiming that Russian audiences did not seek objectivity from their journalists but rather "a sense of pride and nationhood in a troubled and chaotic environment" (p. 20), then what liberal journalists offered them was exactly the opposite of what the majority of Russians expected from them. Journalists in liberal media realised that the majority of Russians did not want to hear their messages and strongly opposed them. As Politkovskaya (International Women's Media Foundation, 2002) herself once said

> It is customary to believe that journalists go to places where wars and catastrophes break out because people and the world want to know the truth and the news about these events. In Russia things are just the opposite today. The people do not want to know the truth about the ongoing war.

Therefore, it was not surprising that their message, especially during the conflict with Ukraine, was met with animosity. Russia's role in Ukraine culminating in the referendum in Crimea was a very important milestone in Putin's nationalistic project. If public opinion surveys are anything to go by, then his strategy was clearly successful in the eyes of the Russian public since support for him soared after the start of the conflict. That made the job of journalists even more difficult because the messages they were conveying did not just contradict Putin's main message propped up by state media but they also challenged Russian audiences' beliefs and expectations. By exposing some of the wrongdoings of their beloved country/president, liberal journalists were questioning the credibility of Putin's nationalistic project and jeopardising its success. That made them "enemies of the people" or in the case of *Radio Svoboda* US/foreign agents, that is, the "voice of the enemy".

This topic has been of particular relevance in the Russian context due to Putin's increased efforts in the process of construction and promotion of a particular type of modern-day Russian national identity, which Hutchings and Tolz (2015) defined as "neo-imperial nationalism" or "isolationist popular nationalism" (p. 9). Hutchings and Rulyova (2009) argued that Putin's "efforts to install a latter-day version of imperial pride in Russian military achievements" were "at the centre of a national identity project amount to a form of remote control" (p. 3). Liberal media often hindered this process, which made them a frequent target for the authorities. The conflict with Ukraine did indeed present opportunities for them to provide an "alternative" framing to the overall pro-Putin chorus led by Russian state broadcast media, but it also led to be a key challenge – the threat of increased marginalisation. Putin's popularity had been soaring in large part due to the strong role he had been perceived to be playing in the process of nation-building and revival of Russia's identity as a superpower on the world stage – a narrative strongly questioned by liberal media's coverage of Ukraine. It was not surprising that Putin had no intention of tolerating any attempts at undermining his project, and the pressures against liberal media significantly intensified over the past few years.

Media Freedom, Russia's Media System, and the Potential for Democratisation

Are media freer in post-Soviet Russia than they were during communism? The legal existence of media organisations such as the three this study focusses on shows that media are indeed freer in post-Soviet Russia than during communism. Nonetheless, media freedom is considerably restrained and the overall trend is of deterioration. That's why I describe Russia's liberal media as handcuffed, but free. While free on paper, the pressures that liberal media experience have significantly intensified in the past few years to such an extent, but their hands are practically tied by the various restrictions and challenges that they face. In addition to that, the identity battles and crises that they have been undergoing, especially since the start of the conflict in Ukraine, have further exacerbated their condition.

The fact that the pressure has indeed intensified is strong evidence of the fact that liberal media such as *Novaya Gazeta, Radio Ekho Moskvy*, and *Radio Svoboda* are much needed in Russia. Oates (2006) argued that "the experience of Russia highlights the fact the mass media are critical factors in halting the slide into authoritarianism" (p. 194). It is hard to claim that liberal media have halted Russia's slide into authoritarianism, given the current state of political freedoms in Russia, but it is clear that they have at least tried their best to reverse or at least slow down this process. As Felgengauer (2014, personal communication) said,

> I know too well how hard it is for us to maintain our positions. There are constant attempts to control us...The pressures are constantly there. That's the process of monopolisation and the attempts to fully control the mass media. It's not a very recent process but it's much more pronounced and visible. There is a definitive trend. In this situation everybody survives the way they can. In this situation we have been lucky. We have a really tough editor-in-chief. He really sort of protects us. And we have a very good constitutional charter so we are as secure as possible but I cannot predict how long this will be sustained for.

The strong protection of their editors-in-chief is a main coping mechanism both for *Radio Ekho Moskvy* and *Novaya Gazeta* journalists. But the two editors disagreed on the issue of whether their continued existence was the result of a deliberate strategy on Putin's side. According to the editor-in-chief of *Ekho Moskvy*, there was no point worrying about the future because if Putin wanted to close them down, he could do that within hours. However, the editor-in-chief of *Novaya Gazeta* said it was wrong to assume that his newspaper existed as a result of Putin's strategy/decision:

> They explain that our peace is very precarious and if *Novaya Gazeta* exists, then Putin must have decided in favour of that. If the

sun rises, then it's Putin's decision. If the river Volga flows into the Caspian Sea, then whose decision it is? Putin's. Why don't you ask me why Volga flows into the Caspian Sea? This is not so. Putin does not decide everything in the world. A lot of children were born without Putin's involvement. *Novaya Gazeta* exists without Putin's involvement. People die without Putin's involvement, people are happy without his involvement. In our state there is this perception of the President as a hero, the President as Batman. There is a difference between Batman depicted in the comic books and in reality. But our society, our people are like children, it's a childish nation. They need to be taken care of. Our President is our babysitter. This is what we are like. This is how we are built.

(Muratov, 2014, personal communication)

Regardless of whether the continued existence of critical media is a deliberate strategy of window-dressing in front of the West or unwillingness to assume full Soviet-style control of the media, Putin's approach towards media management appears to be very effective. On the one hand, as long as critical media outlets such as *Ekho Moskvy* and *Novaya Gazeta* exist in Russia, no one can accuse Putin of being a full-fledged dictator who has stifled all critical voices and is censoring the media. On the other hand, these media organisations are indeed handcuffed – they are considerably restricted in their activities to the point where it is difficult for them to conduct their day-to-day job and accomplish their mission. Marginalising and constantly undermining their credibility is a much cleverer strategy than banning them outright. These journalists are determined, driven, and resistant. An official ban would not stop them from working unofficially. Paradoxically, this might actually provide them with a much clearer mission and identity. Putin does not, therefore, have a strong incentive to totally ban them.

While it is beyond the scope of this book to offer a thorough investigation into Russia's media system, the evidence suggests that Becker (2014) was right in claiming that Russia had "adopted a neo-authoritarian media system that has more in common with similar non-democratic systems around the world than with the Soviet system that once prevailed on the same territory" (p. 191). The approach adopted was indeed of eliminating critical convent without actually eliminating the media outlets themselves (Lipman & McFaul, 2001). Putin's handling of liberal media sets a good example for other neo-authoritarian leaders (Becker, 2014), especially those who want to reap the benefits of capitalism without paying the hefty price that democratic systems demand. His approach to media management and control looks ad hoc and sporadic at times, but it has certainly become much more confident and stringent with time, and thus more successful for his own image, popularity, and credibility. I started my book by saying that Russia's road to democratisation has been thorny. After reviewing and presenting all the evidence, this claim sounds like an understatement. Russia's journey during Putin's three terms as president has not been towards democratisation. Based on the evidence in this book, it is highly questionable whether we should continue using the terms democratisation and democracy in the Russian context.

By completely abandoning them, however, we are running the risk of doing a disservice to the brave, courageous, and highly motivated liberal journalists and their murdered colleagues who persevere in their mission to democratise Russian society. The journalists I interviewed and their murdered colleagues were no saints. Politkovskaya herself was a notoriously difficult person to work with who had been repeatedly warned that her life would be in danger if she continued working on Chechnya, but the numerous threats and intimidations she received did not deter her. As one of her colleagues (Dubov, 2014, personal communication) said, Politkovskaya was like "a drug addict". The same can be said about most of her colleagues who were equally undeterred even when the editor-in-chief wanted to close down their newspaper because of the dangers. As Prusenkova (2014, personal communication) put it, they were not suicidal, but for them their job was a way of life, not a living. A few journalists even used the word "doctor" to describe their role in Russian society – a society in need of treatment, which they were attempting to provide. Fundamentally, the actions of the journalists in my sample were driven by the different vision of Russia they shared in comparison with Putin. Like Putin, most of them claimed that they were motivated by their love for their country. Unlike Putin, they were not dreaming of Russia's imperial grandeur and world leadership, but they believed that Russia's future should be of a global, democratic, and peaceful nation and should not involve the invasion of foreign territories or indeed the imperial grandeur of the past.

What is the role of the international community in that situation and why are news outlets such as *Novaya Gazeta* and *Radio Echo of Moscow* left to fight these battles on their own? After all, the controversial role Russia played in Ukraine and Syria and even in the USA reminds us acutely of the need to refocus our attention to Russia. The international community can do considerably more than it currently does to support liberal journalists in Russia. Any state interventions would not be looked upon favourably by the Russian state, as the new law on foreign agents clearly shows. However, there is considerably more scope for organisations such as the UN, UNESCO, and to a lesser extent the EU to put pressure on Russia to fulfil its commitments in relation to freedom of expression and the safety of journalists. Non-governmental organisations, media organisations, and journalistic unions can also play a much stronger role in supporting their Russian colleagues. Any new measures would only be successful if they are conceived and implemented in close collaboration with the editors and journalists at these media outlets because they are not students who should be taught how to practise journalism, but they are experienced professionals who know best what measures would truly help them and what limitations they are likely to face.

Finally, this book is an attempt to offer a glimpse into the history and the current state of three liberal media outlets in Russia, but it is not a comprehensive summary of the state of Russian media and journalism as a whole nor does it include any form of textual analysis of the actual media publications. Future work can much more closely investigate the link between those texts, the actual production practices, and journalists' own accounts of their work. It would also be of great value if further research is conducted into other liberal media, especially online publications. A thorough re-conceptualisation of the Russian media system and for that matter of Russia's political system would also be pertinent in the wake of the next presidential elections and the evolving relationship with the USA.

Bibliography

Agence France-Presse. (2016). Russia's conviction of opposition leader Alexei Navalny 'arbitrary', *European court says*. Retrieved from www.theguardian. com/world/2016/feb/24/russias-conviction-of-opposition-leader-alexei-navalny-arbitrary-european-court-says (Accessed 4 December 2017).

Allan, S., & Zelizer, B. (2004). Rules of engagement: Journalism and war. In: Allan, S., & Zelizer, B. (eds.), *Reporting War: Journalism in Wartime*, pp. 3–23. New York and London: Routledge.

Anderson, B. (1983/1991). *Imagined communities: Reflections on the origins and spread of nationalism.* London: Verso.

Anikina, M., Frost, L., & Hanitzsch, T. (2017). Journalists in Russia. *Worlds of Journalism.* Retrieved from https://epub.ub.uni-muenchen.de/35063/1/ Country_report_Russia.pdf (Accessed 4 December 2017).

Anishchuk, A. (2014, 31 October). Russian media watchdog blasts radio station over Ukraine coverage. *Reuters.* Retrieved from http://uk.reuters.com/article/uk-ukraine-crisis-russia-media/russian-media-watchdog-blasts-radio-station-over-ukraine-coverage-idUKKBN0IK1YG20141031 (Accessed 31 October 2017).

Arias-King, F. (2004). Yuri Shchekochikhin: A tribute. *Demokratizatsiya: The Journal of Post-Soviet Democratization, 12*(1), 1–4. Retrieved from www2. gwu.edu/~ieresgwu/assets/docs/demokratizatsiya%20archive/GWASHU_ DEMO_12_1/PJ577098V2207162/12_1_ARIAS-KING.pdf (Accessed 4 December 2017).

Arutunyan, A. (2009). *The media in Russia.* Maidenhead: Open University Press.

Åslund, A., & Kuchins, A. (2009). *The Russia balance sheet.* Washington, DC: Peterson Institute for International Economics.

Associated Press. (2017, 30 October). Russian journalist thanks supporters after stabbing attack. Retrieved from https://uk.news.yahoo.com/russian-journalist-thanks-supporters-stabbing-112126344.html (Accessed 13 December 2017).

Azhgikhina, N. (2007). The struggle for press freedom in Russia: Reflections of a Russian journalist. *Europe-Asia Studies, 59*(8), 1245–1262.

Balmforth, T. (2016, 18 January). In Latest Salvo, Kadyrov Ally Threatens to Sic attack dog on Russian opposition. *Radio Free Europe/Liberty.* Retrieved from www.rferl.org/a/chechnya-kadyrov-instagram-threats-attack-dog-russian-opposition/27494978.html (Accessed 3 November 2017).

Baysha, O. (2014). On the dichotomy of corporate vs. alternative journalism: OWS as constructed by Echo of Moscow. *International Journal of Communication, 8*, 2899–2922.

BBC News. (2011, 15 June). Chechnya: Kadyrov loses Memorial defamation case. Retrieved from www.bbc.co.uk/news/mobile/world-europe-13775877 (Accessed 4 December 2017).

BBC News. (2012, 6 March). Putin accuses Echo Radio of pouring 'diarrhoea' on him. Retrieved from www.bbc.co.uk/news/world-europe-16627415 (Accessed 1December 2017).

BBC News. (2014, 18 February). Russian Ekho Moskvy radio director Fedutinov dismissed. Retrieved from www.bbc.co.uk/news/world-europe-26239715 (Accessed 31 October 2017).

Becker, J. (2004). Lessons from Russia: A neo-authoritarian media system. *European Journal of Communication, 19*(2), 139–163.

Becker, J. (2014). Russia and the new authoritarians. *Demokratizatsiya: The Journal of Post-Soviet Democratization, 22*(2), 191–206.

Bidder, B. (2012). Echo of Moscow under pressure in Russia. *Spiegel Online*. Retrieved from www.spiegel.de/international/world/controlling-the-press-echo-of-moscow-under-pressure-in-russia-a-815731.html (Accessed 4 December 2017).

Billig, M. (1995). *Banal nationalism*. London: Sage.

Brenton, T. (2011). Russia's media: Freedom isn't dead. *British Journalism Review, 22*(1), 33–39.

Bromley, M., & Slavtcheva-Petkova, V. (In press). *Global journalism: An introduction*. Basingstoke: Palgrave.

Burrett, T. (2011). *Television and presidential power in Putin's Russia*. New York and London: Routledge.

Butterfield, J., & Levintova, E. (2011). Academic freedom and international standards in higher education: Contestation in journalism and political science at Moscow State Universit. *Communist and Post-Communist Societies, 44*(4), 329–341.

Charmaz, K. (2006). *Constructing grounded theory*. London: Sage.

Clark, L. S. (2012). *The parent app: Understanding families in the digital age.* Oxford: Oxford University Press.

CNN. (2001, 6 July). Resignations rock Russian radio. Retrieved from http://edition.cnn.com/2001/WORLD/europe/07/06/russia.radio/ (Accessed 4 December 2017).

Commissioner for Human Rights. (2016). Third party intervention by the council of Europe commissioner for human rights. *Council of Europe*. Retrieved from https://rm.coe.int/ref/CommDH(2016)18 (Accessed 26 September 2017).

Corley, F. (2003, 9 July). Yuri Shchekochikhin. *The Guardian*. Retrieved from www.theguardian.com/news/2003/jul/09/guardianobituaries.russia (Accessed 4 December 2017).

Cottiero, C., Kucharski, K., Olimpieva, E., & Orttung, R. W. (2015). War of words: The impact of Russian state television on the Russian Internet. *Nationalities Papers, 43*(4), 533–555, DOI: 10.1080/00905992.2015.1013527.

Cottle, S. (2006). *Mediatized conflict: Developments in media and conflict studies*. Maidenhead: Open University Press.

CPJ. (2003, 3 July). Yuri Shchekochikhin. Retrieved from https://cpj.org/killed/2003/yuri-shchekochikhin.php (Accessed 11 December 2017).

CPJ. (2007, 30 August). In a benchmark verdict, Russian court convicts 5 in reporter's murder. Retrieved from https://cpj.org/2007/08/in-a-benchmark-verdict-russian-court-convicts-5-in.php (Accessed 11 December 2017).

CPJ. (2017). Journalists killed between 1992 and 2007. Retrieved from https:// cpj.org (Accessed 13 December 2017).

Deacon, D., & Stanyer, J. (2014). Mediatization: Key concept or conceptual backwagon? *Media, Culture & Society, 36*(7), 1032–1044.

Deibert, R., & Rohozinski, R. (2010). Liberation vs. control: The future of cyberspace. *Journal of Democracy, 21*(4), 43–57.

De Smaele, H. (1999). The applicability of Western media models on the Russian media system. *European Journal of Communication, 14*(2), 173–189.

De Smaele, H. (2009). In search of a label of the Russian media system. In: Dobek-Ostrowska, B., Głowacki, M., & Jakubowicz, K. (eds.), *Comparative Media Systems: European and Global Perspectives*. Budapest: Central European University Press, pp. 41–62.

Dimarsky, V. (2015). Французский связной. In: Ryabtseva, L. (ed.), *Эхо Москвы. Непридуманная история. 25 лет в эфире*, pp. 97–98. AST: Moscow.

Donskih, I. (2009, 21 January). Такой она была. *Novaya Gazeta*. Retrieved from http://old.novayagazeta.ru/society/46446.html (Accessed 11 July 2017).

Dye, J., Schatz, I., & Rosenberg, B. (2000). Constant comparison method: A kaleidoscope of data. *The Qualitative Report, 4*(1–2). Retrieved from http:// nsuworks.nova.edu/tqr/vol4/iss1/8/ (Accessed 4 December 2017).

Dzyadko, T. (2014). Triumph of the will: Putin's war against Russia's last independent TV channel. *The Guardian*. Retrieved from www.theguardian. com/commentisfree/2014/apr/10/putin-war-dozhd-russias-last-independent-tv-channel (Accessed 6 December 2017).

Encyclopaedia Britannica. (2000). Vladimir Gusinsky. Retrieved from www. britannica.com/biography/Vladimir-Gusinsky (Accessed 30 October 2017).

Estemirova, N. (2009, 21 January). Тысячи палачей гуляют на свободе. *Novaya Gazeta*. Retrieved from http://old.novayagazeta.ru/society/46443.html (Accessed 5 July 2017).

Euromaidan Press. (2014, 7 November). The story of Ukrainian soldiers at the Donetsk airport; censored in Russia. Retrieved from http://euromaidanpress. com/2014/11/07/the-story-of-donetsk-airport-cyborgs-that-was-censored-by-russias-roskomnadzor/#arvlbdata (Accessed 1 November 2017).

European Union External Action. (2015). Questions and answers about the East StratCom Task Force. Retrieved from https://eeas.europa.eu/headquarters/ headquarters-Homepage/2116/questions-and-answers-about-east-stratcom-task-force_en (Accessed 8 December 2017).

Fedutinov, Y. (2015). Радио меня интересует только как бизнес. In: Ryabtseva, L. (ed.), *Эхо Москвы. Непридуманная история. 25 лет в эфире*, pp. 189–195. AST: Moscow.

Felgengauer, T. (2015). У нас тут целое поколение next. In: Ryabtseva, L. (ed.), *Эхо Москвы. Непридуманная история. 25 лет в эфире*, pp. 197–198. AST: Moscow.

Fielding, N. (2001). Ethnography. In: Gilbert, N. (ed.), *Researching Social Life*. London: Sage, pp. 145–163.

Filipov, D. (2017, March). Here are 10 critics of Vladimir Putin who died violently or in suspicious ways. *The Washington Post*. Retrieved from www. washingtonpost.com/news/worldviews/wp/2017/03/23/here-are-ten-critics-of-vladimir-putin-who-died-violently-or-in-suspicious-ways/?utm_term=. 020426a2dc90 (Accessed on 4 December 2017).

Filippova, Y. (2003). Юрий Щекочихин: Меня научили никого не обманывать и ничего не бояться. *Novaya Gazeta*. Retrieved from http://ys.novayagazeta. ru/text/2003-08-11-03.shtml (Accessed 6 December 2017).

Finkelstein, D. (2008). Investigative journalism. *Journalism Practice* 2(1), 130–134.

Freedom House. (2015, August 11). *Freedom of the Press: Russia*. Retrieved from https://freedomhouse.org/report/freedom-press/2015/russia (Accessed on 29 November 2017).

Ganapolsky, M. (2015). "…мы просто показали им пример естественности". In: Ryabtseva, L. (ed.), *Эхо Москвы. Непридуманная история. 25 лет в эфире*, pp. 61–73. AST: Moscow.

Ganapolsky, M. (2016). Владимир Владимирович, почему вы молчите? *Ekho Moksvy*. Retrieved from https://echo.msk.ru/blog/ganapolsky/1695960-echo/ (Accessed 3 November 2017).

Glaser, B. (1965). The constant comparative method of qualitative analysis. *Social Problems, 12*(4), 436–445.

Glasnost Defence Foundation. (2009). Criminal investigation into suspected murder of journalist Yuri Shchekochikhin closed. Retrieved from www.ifex.org/ russia/2009/04/21/shchekochikhin_investigation_closed/ (Accessed 11 December 2017).

Golubev, A. (2015). Лайв с пожара – это символично. In: Ryabtseva, L. (ed.), *Эхо Москвы. Непридуманная история. 25 лет в эфире*, pp. 74–80. AST: Moscow.

Gorbachev, M. (2000, 9 June). Письма президентов. *Novaya Gazeta*. Retrieved from http://ys.novayagazeta.ru/text/2000-06-15.shtml (Accessed 6 December 2017).

Grozev, C. (2014). For Russian media, it's "No-Truth, No-Dare". Retrieved from https://cgrozev.wordpress.com/2014/08/23/for-russian-media-its-un-truth-or-dare/ (Accessed 31 October 2017).

Gutiontov, P. (2003, 7 July). Без него нас стало неисправимо мало. Уже навсегда. *Novaya Gazeta*. Retrieved from http://ys.novayagazeta.ru/text/2003-07-07-01. shtml (Accessed 6 December 2017).

Hallin, D. C., & Mancini, P. (2004). *Comparing media systems: Three models of media and politics*. Cambridge: Cambridge University Press.

Harding, L. (2009). Anna Politkovskaya trial: Four accused found not guilty. *The Guardian*. Retrieved from www.theguardian.com/media/2009/feb/19/ anna-politkovskaya-verdict (Accessed 5 July 2017).

Hearst, D. (2006, 9 October). Anna Politkovskaya. *The Guardian*. Retrieved from www.theguardian.com/news/2006/oct/09/guardianobituaries.russia (Accessed 5 July 2017).

Heinrich, H. G., & Tanaev, K. (2009). Georgia and Russia: Contradictory media coverage of the August war. *Caucasian Review of International Affairs, 3*(3), 244–260.

Herman, E., & Chomsky, N. (1988). *Manufacturing consent: The political economy of the mass media*. New York: Pantheon Books.

Horbyk, R. (2015). Little patriotic war: Nationalist narratives in the Russian media coverage of the Ukraine-Russia crisis. *Asian Politics & Policy, 7*(3), 505–511.

Hoskins, A., & O'Loughlin, B. (2010). *War and media: The emergence of diffused war*. Cambridge: Polity.

Hutchings, S., & Rulyova, N. (2009). *Television and culture in Putin's Russia*. New York and London: Routledge.

Hutchings, S., & Tolz, V. (2015). *Nation, ethnicity and race on Russian television: Mediating post-Soviet difference (BASEES/Routledge series on Russian and east European studies)*. New York and London: Routledge.

International Women's Media Foundation. (2002, 16 October). Anna Politkovskaya/2002 Courage in Journalism Award. Retrieved from www.iwmf.org/blog/2002/10/14/anna-politkovskaya-2002-courage-in-journalism-award/ (Accessed 5 July 2017).

Internet Encyclopedia of Ukraine. (n.d.). Banderites. Retrieved from www.encyclopediaofukraine.com (Accessed 27 September 2017).

Izmailov, V. (2006, 12 October). Она поднималась первой. *Novaya Gazeta*. Retrieved from http://2006.novayagazeta.ru/nomer/2006/78n/n78n-s09.shtml (Accessed 27 June 2017).

Izmailov, V. (2009, 21 January). Последнее «чеченское» дело Станислава Маркелова. *Novaya Gazeta*. Retrieved from http://old.novayagazeta.ru/society/46442.html (Accessed 11 July 2017).

Johnson, A. R. (2010). *Radio Free Europe and Radio Liberty: The CIA years and beyond*. Stanford, CA: Stanford University Press.

Kadyrov, R. (2006, 12 October). Горе. Без границ. Retrieved from http://2006.novayagazeta.ru/nomer/2006/78n/n78n-s05.shtml (Accessed 27 June 2017).

Kanygin, P. (2014, 16 May). This is not a ransom, it's your contribution into our war. *Novaya Gazeta*. Retrieved from https://maidantranslations.com/2014/05/26/kidnapped-russian-journalist-pavel-kanygin-on-his-own-abduction-this-is-not-a-ransom-this-is-your-contribution-to-our-war/ (Accessed 23October 2017).

Kashin, O. (2011, 6 July). История русских медиа 1989–2011. *Afisha Live*. Retrieved from www.afisha.ru/article/mediahistory/page10/ (Accessed 6 December 2017).

Khlebnikov, O. (2001, 14 May). Поправки к общеизвестному. *Novaya Gazeta*. Retrieved from http://domnikov.novayagazeta.ru/hlebn.shtml (Accessed 6 December 2017).

Klimentov, V. (2010, 13 October). Novaya Gazeta: The last bastion for political opposition in Russia? *Ina Global*. Retrieved from www.inaglobal.fr/en/press/article/novaya-gazeta-last-bastion-political-opposition-russia (Accessed 11 December 2017).

Koltsova, O. (2006). *News media and power in Russia*. New York and London: Routledge.

Korkonosenko, S. G. (2011) Journalism in Russia as a national cultural value. *Russian Journal of Communication*, 4(3–4), 159–176.

Korzun, S. (2015a). In: Апокрифы. Ryabtseva, L. (ed.), *Эхо Москвы. Непридуманная история. 25 лет в эфире*, pp. 197–198. AST: Moscow.

Korzun, S. (2015b, 23 May). Эхо Москвы 1990–2015 R.I.P. *LiveJournal*. Retrieved from https://bez-durakoff.livejournal.com/?skip=30 (Accessed 3 November 2017).

Lenta.ru. (2017, 23 October). Ведущая «Эха Москвы» обвинила Соловьева в провокации нападения на Фельгенгауэр. Retrieved from https://lenta.ru/news/2017/10/23/provocation/ (Accessed 13 December 2017).

Levada-Center. (2015, 26 October). Trust in the mass media. Retrieved from www.levada.ru/en/2015/10/26/trust-in-the-mass-media/ (Accessed 11 December 2017).

Levada-Center. (2016a, 18 November). Доверие СМИ и цензура. Retrieved from www.levada.ru/2016/11/18/doverie-smi-i-tsenzura/ (Accessed 6 December 2017).

Levada-Center. (2016b, 22 June). Russia Ukraine relations. Retrieved from www. levada.ru/en/2016/06/22/russia-ukraine-relations-2/ (Accessed 6 December 2017).

Levada-Center. (2017, 20 March). Aleksey Navalny. Retrieved from www. levada.ru/en/2017/03/20/aleksey-navalny/ (Accessed 11 December 2017).

Lipman, M. (2010). Freedom of expression without freedom of the press. *Journal of International Affairs, 63*(2), 153–170.

Lipman, M. (2014). Russia's nongovernmental media under assault. *Demokratizatsiya, 22*(2), 179–190.

Lipman, M., & McFaul, M. (2001). "Managed democracy" in Russia: Putin and the press. *The International Journal of Press/Politics, 6*(3), 116–127.

Lokshina, T. (2009, 21 July). Natalia Estemirova. *The Guardian*. Retrieved from www.theguardian.com/world/2009/jul/21/obituary-natalia-estemirova (Accessed 12 July 2017).

Luhn, A. (2015, 19 May). Russia bans 'undesirable' international organisations ahead of 2016 elections. *The Guardian*. Retrieved from www.theguardian. com/world/2015/may/19/russia-bans-undesirable-international-organisations-2016-elections (Accessed 13 December 2017).

Markin, V. I. (2013, 16 October). Pavel Sopot accused of inciting attack on journalist Igor Domnikov to stand trial in Moscow. *The Investigative Committee of the Russian Federation*. https://archive.fo/aTUqn#selection-277.0-276.1 (Accessed 13 December 2017).

Markin, V. I. (2015, 3 April). Sergey Dorovsky charged with attack on Novaya Gazeta reporter Igor Domnikov to face trial in Moscow. *The Investigative Committee of the Russian Federation*. Retrieved from http://en.sledcom.ru/ news/item/912022 (Accessed 8 December 2017).

Mathews, O. (2010). The real reasons Newsweek Russia folded. *Newsweek*. Retrieved from www.newsweek.com/real-reasons-newsweek-russia-folded-73747 (Accessed 8 December 2017).

McNair, B. (2000). Power, profit, corruption, and lies: The Russian media in the 1990s. In: Curran, J., & Park, M.-J. (eds.), *De-Westernizing Media Studies*, pp. 79–93. New York and London: Routledge.

Meek, J. (2004). Dispatches from a savage war. *The Guardian*. Retrieved from www.theguardian.com/world/2004/oct/15/gender.uk (Accessed 5 July 2017).

Merriam-Webster Dictionary. (2017). Patriotism. Retrieved from www. merriam-webster.com/dictionary/patriotism (Accessed 13 December 2017).

Mickiewicz, E. (1999). *Changing channels: Television and the struggle for power in Russia*. Durham & London: Duke University Press.

Mickiewicz, E. (2008). *Television, power and the public in Russia*. Cambridge: Cambridge University Press.

Milashina, E. (2009a, 21 January). Страха нет. *Novaya Gazeta*. Retrieved from http://old.novayagazeta.ru/society/46441.html (Accessed 5 July 2017).

Milashina, E. (2009b, 20 July). Учительница, которую не хотели слушать. *Novaya Gazeta*. Retrieved from http://old.novayagazeta.ru/society/44273. html (Accessed 14 July 2017).

Milashina, E. (2011, 17 May). Очная ставка провалилась. *Novaya Gazeta*. Retrieved from http://old.novayagazeta.ru/politics/5719.html (Accessed 26 September 2017).

Milashina, E. (2015, 11 March). In landmark case, Russia charges alleged mastermind in Domnikov murder. *Committee to Protect Journalists*. Retrieved from https://cpj.org/blog/2015/03/in-landmark-case-russia-charges-alleged-mastermind.php (Accessed 11 December 2017).

Mineev, A. (2006, 14 December). "Газета, в которой работала Анна." *Novaya Gazeta*. Retrieved from http://2006.novayagazeta.ru/nomer/2006/95n/n95n-s09.shtml (Accessed 3 July 2017).

Mortensen, M. (2015). *Journalism and eyewitness images: Digital media, participation and conflict*. New York and London: Routledge.

Moscow Times. (2016, 27 January). Article on Russian-Chechen tensions draws Chechen ire. Retrieved from https://themoscowtimes.com/news/article-on-russian-chechen-tensions-draws-chechen-ire-51592(Accessed 3 November 2017).

Muratov, D. (2006, 16 October). Что худо для расследования. Retrieved from http://2006.novayagazeta.ru/nomer/2006/79n/n79n-s01.shtml (Accessed 27 June 2017).

Myers, S. L. (2002, 5 October). Putin annuls decree allowing Radio Liberty's broadcasts. *The New York Times*. Retrieved from www.nytimes.com/2002/10/05/world/putin-annuls-decree-allowing-radio-liberty-s-broadcasts.html (Accessed 24 November 2017).

Nemtsova, A. (2015, 6 May). Confessions of Moscow's last independent radio newsman. *The Daily Beast*. Retrieved from www.thedailybeast.com/confessions-of-moscows-last-independent-radio-newsman (Accessed 30 October 2017).

Novaya Gazeta. (2000, 20 July). *Novaya Gazeta's* journalist Igor Alexandrovich Domnikov: 29.05.59 – 16.07.00. Retrieved from http://domnikov.novayagazeta.ru/1polosa.shtml (Accessed 8 December 2017).

Novaya Gazeta. (2006). 7 октября 2006 года, в подъезде своего дома была убита обозреватель «Новой газеты» Анна Политковская. Retrieved from http://politkovskaya.novayagazeta.ru/ (Accessed 14 December 2017).

Novaya Gazeta. (2007, 9 October). Боялись, поэтому и убили. Retrieved from http://2006.novayagazeta.ru/nomer/2006/77n/n77n-s04.shtml (Accessed 27 June 2017).

Novaya Gazeta. (2008a, 4 April). По факту смерти Юрия Щекочихина возбуждено уголовное дело. Retrieved from http://old.novayagazeta.ru/news/29713.html (Accessed 8 December 2017).

Novaya Gazeta. (2008b, 9 June). День Юры. Retrieved from http://old.novayagazeta.ru/society/39890.html (Accessed 8 December 2017).

Novaya Gazeta. (2009a, 21 January). Таким он был. Retrieved from http://old.novayagazeta.ru/society/46447.html (Accessed 11 July 2017).

Novaya Gazeta (2009b, 15 July). «Круг стал совсем узким». Retrieved from http://old.novayagazeta.ru/society/44358.html (Accessed 13 July 2017).

Novaya Gazeta. (2009c, 17 July). Три смертельных выстрела. Retrieved from http://old.novayagazeta.ru/society/44309.html (Accessed 14 July 2017).

Novaya Gazeta. (2009d, 20 July). Наталья Эстемирова: «Пора вернуть многим словам их изначальный смысл» (Accessed 22 September 2017).

Novaya Gazeta. (2010, 15 July). Открытое письмо Президенту РФ в связи с годовщиной гибели Натальи Эстемировой от ее друзей (Accessed 25 September 2017).

Novaya Gazeta. (2011a, 19 January). Как убивали Стаса и Настю. *Novaya Gazeta*. Retrieved from http://old.novayagazeta.ru/politics/7500.html (Accessed 12 July 2017).

Novaya Gazeta. (2011b, 15 July). Два года после убийства Натальи Эстемировой: Следствие идет по ложному пути. *Novaya Gazeta*. Retrieved from http://old. novayagazeta.ru/inquests/47217.html (Accessed 26 September 2017).

Novaya Gazeta. (2016, 6 October). Не смейте говорить, что убийство раскрыто. Видеообращение редакции. Retrieved from www.novayagazeta.ru/articles/2016/10/06/70089-ne-smeyte-govorit-chto-ubiystvo-raskryto-video (Accessed 11 December 2017).

Oates, S. (2006). *Television, democracy and elections in Russia*. New York and London: Routledge.

Oates, S. (2013). *Revolution stalled: The political limits of the Internet in the post-soviet sphere*. New York: Oxford University Press.

Orekh, A. (2015). Я знаю, что мы делали прошлых 25 лет. In: Ryabtseva, L. (ed.), *Эхо Москвы. Непридуманная история. 25 лет в эфире*, pp. 128–129. AST: Moscow.

Osborn, A. (2017, 5 December). Russia designates Radio Free Europe and Voice of America as 'foreign agents'. *Reuters*. Retrieved from https://af.reuters.com/article/worldNews/idAFKBN1DZ0PR (Accessed 14 December 2017).

Parfitt, T. (2011). Russian neo-Nazi gets life sentence for murdering lawyer and journalist. *The Guardian*. Retrieved from www.theguardian.com/world/2011/may/06/russian-neo-nazi-life-sentence-murder (Accessed 5 July 2017).

Parta, R. E. (2007). *Discovering the hidden listener: An assessment of Radio Liberty and Western broadcasting to the USSR during the Cold War*. Stanford, CA: Hoover Institution Press.

Pasti, S., Chernysh, M., & Svitich, L. (2012). The Russian journalists and their profession. In: Weaver, D., & Willnat, L. (eds.), *The Global Journalist in the 21st Century*, pp. 267–282. New York and London: Routledge.

Politkovskaya, A. (2006, 12 October). Назначаем тебя террористом. *Novaya Gazeta*. Retrieved from http://politkovskaya.novayagazeta.ru/pub/2006/2006-90.shtml (Accessed 11 December 2017).

Pomerantsev, P. (2014). *Nothing is true and everything is possible: The surreal heart of the New Russia*. New York: Public Affairs.

Popova, N. (2017, 9 October). "Теперь у нас есть скафандры". *Versia*. Retrieved from https://versia.ru/radiostanciya-yexo-moskvy-otprazdnovala-svoj-27-j-den-rozhdeniya (Accessed 8 November 2017).

Price, M. (1995). Law, force, and the Russia media. *Cardozo Arts and Entertainment Law Journal*, 13(3), 795–846. Retrieved from http://repository. upenn.edu/asc_papers/118 (Accessed 11 December 2017).

Puddington, A. (2000). *Broadcasting freedom: The Cold War Triumph of Radio Free Europe and Radio Liberty*. Lexington, KY: The University Press of Kentucky.

Putin, V. (2000). Письма президентов. *Novaya Gazeta*. Retrieved from http://ys.novayagazeta.ru/text/2000-06-15.shtml (Accessed 6 December 2017).

Radio Ekho Moskvy. (n.d.). Хронология. Retrieved from https://echo.msk.ru/about/history/timeline.html (Accessed 11 December 2017).

Radio Free Europe/Radio Liberty (RFE/RL). (n.d.). History. Retrieved from https://pressroom.rferl.org/p/6092.html (Accessed 14 December 2017).

Radio Free Europe/Radio Liberty (RFE/RL). (2006, 10 October). Russia: Where is Putin? Retrieved from www.rferl.org/a/1071936.html (Accessed 11 December 2017).

Radio Free Europe/Radio Liberty (RFE/RL). (2014a, 7 November). Russian radio station editor defies order to dismiss host. Retrieved from www.rferl. org/a/russian-radio-editor-defies-order-dismissing-host/26678974.html (Accessed 31 October 2017).

Radio Free Europe/Radio Liberty (RFE/RL). (2014b, 19 November). Crucial vote on Russia's Ekho Moskvy's future canceled. Retrieved from www.rferl. org/a/26700463.html (Accessed 31 October 2017).

Radio Free Europe/Radio Liberty. (2016, 6 October). Anna Politkovskaya's last interview. Retrieved from www.rferl.org/a/russia-politkovskaya-last-interview-10th-anniversary/28035942.html (Accessed 27 June 2017).

Radio Free Europe/Radio Liberty (RFE/RL). (2016, 10 October). Russia: Where's Putin. Retrieved from www.rferl.org/a/1071936.html (Accessed 27 June 2017).

Radio Free Europe/Radio Liberty (RFE/RL). (2017, 26 November). EU criticizes Russia's 'Foreign Agents' Media Law. Retrieved from www.rferl. org/a/russia-putin-signs-foreign-agent-media-law-rferl-voa-cnn-deutsche-welle/28876680.html (Accessed 14 December 2017).

Remnick, D. (2008, 22 September). Echo in the dark. *The New Yorker*. Retrieved from www.newyorker.com/magazine/2008/09/22/echo-in-the-dark (Accessed 11 December 2017).

Rollberg, P. (2014). Media democratization in Russia and Eurasia. *Demokratizatsiya: The Journal of Post-Soviet Democratization, 2*, 175–177.

Roman, N., Wanta, W., & Buniak, I. (2017). Information wars: Eastern Ukraine military conflict coverage in the Russian, Ukrainian and U.S. newscasts. *International Communication Gazette, 79*(4), 357–378.

Rosenstiel, T. B. (1991, 29 August). Radio Liberty to get a Moscow bureau: Broadcasting: Yeltsin also gives go-ahead to Radio Free Europe. Services may go on AM or FM. *Los Angeles Times*. Retrieved from http://articles.latimes. com/1991-08-29/news/mn-1840_1_radio-liberty (Accessed 24 November 2017).

Rostova, N. (2006, 16 October). Молитвы, заслоняющие главу. *Novaya Gazeta*. Retrieved from http://2006.novayagazeta.ru/nomer/2006/79n/n79n-s02. shtml (Accessed 27 June 2017).

Rostova, N. (2010, 15 December). История "Новой Газеты". *Slon.ru*. Reprinted by *Novaya Gazeta*. Retrieved from http://old.novayagazeta.ru/history.html (Accessed 13 December 2017).

Roth, A. (2017, 29 November). "I love journalism": Russian journalist vows return after surviving brutal knife attack. *The Washington Post*. Retrieved from www.washingtonpost.com/world/russian-reporter-gravely-hurt-in-knife-attack-vows-to-return-to-journalism/2017/11/28/5b042d4a-d3a3-11e7-9ad9-ca0619edfa05_story.html?tid=ss_tw&utm_term=.b1225ef9dfc9 (Accessed 4 December 2017).

Rozhnov, G. (2001, 16 July). Кто убил нашего друга? *Novaya Gazeta*. Retrieved from http://domnikov.novayagazeta.ru/kto.shtml (Accessed 11 December 2017).

Russia Insider. (2016, 22 February). Putin roasts clueless 5th column propagandist Venediktov – YouTube. Retrieved from www.youtube.com/watch?v=_yo4ilzvB7o&list...7 (Accessed 11 December 2017).

Ruvinsky, V. (2015). "Я привык каждый день получать письма, в которых меня обещают физически уничтожить". In: Ryabtseva, L. (ed.), Эхо Москвы. Непридуманная история. 25 лет в эфире, pp. 197–198. AST: Moscow.

Ryabtseva, L. (2015a, 15 May). Демокраклы. *Ekho Moskvy*. Retrieved from https://echo.msk.ru/blog/lejsya/1548974-echo/ (Accessed 8 November 2017).

Ryabtseva, L. (2015b, 20 May). Слово с тремя точками. *Ekho Moskvy*. Retrieved from https://echo.msk.ru/blog/lejsya/1551966-echo/ (Accessed 8 November 2017).

Ryzhkov, V. (2015). "'Эхо' – это маленький средневековый цех радиокулинарии". In: Ryabtseva, L. (ed.), *Эхо Москвы. Непридуманная история. 25 лет в эфире*, pp. 197–198. AST: Moscow.

Sannikova, E. (2009). Убили женщину. *Novaya Gazeta*. Retrieved from http://old.novayagazeta.ru/society/44359.html (Accessed 13 July 2017).

Shane, S. (2012, 13 January). In Russia, echoes of revolution. *The New York Times*. www.nytimes.com/2012/01/15/sunday-review/in-moscow-echoes-of-the-91-communist-overthrow.html (Accessed 11 December 2017).

Sheftelevich, Y. (2009). The state of the media law in the Russian federation: A difficult past, an interesting present, an uncertain future. *Touro International Law Review, 12*, 88–106.

Shmaraeva, E. (2014, 18 June). Politkovskaya killers sentenced, but who hired them? *openDemocracy*. Retrieved from www.opendemocracy.net/od-russia/elena-shmaraeva/who-really-killed-anna-politkovskaya (Accessed 5 July 2017).

Siebert, F. S., Peterson, T., & Schramm, W. (1956). *Four theories of the press: The authoritarian, libertarian, social responsibility, and Soviet communist concepts of what the press should be and do*. Urbana, IL: University of Illinois.

Slavtcheva-Petkova, V. (2017). Fighting Putin and the Kremlin's grip in neo-authoritarian Russia: The experience of liberal journalists. *Journalism: Theory, Practice and Criticism*. DOI: 10.1177/1464884917708061.

Sokolov, S. (2009, 21 January). Страха нет. *Novaya Gazeta*. Retrieved from http://old.novayagazeta.ru/society/46441.html (Accessed 5 July 2017).

Sokolov, S. (2013). Мы ставим точку. *Novaya Gazeta*. Retrieved from http://old.novayagazeta.ru/inquests/58870.html (Accessed 11 December 2017).

Sokolov, S. (2016, 6 October). Не смейте говорить, что убийство раскрыто. Видеообращение редакции. *Novaya Gazeta*. Retrieved from www.novayagazeta.ru/articles/2016/10/06/70089-ne-smeyte-govorit-chto-ubiystvo-raskryto-video (Accessed 4 July 2017).

Sokolova, K. (2015, 29 May). Леся Рябцева: Я переросла уровень, когда носила за Венедиктовым чемоданы, как Путин за Собчаком. *Snob*. Retrieved from https://snob.ru/selected/entry/93140 (Accessed 8 November 2017).

Sosin, G. (1999). *Sparks of liberty: An insider's memoir of Radio Liberty*. University Park, PA: Pennsylvania State University Press.

Sparks, C. (2008). Media systems in transition: Poland, Russia, China. *Chinese Journal of Communication, 1*(1), 7–24.

Starobin, P. (2012, May/June). Muscovy pluck. *Columbia Journalism Review*. Retrieved from http://archives.cjr.org/feature/muscovy_pluck.php (Accessed 11 December 2017).

Stine, R. J. (2012, 19 December). RFE/RL ends Radio Svoboda on AM. *Radio World*. Retrieved from www.radioworld.com/business-and-law/0009/rferl-ends-radio-svoboda-on-am/329468 (Accessed 24 November 2017).

The Economist. (2012, February 18). Echo no more? Retrieved from www.economist.com/node/21547868 (Accessed 31 October 2017).

The Times. (2015). Russia falling to dark forces beyond Putin's control. Retrieved from www.alebedev.org/media/9887.html (Accessed 23 October 2017).

Thussu, D., & Freedman, D. (2003). *War and the media: Reporting conflict 24/7.* London: Sage.

UPI (2000, September 22). Russian media minister in hot water over scandal. Retrieved from www.upi.com/Archives/2000/09/22/Russian-media-minister-in-hot-water-over-scandal/8410969595200/ (Accessed 31 October 2017).

Urban, G. R. (1997). *Radio Free Europe and the pursuit of democracy: My war within the Cold War.* New Haven, CT/London: Yale University Press.

Vartanova, E. (2012). The Russian media model in the context of post-Soviet dynamics. In: Hallin, D. C., & Mancini, P. (eds.), *Comparing Media Systems beyond the Western World,* pp. 119–142. Cambridge: Cambridge University Press.

Venediktov, A. (2014). On the warning issued to Ekho Moskvy by Roskomnadzor, the Russian Telecom Regulator (Echo of Moscow). Human Rights in Russia, 9 November. Retrieved from www.rightsinrussia.info/russian-media/echoofmoscow-11 (Accessed 4 December 2017).

Venediktov, A. (2015). "Нас трижды выключали, четырежды включали." In: Ryabtseva, L. (ed.), *Эхо Москвы. Непридуманная история. 25 лет в эфире,* pp. 52–58. AST: Moscow.

Venediktov, A. (2017a, 8 August). Без посредников / Алексей Венедиктов // 06.08.17. Retrieved from www.youtube.com/watch?v=ZUGVssLG9E4 (Accessed 31 October 2017).

Venediktov, A. (2017b, 24 October). Разворот (Утренний). *Ekho Moskvy.* Retrieved from https://echo.msk.ru/programs/razvorot-morning/2079324-echo/ (Accessed 3 November 2017).

Venediktov, A., & Ryabtseva, L. (2015). Серебраная ложечка. In: Ryabtseva, L. (ed.), *Эхо Москвы. Непридуманная история. 25 лет в эфире,* pp. 5–19. AST: Moscow.

Von Seth, R. (2012). The language of the press in Soviet and post-Soviet Russia: Creation of the citizen role through newspaper discourse. *Journalism: Theory, Practice and Criticism, 13*(1): 53–57.

Vorobieva, I. (2015). "У каждого свое 'Эхо'". In: Ryabtseva, L. (ed.), *Эхо Москвы. Непридуманная история. 25 лет в эфире,* pp. 59–60. AST: Moscow.

Waisbord, S. (2013). *Reinventing professionalism: Journalism and news in global perspective (key concepts in journalism).* Cambridge: Polity Press.

Walker, S. (2015, 9 June). TV rain: Inside Russia's only independent television channel. *The Guardian.* Retrieved from www.theguardian.com/cities/2015/jun/09/tv-rain-russia-only-independent-television-channel (Accessed 11 December 2017).

Walker, S. (2016a, 5 June). Russia's 'valiant hero' in Ukraine turns his fire on Vladimir Putin. *The Guardian.* Retrieved from www.theguardian.com/world/2016/jun/05/russias-valiant-hero-in-ukraine-turns-his-fire-on-vladimir-putin (Accessed 27 September 2017).

Walker, S. (2016b, 5 October). The media that killed free media in Russia. *The Guardian.* Retrieved from www.theguardian.com/world/2016/oct/05/ten-years-putin-press-kremlin-grip-russia-media-tightens (Accessed 4 December 2017).

Walker, S. (2017, 23 October). 'Nobody defends us': Russian journalists respond to knife attack. *The Guardian.* Retrieved from www.theguardian.com/

media/2017/oct/23/russian-radio-journalist-tatyana-felgenhauer-stabbed-in-neck-at-her-moscow-office (Accessed 3 November 2017).

Watson, G. (2006, 20 October). Открытое письмо Президенту Российской Федерации Владимиру Путину. *Novaya Gazeta.* Retrieved from http://2006. novayagazeta.ru/nomer/2006/80n/n80n-s19.shtml (Accessed 30 June 2017).

Witchel, E. (2015). Getting away with murder. *The Committee to Protect Journalists.* Retrieved from https://cpj.org/reports/2015/10/impunity-index-getting-away-with-murder.php#more (Accessed 11 December 2017).

Witchel, E. (2017, 31 October). Getting away with murder. *CPJ.* Retrieved from https://cpj.org/reports/2017/10/impunity-index-getting-away-with-murder-killed-justice.php (Accessed 11 December 2017).

Yabloko. (2017). About us. Retrieved from http://eng.yabloko.ru/?page_id=12427 (Accessed 11 December 2017).

Zassoursky, I. (2004). *Media and power in post-soviet Russia.* Armonk, NY: ME Sharpe.

Index

Taylor & Francis Group
an **informa** business

Taylor & Francis eBooks

www.taylorfrancis.com

A single destination for eBooks from Taylor & Francis
with increased functionality and an improved user
experience to meet the needs of our customers.

90,000+ eBooks of award-winning academic content in
Humanities, Social Science, Science, Technology, Engineering,
and Medical written by a global network of editors and authors.

TAYLOR & FRANCIS EBOOKS OFFERS:

A streamlined
experience for
our library
customers

A single point
of discovery
for all of our
eBook content

Improved
search and
discovery of
content at both
book and
chapter level

REQUEST A FREE TRIAL
support@taylorfrancis.com

 Routledge
Taylor & Francis Group

 CRC Press
Taylor & Francis Group